Constructing Fatherhood

Constructing Fatherhood

Discourses and Experiences

Deborah Lupton and Lesley Barclay

SAGE Publications
London • Thousand Oaks • New Delhi

First published 1997

 SAGE Publications Ltd
6 Bonhill Street
London EC2A 4PU

SAGE Publications Inc
2455 Teller Road
Thousand Oaks, California 91320

SAGE Publications India Pvt Ltd
32, M-Block Market
Greater Kailash – I
New Delhi 110 048

British Library Cataloguing in Publication data

A catalogue record for this book is
available from the British Library

ISBN 0 7619 5340 X
ISBN 0 7619 5341 8 (pbk)

Library of Congress catalog card number 97–067292

Typeset by M Rules
Printed in Great Britain at the University Press, Cambridge

Contents

Acknowledgements

We thank the Australian Research Council for funding our interview study of first-time parents, the preliminary findings of which we draw upon in this book. We thank Dianne Kent, Kate Barclay, Jenny Fenwick, Murray Lean, Leanne Sullivan of the South Eastern Sydney Area Health Service and the Family Health Research Unit, St George Hospital, Sydney, and Ann Colhoun, Deborah Galloway and Mark Amey of the John Hunter Area Health Service, Newcastle, for their helpful research assistance. Virginia Schmied and Greg Fairbrother deserve special thanks for their interviewing work and general contribution to the parenting study. We are also grateful to the study participants, who kindly agreed to be interviewed on a number of occasions about their parenting experiences at a time in which many other things were happening in their lives. Finally, Deborah thanks Gamini Colless and Lesley thanks Kate Barclay for their personal support.

Introduction

Over the past few decades, both motherhood and fatherhood has received increasing attention in social policy and social scientific writings, the medical, nursing and public health literature and popular forums. Debates about what parenthood should entail, its rights and responsibilities, and how mothers and fathers should define and conduct themselves with their children and partners are frequently expressed in a range of media, from medical journals to television talk shows. Motherhood and fatherhood both as abstract socio-cultural concepts and as lived experiences are replete with competing imperatives in western societies at the end of the twentieth century. A series of important social changes have begun to have an impact in terms of renegotiating the meanings of parenthood. In particular the second-wave feminist movement, the entry of larger numbers of women into the workforce, their continuing participation in paid employment after having children and a decrease in the size of families have instigated a reassessment of the nature of both motherhood and fatherhood and how each should be conducted in relation to the other. So too, the continuing development and use of new reproductive technologies have raised issues around the definitions, rights and responsibilities of parents. In this book we focus specifically upon fatherhood. While we recognize that motherhood is equally interesting for analysis and critique, much less has been written thus far on the sociocultural meanings and experiences of fatherhood compared with motherhood.

In contemporary western societies there are several paradoxes and tensions inherent in the meanings of fatherhood that have implications for the ways in which men may see themselves as fathers and practise fatherhood. These are evident in a range of representations of fathers and fatherhood. Fatherhood, for example, is commonly portrayed as a major opportunity for modern men to express their nurturing feelings in ways that their own fathers supposedly did not, and to take an equal role in parenting with their female partners. This is the archetype of the 'new' father which, many argue, is changing family lives and challenging traditional notions of masculinity. As the writer of the foreword to one recent academic book on fatherhood argued, 'Today, involved fathers need not see themselves as weak or maternal. In contrast to the standoffish image of the "strong father", today's nurturing father adds much more strength to the family than his old-style counterpart . . . There is no doubt . . . that at least in America, the father as an involved parent is the wave of the future' (Pouissant, 1995: xxi). This 'new' father archetype, however, is only one of the dominant notions circulating in relation to how men are expected to fashion and present themselves. Men are generally still expected to participate fully in the economic sphere, to act as providers for their families, and are encouraged to construct their self-identities as masculine subjects through their work role.

The current debates on fatherhood emerge from a variety of political positions. From the right-wing approach, concern has been expressed about apparently declining paternal authority related to higher divorce rates and greater numbers of single mothers. Fathers' rights groups have taken up 'fatherless family' arguments to rail against what they see as the strident demands of 'radical feminism' and to call for the increased access of men to their children. Such groups seek to position men as oppressed by the social changes that have taken place over the past two decades since the emergence of the second-wave feminist movement. They are generally insistent about the need for 'families' to be defined as including two biological parents of different gender, thereby seeking to deny the possibility that other types of family arrangements may work as well as, if not better than, the nuclear family. A moral panic about the supposed burden single mothers place on the welfare system has also emerged from conservative critics, and 'deadbeat dads' (in the United States) or 'feckless fathers' (the equivalent British term) have been subjected to criticism for failing to meet their child-support obligations.

The thesis of the 'fatherless family' has been taken up by such powerful men as American President Bill Clinton, who announced in a speech in October 1995 that 'The single biggest social problem in our society may be the growing absence of fathers from their children's homes because it contributes to so many other social problems' (quoted in Fost, 1996: 16). Similarly, the 1996 version of the annual presidential proclamation of Father's Day signed by Clinton was overt in its portrayal of fathers as the stabilizing, strong influence upon their children, providing a means by which children may face the outside world with confidence. According to this proclamation, America owes a debt of gratitude to fathers because 'They share with us their experiences and energies, creating the strong foundation on which our children build their lives. A father's arm is there to protect and steer – whether cradling a newborn baby, steadying the rider of a first two-wheeler, or walking his child down the aisle.' The language here is interesting in its attempts to combine the notion of the affectionate, tender father with images of strength. It is this combination that Clinton himself has sought to present, both as attentive father of his adolescent daughter Chelsea and as the nation's symbolic 'Father'.

From the other side of the political spectrum, since the 1970s participants in the feminist movement have directed critical attention towards the role played by men as fathers in the domestic setting and in perpetuating the social and economic inequality of women. The trend towards women returning to the paid workforce after having children has at least partly destabilized previous assumptions about the gendered division of labour and raised questions about men's participation in domestic and childcare tasks. Even among feminist writers, however, there are at least two competing positions. For some feminists, advocating men's increased participation in child care bespeaks a move towards gender equity by removing the burden from women. For others, it is evidence of men's tendency to take over areas that have traditionally been a female preserve and a source of power for some women.

Fatherhood at the end of the twentieth century, thus, is a rather amorphous phenomenon. Fatherhood is also the site of intensely political debate, and a focus for a number of tensions around notions of gender and intimate relationships and the role of the state in 'private' life that have emerged in the wake of second-wave feminism and changing economic conditions in western societies. It is therefore not surprising that one concern in both the popular media and the social scientific literature has been the need to establish boundaries around the contemporary concept of fatherhood. How should a 'father' be defined – what should his roles and responsibilities be? In addressing these questions, emphasis has been placed on the evolution of the role of fatherhood over time, often with the implication that contemporary fathers are (or at least should strive to be) 'better' in some ways than previous fathers.

In the 1990s there is evidence of a growing interest in both academic and popular forums in masculinity, including a plethora of books examining the contemporary position of men in response to the changes wrought by the feminist movement. Academic writing on masculinity, much of it written by men themselves, has largely been instigated by feminist critiques of gender. Connell (1993: 589) has referred to a subsequent 'cultural turbulence around themes of masculinity' that has developed, calling into question previously taken-for-granted assumptions about how masculinity should be defined and understood. Despite this, much of the literature tends to universalize men's bodily experiences and the construction and experience of masculinity, not taking into account contradictions and divisions between men themselves in their taking-up of masculinities and the different relationships of power involved (Ramazanoglu, 1992: 342).

Further, one would expect that fatherhood would be a pivotal focus of such writing, but this seems not to be the case thus far. Many influential book-length academic works that feature extended discussions of masculinity (now commonly referred to in the plural as 'masculinities', for reasons outlined in Chapter 1) either ignore fatherhood altogether or mention it only briefly. Bob Connell's oft-cited and influential *Gender and Power* (1987) is one of these books. The categories of 'father' or 'fatherhood' do not appear in his index and there are but fleeting references in relation to men and parenting under the 'family' entry. His later book *Masculinities* (1995), as the title suggests, is focused in even greater detail on men. While there are a few references under 'father' and 'fatherhood' in the index, the book contains no extended discussion of fatherhood. Likewise, David Morgan's *Discovering Men* (1992) contains very few mentions of fatherhood, describing fathers largely in terms of their 'breadwinner' role. So too, the more recent edited book *Understanding Masculinities* (Mac an Ghaill, 1996) neglects detailed discussion of fatherhood. While this book does includes a chapter on fathers and the state and another on the experiences of men in their family of origin, the experiences of fathers themselves are not explored. Far more attention is paid in the book to employment issues, male sexuality, violence, crime, sport and race/ethnicity. It appears that for many of the growing number of academics who have written on men and masculinities over the past decade, issues dealing with sporting prowess, schooling, work and sexual activity are far more central to masculinities than is the experience of fatherhood.

In its neglect of fatherhood this literature, particularly as written by men, tends to reproduce a limited notion of the problematic of masculinities. Masculinities, this absence implies, revolve around bodily power and action, physical strength and engagement in education and paid labour. As such, much academic writing on masculinities tends to support the notion that men's lives and senses of self are centrally located in the 'public' rather than the 'domestic' or 'private' sphere. We would by no means deny that these aspects are important and acknowledge the usefulness of some of this literature in casting light on certain dimensions of masculinities. Nonetheless, we would question the implication that early and adult relationships with family members and significant others, work in the home and interaction as a father with infants or children are not equally, or in some cases more, important to the construction and maintenance of masculinities. It is difficult to imagine a book addressing femininities with such limited references to the role and experiences of motherhood (or indeed, non-motherhood) and their meaning for women's experiences.

Little attention has been focused on the social, cultural and symbolic dimensions of fatherhood. Nor have contemporary writings on subjectivity (notions of selfhood) and gender been adequately employed to theorize the ontology of fatherhood. In response to this hiatus, a major focus of our writing is in developing an understanding of fatherhood that sees it as a sociocultural phenomenon. In doing so, society and culture are not seen as things that exist outside fatherhood, shaping it externally, but rather as central to and productive of its very nature. That is, we assume that fatherhood does not exist apart from social and cultural processes; instead, it is viewed as existing *through* these processes. Our analysis is conducted in a theoretical context that recognizes the inevitable interrelationships between motherhood and fatherhood, and that each category draws at least part of its meaning from opposition against, as well as alignment with, the other. Indeed, we have found that the writings of feminist critics on femininities and motherhood have been particularly valuable in providing insights into the nature of masculinities and fatherhood.

Our emphasis in this book on the 'construction' of fatherhood points to the process by which we 'deconstruct' fatherhood. In deconstructing fatherhood, we draw upon poststructuralist perspectives in recognizing the importance of language and visual images for constructing and constituting understandings of reality and subjectivity. We seek to identify the dominant discourses that contribute to understandings and experiences of fatherhood. Discourses, as we use the term here, are understood as ways of representing – talking, writing about or visually portraying – phenomena and the practices or material conditions associated with these representations. Discourses are expressed both in texts (whether written, oral or visual) and in social and embodied practices. The discourses available at a certain historical moment construct the ways that we can think or talk about, or respond to, phenomena. As such, they are both enabling and constraining of human action and notions of reality. Discourses may be regarded as assemblages of knowledges that serve to produce notions of the human subject.

From this perspective, language and visual imagery do not simply 'reflect' or describe reality, but play an integral and inextricable role in *constituting* reality, our knowledge of the world. As Fairclough has put it, such a view sees language as not simply 'in a passive relation to reality, merely referring to objects which are taken to be given in reality'. Rather, 'discourse is in an active relation to reality . . . language signifies reality in the sense of constructing meanings for it' (1992: 42). We argue that these representations are integral to the constitution and reproduction of meanings and knowledges about fathers and fatherhood. Consequently the meanings of fatherhood are dependent on which discourses are being used to represent it. Part of the process of critically analysing discourses is to pay attention to the broader sociocultural context in which discourses are generated and are reproduced. This analysis includes exploring the political context, and asking such questions as: Whose interests are served by the use of specific discourses? How do elite groups, institutions and social structures shape discourses and favour some discourses over others? How are power relations sustained and justified by discursive choices? What types of resistances and alternative discourses are generated in response to dominant discourses? It is upon these issues that we focus in the chapters that follow.

In Chapter 1 we provide a detailed discussion of poststructuralist theoretical perspectives and how they might be taken up to understand the ontology of fatherhood. In this chapter, the integral concepts of discourse, subjectivity and gender are further elaborated, and the notion of the project of the self and psychoanalytic insights into subjectivity, gender and relations with others are introduced. The chapter discusses how subjectivity may be understood to be dynamic, contextual and a continuing project, something that requires work and thoughtful practice and is therefore created through social and cultural processes. We also argue that subjectivity may be understood as a site of conflict at both the conscious and the unconscious levels, while still retaining some degree of cohesion. So too, we raise the notion of gender as a series of embodied and cognitive practices and discourses that in western societies is a strong focal point around which subjectivity is understood and maintained. This chapter serves to site our own preferred approach to developing an analytical critique of representations of fatherhood and undertaking phenomenological research with men themselves about fatherhood.

The next two chapters seek to identify the ways that fatherhood and fathers are constructed in a range of literature. In Chapter 2 we review the range of academic or 'expert' literature that has previously discussed issues to do with fatherhood, focusing in particular on developmental and social psychology, the family health and welfare literature, applied sociological research and recent academic writings on masculinity. This chapter serves two major purposes. First, in the tradition of a literature review of previous empirical research, it provides the context into which our own research fits and to which it responds. Second, the analysis presented in this chapter allows us to identify some of the ways in which academic research has constructed certain ways of thinking about and dealing with fathers; that is, the major discourses on fatherhood circulating in these texts. Because academic research occupies a particularly powerful position as authoritative knowledge, this literature has provided a source of understanding fathers and fatherhood that has been taken up in other forums – in popular texts such as self-help books and newspaper and magazine articles, for example, which potentially reach a much greater readership than does the academic literature itself.

It is to such popular texts on fatherhood that we turn in Chapter 3, reviewing media as diverse as television, popular film, news reports, self-help books and child-rearing and parenting manuals. As we show, while the debt to the academic or 'expert' literature reviewed in Chapter 2 is obvious in these textual accounts of fatherhood, popular representations tend to highlight an aspect of fatherhood that is conspicuous by its absence in much of the 'expert' literature; that is, the heightened emotional dimensions of fatherhood, with all its hopes, joys and pleasures as well as its anxieties. This aspect of fatherhood emerges particularly in men's own accounts of their experiences published in popular texts. We would emphasize, however, that while for the purposes of this analysis we have defined boundaries between the 'expert' academic literature and the popular literature, these boundaries are somewhat permeable. Some texts traverse the boundaries and are not easily defined as either academic or popular. These include some self-help books and childcare manuals or newspaper or magazine articles on fatherhood written by academics or university researchers for a readership extending beyond the tight circle of other academics working in the area.

Written texts or visual images, of course, are not the only sources that shape the meanings and experiences of fatherhood. Little research that we have come across in the Anglophone literature, even within sociology, has attempted a detailed analysis of fatherhood using interview data with men themselves. Further, while some academic writers have acknowledged the importance of relating the sociocultural meanings surrounding fatherhood to men's own experiences, this area remains largely underdeveloped. Few writers have addressed in depth the discourses that men themselves draw upon when relating their own experiences as fathers, or have attempted to explore fatherhood as embodied and emotional subjectivity.

To explore this question of how men talk about fatherhood, we draw in Chapters 4 and 5 upon our own empirical research using a series of one-to-one interviews with 16 first-time Australian fathers. In this longitudinal project, which began recruiting participants in late 1994, each man (as well as his female partner) is interviewed several times, from just before the birth of his first child until the child reaches three years of age. As this project is not yet finished, but is continuing into the next few years, we concentrate here mainly on analysing the interview data from the first 18 months of fatherhood. Our intention in this study was to elicit these men's practices and feelings in relation to their experiences of becoming fathers, and to seek to explore the ways that they may take up, negotiate, reshape or reject the discourses on fatherhood emerging from popular and 'expert' texts and other sources.

Chapter 4 presents the individual case studies of four men, chosen because they represent positions on the continuum of the experiences of fatherhood articulated by the group of fathers in our study. Their narratives of early fatherhood demonstrate positions that range from resentment of the 'new' father archetype to the full embracement of this approach. Chapter 5 moves on to discuss the larger group of men's experiences in relation to three major issues: their anticipation of fatherhood, their negotiation with their partner of domestic and caring labour after the birth of their children and the men's relationship with their children.

In the Conclusion, we return to broader issues to do with the sociocultural dimension of contemporary fatherhood. We pursue the theoretical issues we raised in Chapter 1, seeking to relate them to the ways in which contemporary parenthood, and in particular fatherhood, is constructed and experienced. In doing so, we bring together the discourses on fatherhood we identified in a range of sources, from 'expert' and popular accounts to interview data with men. The discussion focuses on issues of the ambivalences and pleasures of parenthood and their link with privileged notions of subjectivity and embodiment, gender and intimate relationships in the context of late-twentieth-century western societies.

Analysis of discourses and the ways in which they operate in relation to individuals' understandings of the self is a means by which transformation in social relations may take place. This is because such an analysis serves to highlight the constantly changing nature of discourses, subjectivity and power relations, demonstrating that, rather than given and irrevocably fixed, they are historically contingent. As Shotter and Gergen have put it, patterns of identities and social practices are always 'in the making' and are therefore 'open'. As such, 'these patterns may be reconstituted if formulated in a different idiom' (1989: x). Our analysis of the discourses of fatherhood seeks to work towards change, to ameliorate the conditions of parenthood for both men and women, by deconstructing and problematizing its taken-for-granted assumptions. This book itself, as an academic text, is, of course, a forum for the articulation of certain discourses and political positions about the subject of fatherhood. We stress the caveat that our arguments are only one version of reality and are inevitably partial in seeking to explore specific dimensions of the sociocultural construction of fatherhood.

1
Theorizing Fatherhood: Poststructuralist Perspectives

In recent times, the poststructuralist perspective, developing from theorists as diverse as Marx, Althusser, Lacan, Freud, Derrida and Foucault, has exerted an enormous influence upon social and cultural theory and research. One major characteristic of poststructuralism is the 'linguistic turn', or drawing attention to the constitutive role played by language in creating notions of reality. The concepts of discourse and subjectivity are central to poststructuralist theorizing, in its focus on the intertwining of textual representations and the construction and delimitation of personal identities.

This chapter reviews the theoretical underpinnings for our analysis of the meanings and experiences of fatherhood. The interlinking of discourse, subjectivity, knowledge and power are explained and their relationships to embodiment, the project of the self and gender practices explored. The discussion ends with an acknowledgement of the emotional and unconscious dimension of human experience, including what might be described as the 'extra-discursive', and how this dimension should also be considered important in understanding how men construct and conduct themselves as fathers, providing important insights on the emotional, conflictual level of meaning in intimate relations with others.

Discourse and Subjectivity

Subjectivity, which is becoming a central problematic in contemporary social and cultural theory, may be defined as the varying forms of selfhoods by which people experience and define themselves. Moving away from the notion of 'the self' as a fixed identity that has tended to dominate the positivist social sciences and health sciences, subjectivity is generally represented in poststructuralist writings as dynamic and heterogeneous within individuals' lifespans: 'Unlike humanism, which implies a conscious, knowing, unified, rational subject, poststructuralism theorizes subjectivity as a site of disunity and conflict' (Weedon, 1992: 21). Michel Foucault's writings on how notions of the human subject are historically contingent and constantly created and recreated through discourse have been extremely influential here. Foucault argued that we cannot accept the notion of selfhood as pre-existing to social and cultural processes. Rather, we need to accept that selfhood is a product of these processes. Foucault's own work was directed to identifying the historical conditions in which particular subject positions are made possible.

Discourse is central to the production and maintenance of subjectivity. When, for example, people draw upon certain discourses in talking about or telling stories about themselves, they do so with the intention of presenting a certain persona or character (although this may not always be a conscious intention). This presentation of the self invariably involves accessing a pool of pre-established discourses that circulate in wider society and within a specific social context. Likewise, people are positioned by others in discursive interactions as particular types of individuals. The use of discourse, therefore, is constitutive of the self and of others. As such, 'human communication cannot be seen simply as a matter of information transfer from one location to another, it must be seen as ontologically *formative*, as a process by which people can, in communication with one another, literally in-form one another's being' (Shotter, 1989: 145; original emphasis).

As we observed in the previous chapter, fatherhood is a phenomenon around which there currently exist many and often competing discourses. Discourses, as ways of framing, speaking about and giving meaning to phenomena, are the sites of struggle, open to challenge from other discourses. Depending on the context, some discourses are hegemonic over others, taking charge over the definition of what is considered to be 'truth'. As Foucault has argued, '"Truth" is linked in a circular relation with systems of power which produce and sustain it, and to effects of power which it induces and which extends it' (1984a: 74). This is particularly the case if discourses issue forth from privileged and authoritative social institutions such as the government, the mass media, the legal system, medicine and public health, religious institutions and the education system (Weedon, 1992: 110). The family, for example, is a prime site for discursive interventions from members of these authoritative institutions, who attempt to frame its meanings and regulate its members in certain ways (see Chapter 2). Even within these institutions there may be a number of competing discourses around a particular phenomenon. As a result, there is never any one, fixed way of thinking about and representing phenomena such as fatherhood. Rather, there may be said to be identifiable hierarchies of discourse, in which at some times some discourses are hegemonic, carrying most credibility and weight in defining a particular phenomenon. The hegemony of any particular discourse, however, is tenuous, continually subject to contestation and new attempts to define meaning.

Discourses and practices are inextricably intertwined and symbiotic in their effects, each shaping the other. Thus, for example, popular and medical texts which emphasize the importance of men participating in the birth of their children, highlighting the need for them to 'bond' with and feel closer to their infant and partner, are likely to be major contributors to a man's decision about whether to be present at the birth of his children. However, practices influence discourses in the same way as discourses influence practices. The more men who are present at the birth of their children, for example, the more textual sources may point to the importance of such participation, identifying a 'norm' or a 'trend', thus perpetuating and supporting the practice.

Poststructuralism takes up many of the concerns of the earlier social constructionist position, which has argued that any type of knowledge and understanding of reality, scientific or otherwise, is inevitably constructed and understood through social and cultural processes (see Berger and Luckmann, 1966, for a classic statement on the social constructionist position in sociology). This recognition has led to the insight that those aspects of human experience that were previously considered to be fixed, natural and immutable, such as gender and the human body, are rather the historical products of shifting social forces and power relations. As such, the social constructionist perspective views both motherhood and fatherhood, rather than being 'instinctive' or 'inherent', inscribed in the genes and biology, as learnt through acculturation into a particular sociocultural and historical context. Thus far, there has been more attention paid to the social construction of motherhood and femininity than to fatherhood and masculinity. In Ann Oakley's book *Housewife* (1974), for example, she criticized the 'myths' surrounding motherhood – that children need mothers, that mothers need their children and that motherhood is both 'natural' and the greatest achievement of a woman's life – for the role these myths play in perpetuating women's disadvantaged status and dependency upon men.

Taken to its extreme, social constructionism can become overly relativist, suggesting that bodies and identities are endlessly malleable or 'written upon' through social and cultural processes. The fleshy body, the body that becomes ill and inevitably dies, becomes somewhat lost in the utopian visions that sometimes emerge from the highly relativist position. The emphasis on the social construction of gendered positions that dominates contemporary perspectives in feminist studies, for example, tends to discount biological explanations for gender differences as essentialist. Other feminists have responded by arguing that even if attributes such as caring and empathy are not identified as specifically or inherently 'feminine', the biological realities of the differences between women's and men's bodies cannot simply be ignored. The different capacities of male and female bodies, some feminists argue, necessarily shape the types of participation women and men have in relation to reproduction. For instance, women, unlike men, have uteruses, the capacity for menstruation, becoming pregnant, giving birth and breastfeeding, and this has profound implications for their life experiences. As Braidotti has argued, it is important for feminist critics to continue to stress 'the specificity of the lived, female bodily experience, the refusal to disembody sexual difference into an allegedly postmodern anti-essentialist subject, and the will to reconnect the whole debate on difference to the bodily existence and experience of women' (1989: 91).

Nonetheless, at its best, the insights offered by social constructionism into the contingent nature of knowledges and notions of reality have much to offer an analysis of phenomena such as fatherhood and motherhood. The notion that there are certain inevitable anatomical features that distinguish men and women from each other may be retained, in concert with the recognition that the *meanings* given to these features are socially constructed and differ historically. Thus, for example, it has been shown that the bodily experiences associated with the phenomenon that has been labelled in western societies as 'menopause' are understood and dealt with differently in contemporary Japanese society. While Japanese women also experience the permanent cessation of menstruation in mid-life, they are far less likely to view this as a negative experience, or to suffer the symptoms which women in western societies often find debilitating and for which they seek medical attention (Lock, 1993). As this suggests, it is not necessarily the case that anatomical phenomena (such as the possession or otherwise of a uterus or penis) have inevitable consequences for embodiment and social experience. Rather, it may be argued that the ways in which these features of anatomy are identified, defined and invested with meaning are culturally specific, with varying consequences.

In our analysis of the interplay of discourse and lived experience, we take the approach to power that is articulated in poststructuralist theory and which depends, in particular, upon the writings of Foucault and his followers. For Foucault, power is everywhere, part of every social relation and representation. Power is not conceptualized simply as an external influence seeking coercively to repress human action (although this remains one important element of power), nor as located solely in institutions, groups or particular individuals, but rather as a system that may also be seen as productive. Power relations, that is, serve to bring things into being. From this perspective, power and discourse are interrelated and work together to constitute subjectivity and social relations. Discourses both reflect and reproduce power relations, while power produces discourses.

The poststructuralist perspective, therefore, with its recognition of the mutually constitutive aspects of power/knowledge and its insistence that subjectivity is multiple, dynamic and constructed through discourse, also moves beyond the traditional agency/structure debate. Power is located very much at the level of the everyday. The Foucauldian understanding of power relations is that central discourses invite and persuade individuals to conform to norms and expectations rather than directly coercing them, appealing to individuals' desires and wants at both the conscious and the unconscious levels. Individuals are neither passively enmeshed in power relations nor are purely free agents, for subjectivity is always produced through power relations which themselves involve resistances. Power cannot simply be removed or stripped away, allowing individuals to be 'free', for power in some form or another is a condition of subjectivity. We are always the subjects of power.

Another reason why power can never be simply oppressive of freedom is because, as explained above, subjectivity is a moving target. Because there are a number of ways of constructing subjectivity, a range of competing discourses and meanings upon which we can draw in understanding the social and material world and ourselves, spaces are produced for individuals to oppose, reject or transform what they perceive to be constraining or reductive subject positions. Weedon has described it thus:

> The individual who has a memory and an already discursively constituted sense of identity may resist particular interpellations or produce new versions of meaning from the conflicts and contradictions between existing discourses. Knowledge of more than one discourse and the recognition that meaning is plural allows for a measure of choice on the part of the individual and even where choice is not available, resistance is still possible. (1992: 106)

This suggests that it is reductive simply to view fathers *qua* men as participating in the oppression of their female partners via their participation (or lack of participation) in the spheres of the family, work and so on. Both women and men actively participate in the reproduction of dominant discourses and practices around parenting, just as both women and men often are acutely aware of their contradictions, sometimes seeking to challenge or subvert them.

Masculinities and Fatherhood

In western and other societies, gender is a central organizing strategy of subjectivity and embodiment. Feminist writers, in particular, have drawn attention to the role played by gender in the process of shaping and directing subjectivity and embodiment for women. Building upon this work, some writers have begun to explore the nature of gender as it is implicated in men's experiences. Discussions now often take up the notion of gender as a dynamic project of the self: the gendered self is conceptualized as a series of constantly shifting practices and techniques (see, for example, Butler, 1990; Connell, 1993; Probyn, 1993). Judith Butler (1990) describes gender identities as performative, learnt through culture. She argues that gender, therefore, does not express an inner core of selfhood but rather is the effect of performative acts. The production and maintenance of gender may be considered forms of work upon the self, including both bodily practices (for example, styles of walking, hair-styles, body shape and dress), communicative practices (ways of interacting with others) and thinking practices (ways of thinking about the self and gendered others). These practices inevitably take place in the context of institutions such as the family, the workplace, the education and legal systems, the governmental apparatuses of the state and the economic context (Connell, 1993: 602).

From this perspective, masculinity is seen not as something that exists apart from the man, but as a phenomenon that is practised or performed and constituted by men. Masculinity is also regarded as highly contextual: 'Men are not simply masculine but, for example in the UK, they "do" African-Caribbean or Asian masculinity, public school masculinity, hypermasculinity, gay masculinity, or regional versions of working class machismo' (Ramazanoglu, 1992: 343). Connell (1993: 606) has similarly argued that the conventional view tends to represent masculinity as a reified property or attribute of an individual that exists in a greater or lesser degree, failing to appreciate the many and varied concepts of masculinity that co-exist and compete even within a similar cultural context at the same historical moment. Indeed, it is now commonplace for writers to insist that rather than there being a sole notion of masculinity, the more appropriate term is 'masculinities', suggesting the diversity of understandings that co-exist.

Even in acknowledging that there are various forms of masculinities, some of which are dominant over others in different contexts, men and the women who know them may find it difficult to identify the specific masculinities they represent. The feminist writer Lynne Segal (1990: 28) recounts the story of how a group of feminists in London once met to discuss their relationships with their fathers, only to find a diverse range of experiences and fatherly 'types' that called into question attempts to pin down 'fatherhood' and 'manhood'. From a male perspective, Jefferson (1996: 339) has commented upon how many men – particularly pro-feminist or gay men – have found it difficult to 'recognize themselves, their mixed experiences, contradictory desires, and simple confusions' in the 'one-dimensional portraits of masculinity' that have circulated in much academic writing on gender.

Jeff Hearn (1996) contends that too rarely is masculinity linked to men's material practices, and that the shifting nature of notions of masculinities even within the course of one man's life tends not to be acknowledged in much writing about masculinity. He argues that notions of masculinity tend to be assumed as pre-existing, which then naturalizes and reifies the dichotomy between masculinity/femininity and the reproduction of gender. Consequently, Hearn asserts that 'it is sensible not to make too many assumptions about what masculinity might be or even whether masculinity is relevant or meaningful in a particular society' (1996: 210). Masculinities are slippery and often contradictory, even within the one individual's life experience.

This approach to masculinity contrasts with previous academic writings, which tended to position it as a 'psychological essence, an inner core of the individual' that was considered to be either inherited or acquired early in life (Connell, 1993: 599). This conceptualization generally ignored the wider social structural and historical aspects shaping gendered subjects, considering 'the social' to extend little beyond the family setting in terms of forming gender. An alternative to this portrayal of masculinity was the 'male sex role' approach that was dominant in the American social scientific literature in the 1970s and early 1980s. In this approach, masculinity was considered to be a product of socialization, formed through social norms and expectations. The concept of the 'male sex role', while adopting more of a social constructionist perspective to gender, is still limited by focusing on individual agency rather than on the power dynamics underlying gender formation (Connell, 1993: 599). Proponents of this approach have tended to suggest that taking on gender 'roles' is largely an unproblematic, indeed almost automatic, process through socialization. As Connell has contended, 'Role theory rests on a superficial analysis of human personality and motives. It gives no grip on the emotional contradictions of sexuality, or the emotional complexities of

gender in everyday life, which are revealed by fine-textured field research'
(1993: 599).

The poststructuralist notion of the interrelationship between discourse and
subjectivity, related contemporary redefinitions of masculinities and the current focus in the academic literature on the performative dimension of gender
have implications for how the concept of 'the father' should be understood
(and by corollary, femininity and 'the mother'). Thus far, however, surprisingly few academic writers have drawn upon these theoretical insights and
developments to write about fatherhood. There is general agreement in the
social historical and social science literature that the expectations and norms
around 'good' fatherhood have changed dramatically over the course of the
twentieth century. Pleck (1987), for instance, identified four 'phases' of
American fatherhood typologies: first, the father as 'authoritarian moral and
religious pedagogue' (eighteenth century to early nineteenth century); second,
the father as 'distant breadwinner' (early nineteenth to mid-twentieth centuries); third, the father as 'sex role model' (1940 to 1965); and fourth, the
'new' father, who is nurturing and interested in his young children as well as
engaged in paid work (late 1960s to the present). These apparent changes in
the 'cultures of fatherhood' have been accompanied by perceived changes in
the 'cultures of motherhood'; from the ideal of the 'stay-at-home' mother
single-mindedly devoting herself to her children that supposedly characterized the first half of the twentieth century, to the growing acceptance that
women could seek paid work outside the home in combination with mothering (the 'dual career') in the late twentieth century.

The difficulty with quite rigid categorizations such as these is that there is
little recognition of differences between men of different social classes, edu-
cational level, ethnicity/cultural background and so on. Fatherhood is
portrayed as dynamic only in the terms in which today's fathers are considered to be different from their own fathers, a change which is viewed as
accompanied by a certain amount of role or identity confusion. This
approach is evident in the claim of feminist critics Knijn and Mulder that
'Fathers are not what they used to be. Fathers do not longer [sic] model themselves on the image of the sovereign patriarch, the head of the family, who
orders his wife and children about, but they have not developed a new identity, either' (1987: 1).

Some academic writers, however, have challenged these assumptions.
Lewis, for example, contends that 'A cursory glance at the literature on marriage indicates that the emergent image of fatherhood – the view that men are
starting to become involved in family life – is as old and perhaps as prominent
as the notion of patriarchy' (1986: 5). He goes on to give examples of academic writers who championed the participation of fathers in family life in the
1930s, 1940s and 1950s. As McKee and O'Brien (1982: 18–19) have noted,
within the same society at the same historical moment a man's occupation,
social position and geographical location are significant to the ways in which
he approaches fathering, and even then there is much diversity in men's experiences. For instance, in Edwardian and Victorian Britain the upper-class

father may have been regarded as 'remote' and may often have been absent on business, but there is also evidence that such fathers were benevolent and affectionate towards their children and held a central authoritative position within the family (McKee and O'Brien, 1982; Tosh, 1996). (See also Griswold (1993) for a more nuanced historical account of fatherhood in the United States.)

LaRossa (1988) argues in relation to the contemporary American context that it is middle-class men who are experiencing the greatest ambivalence, guilt and confusion around fatherhood, as they ascribe more closely to the ideals of the 'new' father. Griswold (1993: 254) also suggests that the contemporary 'new' father is a very middle-class phenomenon, used by men as a marker of their sensitivity and refinement, their willingness to incorporate the ideals of liberal feminism and their distance from the stereotype of the crude, sexist working-class man. In contrast to this ideal of the 'new' father is that of the 'dangerous' father, the father who abuses and neglects his children, who has recently become a figure of moral panic. This father is frequently designated as poor, working-class or of non-European ethnicity, preserving the 'new' father image as predominantly white and middle-class (Messner, 1993).

The 'new' father archetype, therefore, tends to elide differences between men. When subcultural groups *are* singled out for attention in relation to the fatherhood debate, they are often positioned as negative counterparts to the bourgeois ideal of the 'new' father; as 'absent' fathers, 'dangerous' fathers or 'deadbeat dads'. The diversity, richness and constantly changing nature of the fatherhood experience for individual men is lost in the use of these categories. They all present somewhat confining and reductive accounts of how men may engage in fatherhood.

The social constructionist perspective has begun to emerge in recent discussions on fatherhood. For instance, one writer has explored what he calls 'the cultural images of fatherhood', or the symbolic representations, ideologies, cultural images, stereotypes, beliefs, norms and values that surround fatherhood (Marsiglio, 1993). Sometimes the phrase 'father role identity' is used to denote these phenomena in the social scientific literature on fatherhood, particularly that published in the United States. While this approach, like the related 'male sex role' concept we discussed above, is vaguely social constructionist in recognizing that fathers are 'made and not born', the 'father role identity' is typically presented as a set of quite fixed and individualistic characteristics. It is described as involving an individual's recognition of specific behaviours that he regards as conforming to 'good' or 'bad' father types or 'scripts', choosing from among these behaviours and then developing a 'father identity'. There is a reliance here upon static and specifically defined models of identity and upon rational choice as a means of constructing subjectivity. Sometimes this use of social constructionism slides into positioning 'the social' or 'the cultural' as separate from and external to the individual. There is an assumption in this writing that masculine identity is pre-existing, and is merely altered in some way as men respond to these expectations.

We would not want to suggest that there is no element of rational choice operating in men's construction of fatherhood. Indeed, as we go on to argue below, parenting for both men and women has become conceptualized and approached as requiring much considered thought and the weighing up of alternatives. The 'father role identity' approach, however, tends not to admit of a less conscious level of experience that contributes to men's conceptualization and presentation of the self as a father. It also implies that once a 'father role identity' is 'chosen' and constructed, it is more or less discrete and fixed, except for shifts that take place over time due to responses to external 'life events'; for example, in the case of marital separation, remarriage or children reaching adulthood and leaving home. In these cases, it is argued, a certain identity changes into another one, and so on. While role theory admits that there are many identities that people enter and leave (the 'work identity', the 'husband identity', the 'father identity' and so on), it tends to suggest that these identities are separate from each other, and are juggled by the individual who takes up one identity at some times, then drops it and takes up another as the context demands.

There is little recognition in this literature that fatherhood is a continually changing ontological state, a site of competing discourses and desires that can never be fully and neatly shaped into a single 'identity', and that involves oscillation back and forth between various modes of subject positions even within the context of a single day. The concept of 'the father' is typically gendered in western societies; it denotes maleness, the possession of a penis and testes in working order, the proven ability to produce viable sperm to impregnate a woman resulting in a child. Yet, as de Kanter (1987: 6) points out, the contemporary concept of 'the father' is far more complex and less unified than this common-sense definition suggests. There are different modes of masculinity expressed between and within fathers. The concept of 'the father' or 'fatherhood' is multiple rather than unitary, changing according to the context even for the individual, as do concepts of 'the mother' or 'motherhood'.

De Kanter (1987) notes that when speaking or writing of 'the father' there is a continual move between at least three different levels of meaning: the person of the father (that is, an individual's embodied presence), the socio-cultural position of the father and the more abstract symbol of the father. As she argues, the term 'father' may be used to describe the individual who provided the biological material, even if he is never known to his child (as in the case of sperm donors), to describe the person who lives in the same household as the child and is the mother's partner but is not biologically related to the child, and the man who is legally the father but does not live in the same household because of marital separation or divorce. So too, a 'father figure' may be a friend of the family or a relative such as an uncle. Indeed, fatherhood need not be linked with maleness or heterosexuality at all. For instance, among lesbian couples with children, a woman may be conceptualized as performing the 'father' role, while gay men can be fathers in any of the above senses. As this suggests, there is no a priori or necessary relationship between maleness, masculinity, heterosexuality and 'the father'.

There is nothing particularly linear or predictable therefore about the inter-action between the subject position of 'father' and discourse and practice. Men will take up and adopt different discourses and practices at different times, perhaps ascribing to contradictory discourses simultaneously. The extent to which men and women may accept the dominant discourses on fatherhood is a highly complex process. That is not to say that there are *no* constraints to the extent to which dominant discourses may be avoided, rejected, or, for that matter, taken up by individuals. There continue to be material as well as ideological constraints to the autonomy of individuals. As Weedon argues, 'How we live our lives as conscious thinking subjects, and how we give meaning to the material social relations under which we live and which structure our everyday lives, depends on the range and social power of existing discourses, our access to them and the political strength of the inter-ests which they represent' (1992: 26). Material conditions must change as well as discourses for some social transformations to take place. Similarly, as we contended above, such features as the differing anatomical capacities of women and men continue to have implications for their life choices. Changes in discursive practices may go some way towards changing the meanings associated with these capacities or perhaps reducing their potency, but they cannot erase them entirely.

Parenting and the Project of the Self

The poststructuralist concept of subjectivity recognizes that it must be worked at on a daily basis, rather than being given or becoming static from a certain point in an individual's development. Rose (1996) has taken up Foucauldian insights to argue that historically there have been different ways available to humans to produce and understand themselves as subjects of a certain type: 'The human being is not the eternal basis of human history and human culture but a historical and cultural artifact' (Rose, 1996: 22). Rose describes the discourses and practices related to subjectivity, after Foucault, as particular 'regimes of the person'. He observes that many such regimes have developed around aspects of everyday life, including parenthood and child rearing, constructing them as problems.

Several sociologists have recently written about the ways in which individ-uals in contemporary societies seek to establish and maintain a sense of identity and set of beliefs in a world that is experienced as rapidly changing and full of uncertainties and risks. Zygmunt Bauman (1996), for example, has described the notion of life as a pilgrimage. He argues that unlike that of the pilgrims of pre-modern times, the pilgrimage of modern individuals is accom-plished without leaving home; they are inner-worldly pilgrims who embark on this journey not through choice but through necessity. This pilgrimage is, in other words, the 'unfinished project of the self', the ever-continuing endeav-our of fashioning self-identity. It is ever-continuing, because 'the rules of the game keep changing in the course of playing' (Bauman, 1996: 24).

The project of the self requires reflexivity, or rationalized attention to how best to deport one's self, how to relate to others and live life wisely and well, accomplishing one's goals. It involves drawing upon and making use of available knowledges about selfhood. In contemporary western societies, such knowledges tend to include the insights offered by the 'expert' knowledges of psychology, sociology and the health sciences and, to a lesser extent, religion. In relation to the contemporary regimes around the project of the self, Gordon argues that the individual is seen to be engaging in a type of enterprise, involving continual reflection upon one's way of life and conduct with others:

> the idea of one's life as the enterprise of oneself implies that there is a sense in which one remains always continuously employed in (at least) that one enterprise, and that it is a part of the continuous business of living to make adequate provision for the preservation, reproduction and reconstruction of one's own human capital. (1991: 44)

It is not only the intangible self that is part of this regime, but also the body, given that there is an inextricable relationship in western notions of subjectivity between the body and the self. Thus practices of the self also involve bodily care and deportment – ways of decorating, grooming, disciplining, moving and presenting the body.

From this perspective, fatherhood may be understood as an entrepreneurial activity, part of the project of shaping one's life as a rational, autonomous, responsible individual seeking to maximize one's potential and achievements as a worthy person. The 'expert' or 'professional' discourses emerging from such fields as medicine, psychology and sociology, as well as those evident in popular forums, are translated into prescriptions for how men should understand and practise fatherhood. In turn, men's experiences, as they are catalogued in clinical and academic research, are transformed into the contentions of 'expert' discourses. Such bodies of knowledge serve to bring phenomena such as fatherhood into being, making them thinkable, knowable and measurable. Fathers, that is, are produced as objects of knowledge through these discourses.

We can point to common discursive patterns in the ways of representing fatherhood in popular and 'expert' texts and the decisions men may make in their practice of fatherhood. Given the sheer volume of textual representations of fathers and fatherhood in contemporary western societies (although this remains small compared to textual representations of mothers and motherhood), it is inevitable that men and women will draw on these in constructing their understandings and experiences of fathers and fatherhood. In some cases this will be a highly conscious and deliberate process, including the purchase and perusal of self-help books on childbirth and parenting, for example. In other cases it will be a less deliberate and far more diffuse process, occurring as an inevitable part of acculturation into society through formal education, participation in family life, discussions with other parents and so on. In seeking to identify the interplay of discourses that constitute fatherhood, we do not wish to imply that men are somehow forced into particular versions of fatherhood via discourse. It is difficult, if not impossible, to iden-tify a 'cause and effect' relationship or to isolate specific forums of discourse as the most influential upon men's own practices and experiences in relation to fatherhood, or vice versa.

In their writings on intimate life and family relationships in the context of late modern societies, Beck-Gernsheim and Beck (Beck, 1992: chapters 4 and 5; Beck and Beck-Gernsheim, 1995; Beck-Gernsheim, 1996) discuss the process of individualization, or the movement in post-industrial societies away from traditional social ties, systems of belief and towards relationships involving not only more flexibility but also new demands and obligations. The creed of individualization is that 'life is what you make it' (Beck-Gernsheim, 1996: 140). As part of individualization, 'Women and men are currently com-pulsively on the search for the right way to live' (Beck and Beck-Gernsheim, 1995: 2). But it is not only this diminishing of general norms about how to live one's life that is part of the growing uncertainties about how family life should be conducted. It is also the discourses that suggest that people should devote time to themselves and should interrogate their relationships for their flaws.

Beck and Beck-Gernsheim (1995) argue that traditional notions around gender-defined roles and expectations have, to some extent, dissolved, and have been replaced by a more androgynous approach, involving a greater need for couples to work out for themselves how their relationship will oper-ate. In contemporary intimate relationships, men are now expected to respond to and provide emotional closeness with others. The ideal notion of marital love is that which expects both partners to develop a fulfilled and independent self, in which family and gender roles are flexible and constantly renegotiated. There is a strong emphasis on individuals seeking to communicate needs and feelings to each other and on openly confronting problems, in 'working' on the marriage (Cancian, 1987; Duncombe and Marsden, 1993; Griswold, 1993). As a result, 'love is more difficult than ever' (Beck and Beck-Gernsheim, 1995: 52). There is more freedom and flexibility to 'choose' how one should behave in an intimate relationship, but this very flexibility brings with it added burdens and uncertainties: 'the more complex the decisions are, the more likely they are to lead to quarrels' (1995: 52).

This increased emphasis on negotiation, egalitarianism and communica-tion in intimate relationships is evident in contemporary discourses on fatherhood. As we will show in Chapters 2 and 3, both 'expert' and more pop-ular discourses on masculinity have tended to argue that men should take on a more 'feminine' approach in interacting with their family, including reveal-ing their emotions to their partners and children, demonstrating their love and affection openly and participating in embodied caring activities with their young children. This is a shift from earlier notions of the role played by 'the home' for men, where it was conceptualized as a place where they could retreat from the burdens of public life and allow themselves to be cared for by their partners. Women, for their part, are expected to behave not only as 'angels of the home', bestowing love and care on their partners and children,

but also to engage as active workers in the paid workforce. They are encouraged to seek emotional companionship from their partners in return for their
own emotional support. A 'developed' person now tends to be described as
'someone who combines feminine intimacy and emotional expression with
masculine independence and competence' (Cancian, 1987: 8).

This intensification of discourse around intimacy and love in the marital
and family context coincides with an increased concern about the vulnerability of the child, and the importance of parental actions in affecting
children's moral, emotional, social, physical and cognitive development.
Individuals in western societies have been constructed to experience and perceive relationships between children and their parents as highly important,
emotionally charged and integral to the sense of self. It is no longer considered enough to do one's duty as a parent, to conform to moral standards.
Rather, the emphasis now is upon individuality and self-development, and
hierarchical relations between parents and children are no longer valued:
'Modern conceptions about good parenthood do not emphasize that parents
have to teach their children societal norms and values; they should relate to
their children in such a way that the individuality of the children can fully
develop' (Verheyen, 1987: 37).

Part of the idea of life as malleable to individual agency is the notion that
children are planning objects, requiring the investment of much care and
attention as well as economic resources on the part of their parents. Parents
actively seek to produce a perfect child, for the child has come to stand as the
tangible outcome of parental labour and care: 'A child, once a gift of God,
sometimes also an unwanted burden, increasingly becomes for parents/moth-
ers "a difficult object for treatment"' (Beck-Gernsheim, 1996: 143–4).
Nippert-Eng has referred to the contemporary dominant concept of children as that of 'sacred children', seen as 'precious entities entrusted to adults'
care, deserving the very best from us' (1996: 203). She goes on to note that 'In
its extreme form, "sacred-child parenting" places children (especially infants)
on a pedestal of the highest magnitude. Here, a parent's life is utterly devoted
to a child's needs and desires, subordinating all other goals, actions, claims,
and people to the child' (1996: 204). Parenting, therefore, is an integral site of
the reproduction of modes of care of the self. It has become important as a
performative practice, with the outcome a child whose demeanour, appearance and achievements are strongly linked to parents' own subjectivity, their
presentation of the self to others *qua* parent.

The practices of the self related to the role of the parent are not simply limited to one's own body or self, although they may include this focus
(particularly during pregnancy), but primarily revolve around the care of the
body and self of another: the child. Clearly, parenting is an important practice of the self for those who have infants or young children, for some people
at some times coming to the fore and virtually overwhelming other practices.
The project of the child begins well before birth, when individuals have to
decide whether or not they even want to have a child, whether their relationship is stable enough, whether their economic resources are robust enough or

whether they feel emotionally ready for the demands of parenthood. Once the difficult decision is made to go ahead, both prospective parents are encouraged to maximize their own state of good health before attempting to conceive. This intensifies for women during pregnancy, when they are offered a battery of prenatal diagnostic tests to measure the health and normality of the foetus. Then follows a whole range of decisions that have to be made and information sought and considered (Beck and Beck-Gernsheim, 1995: chapter 4). An important part of these decisions is how the father will conduct himself in his parental role. Fathers are encouraged to negotiate with their partners about how child care will be undertaken, to attend antenatal classes with their partners, to be present at the birth of the child and to consider the nature of their relationship with their child and how best to achieve this.

Emotions and the Inner World

One area which discourse theory has tended to overlook is an understanding of the inner world of the subject and the importance of emotional states, mutuality and intimate relationships between people, including those between parents and their children, as contributing to subjectivity. Feminist critics in particular have drawn attention to these absences in Foucault's work, as well as to his tendency to construct a masculinist concept of subjectivity (see, for example, the chapters collected in Ramazanoglu, 1993). Foucault and his followers have also been charged with neglecting the ways in which subjectivity is also shaped via the pre-discursive, or that part of existence that develops in earliest infancy before the subject is aware of language, and the extra-discursive, or those elements that go beyond language and visual representation, such as spatial, embodied and sensual experiences (smell, touch, taste and so on), feelings and emotional states and relations to other bodies and material objects. For instance, Cain (1993) argues that is possible to *feel* something before this feeling is translated or expressed into language or visual imagery; feelings, indeed, may remain imperfectly expressed in discourse or not expressed discursively at all. An over-emphasis on discourse, thus, may descend into 'discourse determinism', and this 'does not account for what we experience as individuality: the fact of each person's uniqueness in relation to language/discourse' (Hollway, 1989: 84).

Social research in general too often ignores the emotional dimension of human action, preferring to turn its attention to documenting and explaining patterns of 'rational' behaviour. The lack of interest in the affective dimensions of fatherhood, or what the writer of one popular book has called 'the passions of fatherhood' (Osherson, 1996), is typical of academic writing in general in the social sciences. As Game and Metcalfe have argued, linking the word 'passionate' with the words 'sociology' or 'psychology' generally is disturbing, for it challenges assumptions about what is proper for social scientists to write about: 'Modern sciences like psychology and sociology rarely talk about passions, and certainly not their own. The closest they come is through the more anaemic concept of emotions. For most psychologists and sociologists, the idea of passion is as imprecise and pre-scientific as humoral understandings of health' (1996: 4).

So too, both psychology and sociology tend to assume the notion of the unified, rational subject, the subject who seeks out knowledge so as to make wise choices. Traditionally, therefore, sociology and psychology have tended to construct a dualism between individual and society, structure and agency. These perspectives are reflected and reproduced in popular and expert writings on fatherhood. As we show in Chapter 2, much of the social scientific literature on fatherhood argues for change, advocating that fathers take a far greater interest in, and provide practical assistance for, their children's care. The writers of this literature mainly rest upon the 'voluntarism' position, implying that as long as men's consciousness is raised, that they are made aware of their inherent potential for nurturing and the rewards that come from close physical contact with infants and children, then they will take steps to alter their lives so as to be more 'involved' fathers. While much sociological writing has drawn attention to the constraints imposed by society on men's ability to change their fathering practices, including such factors as gendered expectations around work and concepts of masculinity and femininity in relation to the care of children, most sociologists argue for change driven by 'rational' action. In their focus on rationality, neither psychologists nor sociologists appear very much interested in the emotional and embodied dimensions of fatherhood; that is, the ways in which the discourses, meanings and practices of fathering are experienced by men themselves at a visceral, sensual and affective level.

What such perspectives do not and cannot account for is the 'extra-rational' aspects of life, including the generation and experience of strong emotional states. We would argue that fatherhood is not only constituted through discursive and conscious processes, but importantly is also constructed through touch and smell and inchoate memories of infancy and early childhood, all of which form part of the realm of knowledge and experience. While many of the everyday activities in which we engage are not particularly invested with emotion, it is clearly the case that familial and other intimate relations, including parenthood, are primary sites for the expression and investment of emotions.

It is here that the psychoanalytic approach provides an alternative perspective. This perspective in general offers the insight that there is much that lies beyond conscious thought, that individuals' sense of their own coherence as an individual, their certainties about self, others and the world are only one part of subjectivity. It differs from mainstream developmental and social psychology in its focus on the emotional, the contradictory, the fragmentary and disordered subject rather than the 'rational', the conscious and the unified subject (Burman, 1994: 13). It recognizes that there is an element of the human psyche, namely the unconscious, that acts as a reservoir for repressed thoughts, phantasies, desires, libidinal drives and motivations which are always potentially rising to the surface and revealing themselves through such outlets as dreams, slips of the tongue, jokes and what might be experienced as 'irrational' emotional reactions. These emotions, phantasies and desires themselves are socially constructed in particular historical settings: 'those processes which position us are also those which produce the desires for which we strive' (Henriques et al., 1984: 205).

The concept of the unconscious highlights the ever-present 'threat' of loss of control over the rational, ordered and reflective self. As Walkerdine and Lucey suggest,

> The psychic dimension of our work – the problems of what people remember and how they interpret situations, mixing fact and fantasy, the defences against pain, the push of wishing, hoping, desiring – are rarely discussed in social analysis. A politics of subjectivity needs this engagement if it is not to succumb to a too simplistic determinism, for it shows the complexity of how we are struggling. (1989: 44)

Although language and culture are important to the construction of subjectivity, the emotional self, the self who has a personal biography of unconscious emotionally imbued phantasies, also plays a part in the shaping and reshaping of meaning for each individual. That is not to say that each is separate from the other. Language, culture and emotional phantasy interact, each shaping the other (Chodorow, 1995a). The unconscious, therefore, may be understood as structuring and reconstructing social relations in certain ways. In turn, the unconscious is constructed through social and cultural processes. The psyche and subjectivity are developed as a product of the social and ideological field but also 'feed back' into the social world, serving to shape social, political and cultural relations.

Psychoanalytic theory is able to provide some insight into the question of why individuals may 'believe' one thing and 'do' or 'feel' another: for example, why strongly feminist women who are critical of what they see as the oppressive aspects of the institution of the traditional family may still want to engage in heterosexual relations, live with a man and bear children. Henriques et al. make use of the notion of 'investment', or 'the emotional commitment, involved in taking up positions in discourses which confer power and are supportive of our sense of continuity' (1984: 205). This notion of investment is useful, for it both recognizes that individuals possess agency in positioning themselves in certain ways, and allows for the affective underpinnings of everyday thoughts and actions. Thus, for instance, men may be conceptualized as taking up certain masculine subject positions as a way of (partially) resolving contradictions, anxieties and uncertainties as well as achieving pleasure and a sense of power (Hollway, 1984; Jefferson, 1996).

By extension, this theoretical point also raises the question of how people who have been 'socialized' into taking up certain discourses and norms of behaviour may instead flout or transform them. Because in psychoanalytic theorizing the self is understood as complex and often unpredictable in responding to unconscious desires, this approach further opens up the potential for social change. Those who have taken up psychoanalytic theory have suggested that social norms are usually 'internalized', but not without struggle and conflict, particularly as norms themselves contradict each other (for example, the conflict between autonomy and dependence that dominates western notions of the ideal self – see further discussion of this below). This internalization, therefore, is never quite complete and closed off.

A focus on analysing discourse remains important, however, not only because of the role of discourse in contributing to the shaping of experience but also its function as the primary means by which we convey to others, however inadequately and clumsily, our feelings and emotional states. Thus the Foucauldian interest in discourse may usefully be brought together with psychoanalytic insights into the meaning and experience of motherhood and fatherhood that are often neglected in other approaches interested in the sociocultural aspects of parenting. Such a perspective is able to delve below the manifest level of meaning to explore the symbolic and emotional dimensions of the parent–child relationship, including the profound ambivalences and contradictions that characterize this relationship (and all other intimate human relationships).

Object Relations Theory, Gender and Intimate Relations

Psychoanalytic theory has provided a number of important insights into the production and shaping of subjectivity and gender. Writers adopting psychoanalytic perspectives have argued that early parent–child relations have significant implications for adult subjectivity, including individuals' relationships with and feelings about their partners and own children. Feminist writers, in particular, have employed insights derived from psychoanalytic perspectives to speculate upon the ways that gender is produced through relations with one's mother and father in early childhood. In the emphasis on unconscious phantasies and desires as they are developed in infancy, the object relations theory is able to raise some questions (and attempt to answer them, albeit partially) about the deeply-felt emotions around childhood and parenting which are often regarded as 'irrational', the investments that people have in taking up gender roles, that external theories of subjectivity are often at a loss to explain (Hollway, 1994: 541).

Early psychoanalytic theory tended to highlight the importance of the father as the primary figure responsible for introducing children into the 'real', external and moral world and shaping their gender identity. Freud, for example, viewed the domestic space, the world of the mother and the infant as a closed circle. He contended that the infant is at first unable to differentiate itself from the maternal body, the provider of pleasure. For Freud, particularly in his earlier writings, the father was of great importance, representing the outside world, its morality, the necessary link the child requires to gain autonomy from the mother and achieve differentiated selfhood and sexual identity.

Freud's major preoccupation in exploring the unconscious dimensions of the relationships between parents and their children was in relation to male children. In what Freud called the Oedipal crisis, he described the situation by which the male child, around the age of three years, first begins to conceptualize himself as separate and different from his mother. At this time, argued Freud, the boy desires his mother, seeking to maintain his sense of psychic union with her, and views his father as an intrusion into his intimate relationship with the mother. The boy therefore sees the father as his rival and wants to usurp him, phantasizing about his death. For the father's own part, he requires that the child renounce the mother as the love object and acknowledge paternal authority, the father's right to the mother. Eventually the boy must learn that his father's authority cannot be usurped, and his forbidden desire for his mother is driven into his unconscious. As part of the process of achieving maturity as an adult, the boy must find his own (ideally female) sexual partner to replace the mother figure, but the forbidden desire for his mother may re-emerge from the unconscious from time to time.

Freudian theory has been widely criticized for its universalizing tendencies and for the stereotypical representations of gender, reflecting the sociocultural context in which Freud was writing (Europe in the late nineteenth century) and his perspective as a privileged middle-class European man. Nonetheless, Freud was the first to establish the concept of the unconscious and to attempt to draw implications for the ontology of human existence and selfhood. Later object relations theory, particularly as it was used by feminist writers, diverted emphasis from the influence of sexual desire and the Oedipus complex in constructing the unconscious, as was the focus in Freudian and Lacanian approaches, to the 'pre-Oedipal' stage, or the maternal–infant relationship. Turning away from the approach that seems to predominate in masculinist psychoanalytic theory, these theorists have adopted a position that both recognizes and celebrates the role of the mother while simultaneously acknowledging the struggles that ensue at the stage of the child's separation and individuation from her.

The work of Melanie Klein, first published in the 1920s, has been taken up as an alternative to simply focusing on boys and their fathers by exploring the unconscious dimensions of the relationship between infants of both sexes and the mother (for a collection of some of her most influential writings, see Klein, 1979). Klein and her followers have pointed out that because only women's bodies have the potential to give birth to children and lactate, it is the woman who gives birth to the infant who tends to take care of it. Therefore, in most situations, individuals' primary identification is with one person: the woman who gave birth to them. Klein focused on infants' intense ambivalent reactions to the powerful mother, including their fears of her omnipotence, which, she argued, shaped subsequent subjectivity. Like Freud, she argues that at the beginning of life, human infants are unable to differentiate themselves from the care-giver, but experience an emotional and physical oneness with this person. Infants are also helpless, utterly reliant upon this care-giver for survival, as they were in the womb.

In the first few months of life, according to Klein, the infant experiences frustration and discomfort in birth and adapting to a new environment out of the womb. This leads to the unconscious feeling that she or he is attacked by hostile forces, which is alleviated by the sensual gratification and comfort provided by feeding and other caring actions provided by the mother figure. For the infant, therefore, the mother figure represents the whole of the external world. As part of normal development, the first object upon which infants fixated, Klein contended, was the mother's breast, which was conceptualized by the child as both 'good' at some times (when it gratified desires) and at others, 'bad' (when frustrating desires or withholding pleasure). So that the infant may preserve the loved aspects of the good mother, a splitting occurs that results in a severance of love and hate.

While these processes emerge in earliest infancy, when infants undergo the psychic processes of differentiation from the maternal body, they continue to work into adulthood in individuals' relationships with other people and with material phenomena and their dealing with ambivalent feelings. Parts of the self (sometimes the 'bad' parts, sometimes the 'good' parts) continue to be split off and projected onto important others, influencing emotional life and relations with other people and things in adult life. Klein argued that sometimes this projection can lead to severe emotional or personality problems, but it is also found in minor degrees in 'normal' people. Hollway (1989) gives the example of the vulnerability and anxiety experienced by adults in their relations with others. She argues that these emotions may be understood as culturally inevitable, developed in infants through their interactions with and positioning by their care-givers, who invest their own anxieties in the infants. As a result, for adults, 'Anxiety thus provides a continuous, more or less driven, motive for the negotiation of power relations' (Hollway, 1989: 85).

Feminist writers drawing upon the foundation work of Klein, such as Dorothy Dinnerstein (1976), Nancy Chodorow (1978, 1989) and Jessica Benjamin (1994) have employed object relations theory to argue that the role differentiation between women and men shapes the ways in which gender is reproduced. They build upon the recognition common to most psychoanalytic approaches that children construct their autonomous self identity by going through the process of separating from their mothers. The feminist object relations school of thought goes on to argue that the process of separation from the mother is both more important and more complete for boys than for girls, underpinning the apparent need for detachment and rationality that supports a masculinist approach to the conduct of the self. These writers suggest that the basis of men's need to dominate women is their early attempts to separate from the mother figure and construct an individual identity. They argue that it is in this process of differentiation that men develop an intense fear, anger and resentment towards women. Boys' rejection of the engulfing, threatening mother and the embracing of the father becomes the rejection of women and things deemed feminine, and hence is the cause of adult men's attempts to dominate women.

In her influential book *The Reproduction of Mothering* (1978) and in a collection of essays, *Feminism and Psychoanalytic Theory* (1989), Chodorow argues that girls also recognize that they must gain autonomy from the maternal body, but feel less inclined to separate themselves because they identify with their mothers as women; they incorporate their mothers into their own identity. Mothers, for their part, treat their children differently according to whether they are male or female. As women, they see their daughters as more like an extension of the self, while their sons are more likely to be perceived as 'other' and are pushed towards differentiation. Chodorow asserts that through their more symbiotic relationships with their mothers, women develop a 'self-in-relation', while men develop a self that tends to deny relatedness. Men remain psychologically defensive and insecure, while women may, at least in favourable circumstances, gain better psychological security for they have less of a need for differentiation from the primary care-giver.

This approach recognizes that both men and women experience the ambivalences around the desire for autonomy and independence and the desire for dependency, connectedness and intimacy with another that produces the same pleasures experienced in infancy with the maternal body. However, the process of becoming a gendered subject subsequently shapes the nature and manifestation of these responses. While both boys and girls go through the psychic processes of individuation in early infancy, due to sociocultural assumptions and expectations around gender boys rather than girls are eventually acculturated to find intimacy, closeness with and dependency upon another more frightening and threatening to their presentation of the self. As part of performing masculinity, boys have more at stake than do girls in constructing and presenting a self that is autonomous. It is later in a child's development, in interactions with others and in the context of institutions such as the family, the mass media and the education system that she or he comes to recognize the gendered meanings around autonomy/intimacy and rationality/emotionality and learns how to phrase her or his own emotional responses through dominant discourses on gender.

There are implications in this work for understanding both the role of fathers in producing gendered subjectivities and men's relationships as adults with intimate others, including their children, although Chodorow tends to focus on the former rather than the latter. In Chodorow's schema it is more difficult for men to take on a caring role because of their more strongly-differentiated sense of self and unconscious need to remain separate from others. As a result, she argues, as fathers men have difficulty in engaging with their children emotionally and understanding their needs in comparison with women's more empathetic, other-centred approaches. Chodorow (1978) contends that changes in the ways in which child care is divided between women and men, with men taking more responsibility, would lead to changes in gender roles for ensuing generations. Boys and girls would first identify equally with both parents and would then go through the process of separation from them both. As such, boys would not need to become so resistant to, afraid, and dismissive of, the mother/femininity in establishing their independence and masculine persona. Both boys and girls could develop an individuated and strong sense of self and secure gender identity that does not involve either defensiveness and denial of connection to others or ego-boundary confusion.

Dorothy Dinnerstein (1976) has taken this approach even further, arguing that mothers produce 'maimed', 'semi-human', 'monstrous' adults who harbour fury against their mothers because of the stifling, absolute power they hold over their helpless children. For Dinnerstein as for Chodorow, the way out is to construct an alternative psychic scenario whereby infants develop the initial relationship with both parents and thereby project their earliest feelings onto both the mother and the father. The consequence of this, she argues, would be that the hostility, dread, rage and frustration inevitably aroused through the psychic separation process would be diverted from women as the sole target.

The object relations approach provides a number of insights for understanding parenthood and gender differentiation and, by extension, fatherhood. However, it has been subject to criticism on several grounds. There is a strong structuralist tendency in this work, at least as it was formulated in the 1970s, with the construction of gender reduced to reproduction via family relationships. Object relations theory has been criticized for its ethnocentricity, ahistoricity and its essentialist tendencies in referring to 'the mother' and 'the child' in the context of the westernized, one-to-one relationship of mothers with their children (Burack, 1992: 500–1; Cornwall and Lindisfarne, 1994: 33). Another criticism is that this perspective privileges such characteristics as separation and individuation, focusing on the conflict, and indeed even hostility, supposedly inherent in breaking the symbiotic maternal–infant attachment rather than the pleasures and benefits of interrelationships and emotional connections with others (Burack, 1992: 500).

Further, there are a number of assumptions made about gender by some proponents of object relations theory that tend to present a homogeneous, universalized account of masculinity and femininity. These include the assertion that men cannot engage in nurturing roles because of their need to defend themselves against what they perceive to be 'feminine' characteristics, and the assumption that women are psychically predisposed towards nurturing, and feel less ambivalence about merging their identities with another individual. There is little examination of how men in different life circumstances based on their socioeconomic status, ethnicity, generational group, sexual preference and so on may respond differently to fatherhood. Nor does this body of literature provide explanations for how individual men may transcend the defensive position into which they are placed as a result of unconscious processes of individuation. Schwartz (1994: 249) asks, for instance, how it is that some men *do* assume the role of primary care-takers and nurturers and how does Chodorow's model apply to gay male couples with children? Such theory tends to imply that neither men nor women can escape the bounds of gender roles; if men are disposed towards differentiation, how can they begin to take on a nurturing response that is expected of them? These criticisms would suggest the need for a less essentialist understanding of how men and women come to develop gendered approaches to intimate relationships.

In her more recent work, Chodorow (1995a, 1995b) has addressed some of these criticisms, moving away from some of her originally essentialist tendencies. She now emphasizes the importance of recognizing the variation and complexity that are evident in the ways that individuals take up gender and engage in intimate relations. Chodorow notes that her own work as a psychotherapist has demonstrated to her that the emotions and fantasies invested in mother–daughter relationships, the symbolizations of the self and the mother, differ widely between her female patients. So too, Chodorow found that for the women she was treating, the personal and cultural meanings of the father were contingent, albeit strongly influenced by dominant sociocultural discourses about gender. Thus, she concludes: 'Anyone's emotionally and linguistically constructed gender, the personally animated gendered self and world she inhabits, is a continuously invoked and reshaped project involving self, identity, body imagery, sexual fantasy, images and fantasies about parents, cultural stories, and unconscious and conscious fantasies about intimacy, dependency, and nurturance' (1995a: 541).

As a feminist who has more recently taken up Kleinian approaches to theorizing gender relations and sexuality, Wendy Hollway similarly rejects a deterministic approach, arguing that individuals experience individuation in different ways, which has implications for their subsequent intimate relationships. She has a somewhat more optimistic approach to how people may deal with the unconscious anxieties produced through individuation, arguing that 'Depending on the quality of early object relations, people can achieve relations in adulthood in which the need for recognition and the wish for autonomy can coexist, albeit in tension' (Hollway, 1995: 96–7).

Both Hollway's and Chodorow's more recent theorizing on subjectivity and intimate relationships underline the importance of avoiding over-generalization and the need to acknowledge the shifting nature of gendered subjectivities. Individuals, they argue, may be understood as constructing, experiencing and understanding their own position as a gendered subject as an individual creation that is personally inflected as well as shaped more broadly through language and culture. As a result, 'there are many individual masculinities and femininities', although these may share some similarities with others (Chodorow, 1995a: 521). This approach recognizes that while there are certain anatomical and sociocultural conditions that tend to structure individuals' responses to others, the nature of individuals' personal biographies – their lived experiences, their observations of the experiences of others, their relationships with others (including their own parents), their sensual, emotional, embodied interactions with the world – mediate the outcome of these conditions. It emphasizes the ways in which different sources of the self intertwine and become important at different times for the same person. In one context, for example, gender may be particularly important for an individual's sense of self and presentation of the self; in another, it may be her or his sexual preference, occupation, position as a parent or non-parent, or as a member of a particular ethnic or cultural group.

Blurring the Boundaries: Pleasures and Anxieties

The anthropologist Clifford Geertz once described the dominant western notion of personhood as 'a bounded, unique, more or less integrated motivational and cognitive universe, a dynamic center of awareness, emotion, judgement and action, organized into a distinctive whole and set contrastively against other such wholes and against a social and natural background' (quoted in Sampson, 1989: 1). As this suggests, in contemporary western cultures one's body is conceptualized as an organism that as one's 'being-to-the-world' is generally kept and understood as separate from other bodies, even as it is established through interrelationships with others. Like the bourgeois subject that is privileged in western notions of personhood, the ideal body is understood to be separate from others, self-contained, autonomous. This ideal body is regarded as 'civilized', as controlled and regulated, its boundaries from others and from 'the outside world' kept firmly policed. The opposition to the 'civilized' body is the 'grotesque' body, the body that is unable to regulate and control its boundaries or behaviour, the body that allows too much in and out (such as bodily fluids, emotions, food and drink). The notion of the 'civilized' body includes keeping a distance from others, avoiding too much emotional or physical contact, remaining aloof (Shilling, 1993).

This concept of the body/self is relatively recent even in western cultures. In early seventeenth-century Europe the body was not yet conceptualized as discrete, isolated from the network of social relations or the physical world surrounding it. Instead, the body was understood as essentially porous, open to the elements, allowing a constant interchange of the elements between inside and outside the body (Duden, 1991: 11). During the course of that century, however, bodies gradually became privatized and, to some degree, invisible and unacknowledged (albeit constrained by a proliferation of sensibilities around their conduct). The broad context for this reformulation of subjectivity was the transition from feudalism to capitalism and the rise of the modern state (Barker, 1984: 10–12). In that period, the subject became 'self censoring'. By the late eighteenth century, the body had become individualized and viewed as 'owned' by the individual, signifying that person's social position (Elias, 1994). For writers such as Descartes and Hobbes, the body was understood as a machine-like object, amenable to domination by the rational power of reason: 'The most superior minds suffer least from the intrusions of the body' (Gatens, 1988: 60).

Despite this privileging of the individuated, autonomous body/self in contemporary western societies, there remain key points at which the experienced reality of the separate embodied self fades and blurs. Pregnancy is one of those points, as is, potentially, the experience of breastfeeding and holding or embracing intimately another person, sexually or otherwise. Feminist scholars have vividly written about the ways in which their bodies are experienced as diversified through pregnancy and childbirth. For instance, Iris Young (1990) has described the unique experience of pregnant embodiment, involving the simultaneous experience of multiplicity as well as continuing singularity, the blurring between 'inside' and 'outside' the self. She argues that the pregnant woman experiences her body as decentred, split or doubled, as herself and not herself. As such, the boundaries of her body are not as confined as are other bodies: 'The integrity of my body is undermined in pregnancy not only by this externality of the inside, but also by the fact that the boundaries of my body are themselves in flux. In pregnancy I literally do not have a firm sense of where my body ends and the world begins' (Young, 1990: 163). In another essay, Young discusses the fluidity of embodiment that is part of the breasted experience for many women: 'Many women's breasts are much more like a fluid than a solid; in movement, they sway, jiggle, bounce, ripple even when movement is small' (1990: 195). Breasts, she argues, are not simply the 'property' of the woman, but are also thought of as belonging to her sexual partner and her suckling infant. They therefore provide another blurring of one's 'own body' and desires and those of others.

While pregnancy, and to some extent breastfeeding, may represent the apotheosis of this self/not self ontology, the practices of parenthood also potentially embrace a decentring of subjectivity. Just as pregnancy may evoke connections to repressed, preconscious aspects of existence, straddling language and instinct (Young, 1990: 166), the parenting body in close contact with an infant or small child may recall early infantile feelings and desires related to one's own relationship with the care-giving body. This blurring of the boundaries between one's body/self and that of another, however, challenges privileged concepts of the autonomous body/self in western societies.

The tension between wanting to maintain a sense of an individuated self and finding oneself physically or emotionally intertwined with another can be confronting and unsettling. Julia Kristeva (1982) has written vividly of the revulsion inspired by the 'abject' body, the maternal body that has blurred boundaries and therefore cannot easily be categorized as 'self' or 'other', as subject or object. The abject threatens self-identity in its lack of boundaries. For Kristeva, the abject

> is an extremely strong feeling which is at once somatic and symbolic, and which is above all a revolt of the person against an external menace from which one wants to keep oneself at a distance, but of which one has the impression that it is not only an external menace but that it may menace us from inside. So it is a desire for separation, for becoming autonomous and also the feeling of an impossibility of doing so. (1982: 135–6)

Kristeva conceptualizes the unconscious approach to the abject maternal body as a combination of both strong revulsion and strong desire. This body provides food and therefore life, but is also threatening because of its very omnipotence and its ownership of one's own body, having produced and nourished it from its own flesh. In its ambiguity, the maternal body revolts a cultural sense of order, but also fulfils a longing for unification with another.

Women who are mothers may find the blurring of boundaries between themselves and their foetuses/infants as confronting as well as pleasurable.

Women who give birth do not 'naturally' experience attachment to their infants as 'mothers'; some feel 'invaded' by the foetal body when pregnant or fear the constraints and demands of mothering. Urwin (1985) notes, for example, that the interests between infants and mothers may be contradictory, that the mother may have conflicting desires, both conscious and unconscious, when interacting with her infant which enter into the constitution of her role as mother. Women may feel symbolically 'devoured' by their children, or may feel antagonistic towards them as they lose their autonomy and sense of individuated self, or resentful that they become portrayed as mere containers for the foetus or providers of food for the infant (Cosslett, 1994: 126–9; see also Walkerdine and Lucey, 1989; Flax, 1993).

While women may well experience these feelings of ambivalence about their children, they are positioned far more as embodied subjects than are men. It may be argued, therefore, that the blurring of body/self boundaries that may be an outcome of parenthood may be experienced as more confronting by men because it challenges specifically dominant ideals of masculinity. These ideals tend to position the male body/self as far more separate and autonomous than the female/body self. Women are conceptualized as lacking the rigidly defined bodily boundaries that men possess, as having 'leaky' bodies through such activities as menstruation, pregnancy and lactation; 'women's corporeality is inscribed as a mode of seepage', linked with the meanings of uncontrollability, contagion and disorder (Grosz, 1994: 203). Grosz argues that because at this stage in human history only women's bodies have had the potential to experience the duality of bodies/selves that pregnancy, childbirth and lactation provide, 'The relations between immanence and transcendence, between owning and being a body, between subject and object or one subject and another, are not the same for women as for men' (1994: 108). The experiences of having breasts and of pregnancy, childbirth and breastfeeding, and perhaps even the assumption or knowledge of their potentiality, are ways of being for women that simply are not accessible to men. Women, indeed, are understood as far more embodied than men; women are constituted as 'bodies' in ways that men are not.

For example, the pregnant woman who is disadvantaged through her social class or ethnic position is often portrayed in legal situations as 'mere body', a 'life-support system for a foetus' subject to court orders enforcing such procedures as prenatal screening, detention and intrauterine transfusions or surgery, with her own wishes discounted in the interest of the wellbeing of her foetus (Bordo, 1993: 76—7). Other disadvantaged women have been subjected to enforced sterilization because of perceptions of them as unruly bodies, as 'promiscuous breeder[s]' (Bordo, 1993: 79), or have been charged with 'abusing' their foetuses by taking drugs (including alcohol). It is this embodied understanding of women that is the source of much of the cultural negativity that surrounds women. As Bordo notes, if '*the body* is the negative term, and if woman *is* the body, then women *are* that negativity, whatever it may be: distraction from knowledge, seduction away from God, capitulation to sexual desire, violence or aggression, failure of will, even death' (1993: 5, original emphases). Given the common conflation between rationality and bodily and emotional containment of the self, women have therefore been historically understood as less rational and less able to ascribe to the ideals of the autonomous body than have men (Lloyd, 1984; Grosz, 1994).

Grosz (1994: 203) has suggested that men's own fears of loss of boundaries, their hatred of liquidities, are projected onto women in men's attempts to resolve these anxieties. Empirical research would seem to suggest that this is indeed the case. Using documentary evidence, Klaus Theweleit (1987) has written about the fears harboured by soldiers who were members of the German Freikorps in the years immediately following the First World War towards what they saw as the seeping, fluid bodies of women, and their own desires to keep their bodies contained. In response to the potential contamination of both women's bodies and the flood of revolution, the soldiers described themselves as stiffening, closing themselves off to form a discrete entity, holding themselves erect to ward off dissolution and stand above engulfment by fluids (Theweleit, 1987: 244). Women were associated, in the domestic sphere, with activity that engaged with hybrid substances: 'They turned solids into liquids when they cooked; and when they washed clothes and dishes, or took care of babies, they worked with, and in, things that were swampy, mushy' (1987: 409). To participate in such activities was considered unmasculine, as was the generation of such substances by the male's body. For the soldier male, 'Anything that affected his boundaries or orifices – anything that exited, entered, became moist, or flowed – was not only "forbidden", but lethal' (1987: 427). Against this the soldier male struggled to achieve the body as hard, cold machine, differentiated from and violent towards the mass that threatened to swallow him.

Such anxieties also emerged in Hollway's (1984) account of interviews with British men in which they expressed their fear of becoming emotionally 'engulfed', being 'sucked in' or 'getting in deep' in their relationships with women. The men experienced themselves as vulnerable in becoming emotionally close to women, positioned as the maternal 'Other'. At the same time they articulated a great desire for such closeness which was able to invoke the pleasures of contact with the mother they experienced in infancy. Hollway argued that the men typically dealt with this contradiction by unconsciously projecting weakness and emotionality onto women and positioning themselves as stronger and more contained, with fewer needs and anxieties.

These theoretical points are integral for understanding both the pleasures and the conflicts that men may experience as fathers. They suggest that because of the sociocultural meanings attributed to the importance of containment of one's body/self, to maintaining hardness and dryness, and because of the deeply gendered nature of these meanings, for men more than women to blur one's boundaries with another, to become plural and interdependent rather than autonomous (whether it be one's sexual partner or child), is potentially to incite anxieties and fears.

Concluding Comments

In drawing upon Foucauldian perspectives on discourse in conjunction with psychoanalytic theories, we can begin to move towards an understanding of the experiential, affective, embodied nature of fatherhood that may perhaps avoid the essentialism of much contemporary writing on the topic. This combination of theoretical perspectives remains a relatively new approach in inquiries into masculinities and male subjectivity and embodiment. As Jefferson recently commented, 'It is an exciting if barely started project' (1996: 342). Nonetheless, it is making itself increasingly known in the literature on masculinity: see, for example, several of the chapters in Mac an Ghaill (1996).

The implications of taking up these theories for our own work on fatherhood is that we seek to explore the biographical dimensions of becoming a father (a process which we would see as open-ended throughout a man's lifespan) as well as acknowledging the broader sociocultural context in which men are situated. We see these two contexts as inevitably interrelated. As Chodorow argues, an individual becomes a person 'in internal relation with the social world . . . People inevitably incorporate one another; our sociality is built into our psychic structure and there is no easy separation of individual and society or possibility of the individual apart from society' (1989: 149). Hence our decision both to investigate the dominant discourses circulating in integral texts, including the 'expert' and 'popular' literature, and to talk to men themselves about their experiences in a longitudinal project that is designed to focus attention on the shifting nature of taking up the father subject position in the context of individuals' specific and personalized life stories.

2

'Expert' Discourses and the Construction of Fatherhood

A central focus of Foucauldian-influenced research into parenting is identifying the ways in which the state and other agencies, supported by expert knowledge systems such as science, medicine and public health and the social sciences, have sought to measure, monitor and hence regulate the physical and mental characteristics of individuals in the attempt to manage and govern populations. As Rose has noted, 'For a domain to be governable, one not only needs the terms to speak and think about it, one also needs to be able to assess its conditions' (1989: 121). Such assessment requires continual monitoring, the recording of facts and figures, statistical calculation, the production of written reports and graphs and so on. These expert techniques and knowledges may be seen as 'techniques for the disciplining of human difference', serving to 'individualize' humans through processes of classification and calibration and developing norms (Rose, 1989: 123).

Over the past half century, the body of academic literature on parenthood and the family has proliferated. Mothers and fathers, and their children, have been major subjects of empirical research in the medical and social sciences, particularly for developmental psychology. Indeed, these bodies of knowledge have been central to the very constitution of the categories of 'mother', 'father' and 'child', particularly in identifying 'normality' and 'abnormality'. In this chapter, we build upon our discussions of the theoretical approaches to understanding fatherhood in the previous chapter to explore some of the dominant ways in which fathers and fatherhood have been studied and represented in the social and health care sciences. As we have noted, the weight of authority carried by 'expert' knowledges means that they play an integral role in shaping contemporary notions of what fatherhood is and how it should be conducted.

The chapter begins with a historical overview of the ways in which these 'expert' knowledges have gradually colonized the family, serving to measure and monitor, and therefore constitute it in certain ways. We then go on to look at the field of psychology and how it has been used to research fatherhood, followed by an analysis of the family health and welfare literature, applied sociological research and academic writings on masculinity. In conducting this analysis, we are assuming that, as the sites for the production of discourses in themselves, the health and social sciences cannot be isolated as separate from the sociocultural context in which they operate and construct certain types of individuals and social groups as 'problems'. None of the knowledges developed from within these disciplines, therefore, is positioned as the essential 'truth' on the matter of fatherhood. Rather, we seek to identify the dominant discourses emerging in this literature in terms of how they construct the phenomenon of fatherhood.

'Experts' and the Regulation of Parenting

In the 1960s and 1970s there was an 'explosion in the production of social–scientific knowledge. Sociologese and psychologese filtered into every discourse of administration and management' (Henriques et al., 1984: 4). Experts stepped in to measure and monitor individuals in virtually every social setting: the workplace, the school, the bedroom, the street corner and the pub as well as the family. This 'explosion', however, had been building to a crescendo as part of broader social changes emerging in the sixteenth century in Europe. At this time, argues Foucault (1984b, 1991), the modern city-states began to take measures of their populations to fulfil the demands of government. With the rapid growth of populations of the European states in the eighteenth century, accompanied by industrialization and urbanization, these strategies of government became more pressing, bolstered by Enlightenment ideals of rationality and the role of knowledge in human progress. Such knowledge systems as medicine, public health and psychiatry flourished as ways of taking stock of particular sub-groups in the population.

This focus on the monitoring and regulation of populations so as to ensure order and prosperity brought with it the strategy of normalization, or the production of norms based on population measures against which individuals were encouraged to measure themselves and to take steps if they were outside the boundaries of the norm (Miller and Rose, 1993). The child became a central site of normalizing strategies. Where once the reproduction of children centred around kinship systems and the transmission of property, childbearing began to be represented as a set of obligations for bodily care requiring expert advice. Beginning in the eighteenth century, Foucault argued,

> The problem of 'children' (that is, of their number at birth and the relation of birth to mortalities) is now joined by the problem of 'childhood' (that is, of survival to adulthood, the physical and economic conditions for this survival, the necessary and sufficient amount of investment for the period of child development to become useful, in brief the organization of this 'phase' perceived as being both specific and finalized). It is no longer just a matter of producing an optimum number of children, but one of the correct management of this age of life. (1984b: 279)

The 'private' world of the family was charged as the site at which the problem of the child was largely dealt, including the maintenance and development of the child's body (Foucault, 1984b: 280). Parents were expected to devote attention to a whole series of obligations in relation to their children: ensuring they were kept clean, warm, fed, in close proximity, engaged in the proper amount of exercise and properly clothed. The health of the child, in particular, was portrayed as a primary objective to be achieved by parents: 'The rectangle of parents and children must become a sort of homeostasis of health' (Foucault, 1984b: 280). To achieve this end, what Foucault describes as a 'great enterprise of acculturation' was directed by medical professionals at the family in relation to the care of infants and children, including the publication of books and professional journals (1984b: 280).

The nineteenth century was characterized by a plethora of studies into the family and the child carried out primarily in Britain, continental Europe and the United States. By the late nineteenth century, the 'child study movement', influenced by Darwin's evolutionary investigations into child development, became a field of 'scientific' study in Britain for the first time. This movement, which included the formation of Child Study Societies, involved the detailed observation of children, including their weight and height, activities, ideas and stages of growth. It is from this movement that the current interest in psychology in child development has evolved (Walkerdine, 1984: 170–1). In the United States in the closing years of the nineteenth century the National Congress of Mothers was formed, its members comprised of mothers, prominent educators, clergymen and politicians. This group was responsible for publishing a journal called *Child Welfare* and advocating parent–teacher associations, and by 1908 boasted a membership of some 100,000 people. The Federation for Child Study was formed in 1908, and by 1919 was in contact with over 30 other child study groups across that country. It eventually became the Child Study Association of America, producing the magazine *Child Study* and establishing institutes and research stations at universities across the United States (Griswold, 1993: 127).

This increasing focus of attention upon the welfare and body of the child was accompanied by transformations in family organization, involving less participation of the father in the rearing of children and more responsibility placed on the mother. The location of both men's and women's work within the home or its close environs that was characteristic of pre-industrial society meant that men were in a position to engage more actively in child rearing. In early modern Europe, fathers were generally considered as more important than mothers in the caring, raising and education of children, including overseeing wet-nursing and feeding of infants and taking primary responsibility for older children's moral and religious instruction, preparing them for their adult duties. At least until the early decades of the eighteenth century it was the father who was considered to shape the child, to be the 'natural parent' (Gillis, 1995: 6–7). As Gillis (1995: 6) observes, 'Caring had not yet undergone feminization' (see also Stearns, 1991; Griswold, 1993: chapter 2). This emphasis on the father's role was underpinned by assumptions about the rationality of men, their representing culture rather than nature and their ability to bestow order, while women were conceptualized as little more than the passive vessels in which the child grew. Fathers were believed to be superior to mothers in providing such guidance because of their greater reason and their ability to control their emotions (Pleck, 1987).

Changes to family life wrought by industrialization and urbanization from the early 1800s onwards, as well as changing ideas about reproduction, pregnancy and the female body, had the eventual effect of altering parental roles in western countries dramatically. With the movement of paid labour out of the home that was the outcome of industrialization, the dichotomy between the sphere of the home as the domain of women and that of the paid workplace as the domain of men was created. By the mid-nineteenth century, many fathers were absent from the home for much of the day, undertaking paid work. For working-class men, working long hours was essential to support the family, while the demands of the career path meant that middle-class men similarly spent little time at home (Stearns, 1991: Griswold, 1993: chapter 2; Gillis, 1995; Tosh, 1996). Parenthood, including the close supervision and rearing of young children, gradually became the province of mothers rather than fathers. Motherhood began to be represented as the 'essence of a woman's being', while men were marginalized as parents (Gillis, 1995: 16). As one English writer of the time claimed of the mother, 'None can supply her place, none can feel her interest; and as in infancy a mother is the best nurse, so in childhood she is the best guardian and instructress' (Elizabeth Sandford, 1839, quoted in Tosh, 1996: 52). It should be noted, however, that many working-class women did engage in the public sphere through paid work in the eighteenth and nineteenth centuries, thus blurring the boundary between the private and the public sphere (Clark, 1992: 193). Indeed, the notion of the wife and mother as the 'angel of the home' was a middle-class and upper-middle-class ideal rather than being universal.

As a result of this shift in notions of parental responsibility from men to women, since the late eighteenth century mothers in particular have been singled out as primarily responsible for the health and 'normal' development of children. Indeed, women have been portrayed as citizens not through the 'public' activities of political involvement or paid labour, but through the 'private' activities of bearing and raising children (Petersen and Lupton, 1996: chapter 3). By the nineteenth century, the role of the mother had been surrounded and constituted by more and more prescriptions around her behaviour. These prescriptions were supported by the development of scientific knowledges on children's health and development, accompanied by regulatory apparatuses directed at families, such as the child welfare system, social work and family health organizations. Mothers were encouraged to engage in self-surveillance and self-regulation by monitoring their own activities and those of their children and comparing them to 'norms' of behaviour, growth and development that had been instituted by expert discourses (Donzelot, 1979; Foucault, 1984a; Urwin, 1985).

At the turn of the twentieth century, the health and physical fitness of the population had become of great concern for Britain, Europe and Australia, including the rates of birth and infant mortality, the fitness of recruits and the physique of children (Hooper, 1992). This led to the instigation of child welfare and protection reforms, 'since children were the raw material to be safeguarded in the name of national efficiency' (Hooper, 1992: 60). Working-class women in particular were targeted as feckless, requiring the advice of professionals to perform their work as mothers adequately. The establishment of the health visitor system in Britain in the late nineteenth century comprised a formalized means of surveilling working-class women's mothering practices. Women's non-compliance to such laws and regulations were punished through humiliation, fines, jail sentences or loss of child custody (Ross, 1993: 197).

The growing body of expert knowledge on the child, the parent and the family developing at this time was taken up in popular forums. In the early nineteenth century and gaining force by the late twentieth century, such publications as popular child-rearing books and pamphlets began to be published and read in large numbers in countries such as the United States, Britain and Australia, providing a set of norms and values for parents to follow in raising their children 'successfully'. The plethora of material available to advise parents in the United States was such by the mid-nineteenth century that one writer on 'child education' 'complained about "the current of popular treatises on this subject that almost daily issues from the press"' (Philipson, 1981: 61). Magazines such as *Parents Magazine* and *Mother's Assistant* were published in that country from the early nineteenth century onwards, directed at a mass audience of middle-class parents.

From the mid-eighteenth century to the mid-nineteenth century, there was a strong focus on 'religious morality' in child care advice texts, with a focus on preparing children for death and life in the hereafter (Burman, 1994: 51). The nineteenth-century literature on child raising was directed at the inculcation of self-discipline and self-control in children, qualities that became increasingly important in the wake of industrialization and what was considered to be a subsequent breakdown in the regulation of individuals by the family and the community (Philipson, 1981: 67). This literature was mostly written by lay people concerned with explaining the basic caretaking of infants and children. Both fathers and mothers were criticized for not paying enough attention to their children. In *Parents Magazine* in 1842, for example, 'Fathers were criticized for their "paternal neglect," being "eager in the pursuit of business, toil(ing) early and late, and find(ing) no time to fulfil their duties to their children"' (Philipson, 1981: 62).

Women, as mothers, were the particular target of these publications. While fathers were still often included in the American child-rearing literature of the early 1800s, by the middle of that century they were rarely mentioned, as it was assumed that mothers had almost sole daily responsibility for child rearing. Fathers were viewed as the economic providers for the family, absent from the home in fulfilling this duty (Philipson, 1981: 1–17; Stearns, 1991: 4–1). Where once fathers had been deemed the appropriate source of moralizing their children, mothers were now understood to be better equipped for this task, by virtue of their 'innate' qualities of purity, lack of aggression and capacity for love and nurturance (Stearns, 1991: 40).

Medicine and psychology as the authoritative knowledge bases for child care had succeeded religion by the years after the First World War. The strict regulatory strategies for child rearing championed by writers such as Truby

King in the 1930s were followed by a more *laissez-faire* and 'permissive' approach advocated in the 1950s. This latter approach emphasized the importance of maternal flexibility to best meet children's 'needs' and 'natural development' (Burman, 1994: 52–3). Despite these shifts in emphasis, as Burman notes, 'all types of advice laid claim to the moral authority to define the requirements not only for good parenting, but also for what made an appropriate child, albeit often concerned with what the children would become rather than how they fared at the time' (1994: 53).

While the absence of most men from the home in the nineteenth century was accompanied by an increasing emphasis on women as child rearers, some historians have noted a change in assumptions about the behaviour and role of fathers by the end of that century. According to Robert Griswold in his history of fatherhood in the United States, the closing decades of the nineteenth century, at least in that country, were characterized by calls on the part of experts for 'a new conception of masculinity [that] called men to the home and to child rearing' (1993: 88). Middle-class men, in particular, were encouraged to work towards a 'new conception of fatherhood that reflected the values of a therapeutic culture dedicated to growth, personality, and self-realization' (1993: 89). An increased focus on the nurturing and involved father, Griswold argues, was part of a broader move towards the expression of the modern companionate marital couple and family, where love, romance, sexual fulfilment, mutual respect, rights and responsibilities and emotional satisfaction were highly valued (see also Cancian, 1987, on the 'feminization of love' in marital relationships). Tosh (1996) argues that there was a similar emphasis in bourgeois Victorian Britain on fathers taking a strong interest in the moral supervision of their children in addition to providing for them economically. He contends that while there is evidence of a valorizing of the mother's moral role during this time, 'In some ways the Victorian era was one of strengthened paternal moral authority' (1996: 51).

Part of the impetus towards focusing more attention on fatherhood into the early twentieth century was a concern that children, particularly boys, were neglected by their fathers and were becoming 'overly feminized' in the hothouse of the mother-dominated family (Griswold, 1993: 89–90; Tosh, 1996: 55). It was seen to be middle-class fathers' role to ensure that their sons acquired proper manliness as they grew into adulthood (Tosh, 1996: 54). For fathers and their children, 'The emphasis was on mutual companionship, growth, and enrichment: men would learn the joys of nurture, children the joys of fatherly solicitude and good cheer. Friendship and play, not obedience and discipline, would define the ideal paternal relationship with children' (Griswold, 1993: 90). According to Griswold, in the early decades of the twentieth century, the writings of the 'family experts' – including social workers, sociologists, psychologists, home economists and psychiatrists – had begun to support and promote the notion of middle-class fatherhood as therapeutic, a source of self-fulfilment and self-expression. They also identified a transitional process for fathers, or even a 'crisis' of masculinity in relation to fatherhood caused by industrialization, the apparent spread and domination of materialist and individualist values and the accompanying 'shrinkage' of the role played by the father in child rearing and a diminishing in his authority as head of the household.

Into the 1930s, in popular forums such as parenting magazines men were constantly urged to spend more time with their children (Griswold, 1993: 98). Many middle-class men as well as women responded by seeking information about child rearing and child development. One study conducted in the late 1920s found that 91 per cent of mothers and 65 per cent of fathers in the 'professional class' read articles in newspapers and magazines about child care, far more than mothers and fathers in the 'day-labouring class' (Griswold, 1993: 103).

Given the emphasis then placed on the importance of the psychological ties in familial relationships and their relation to individual happiness and maintenance of the social order, bourgeois fathers could now no longer simply act as breadwinners. Rather, they were expected to contribute actively to their children's psychological and emotional development, particularly by fostering their independence and providing an ideal-type masculine 'role model' for both boys and girls (Griswold, 1993: 91–3). The emphasis, therefore, was on the difference between mothers and fathers in their dealings with and influence upon their children. Both were considered important to the child's development, but in different ways. As one 'expert' asserted in a parenting magazine published in the 1930s: 'From the time a father first holds his child in his arms and talks to him [*sic*], the child senses that he is being handled and talked to in a manner different from that of the mother' (quoted in Griswold, 1993: 96).

As this suggests, men as fathers have not been ignored by 'expert' or popular discourses, even though in recent times their positioning as responsible, nurturing fathers may have taken place at a somewhat less intense level than the positioning of women as mothers. In the context of the spread of 'expert' knowledges on child rearing in western countries throughout the late nineteenth and twentieth centuries, both fathers and mothers have been portrayed as requiring professional assistance to carry out their parenting role, and as possibly neglectful if they fail to do so. Nor is the contemporary notion of the 'new' father particularly novel at the end of the twentieth century, despite regular claims to the contrary. It would seem that a century ago, the same types of anxieties and concerns around the need for an involved and nurturing father were articulated in both 'expert' and popular texts, and by fathers themselves, albeit those mainly from a middle-class background. Such men, it seems, were often torn between the expectation that they should support the family economically and be successful in their career, and the expectations of them in relation to participative fatherhood.

Psychological Research

By far the bulk of academic research into fatherhood has been published by psychologists interested in child development. Understanding the role played by developmental psychology in the construction of notions of the ideal-type father is vital to understanding popular ideas about fatherhood, because of the powerful impact that the theories about parenting and child welfare developed by researchers in this field have had outside the academy. This impact has included not only shaping popular knowledges but also modern state interventions into the family (Burman, 1994: 2). Since the middle of the twentieth century it has been assumed that the maternal–child relationship has immense significance for the later psychological and emotional develop-ment of the child. This assumption has often led 'to a psychological determinism and reductionism that argues that what happens in the earliest mother–infant relationship determines the whole of history, society, and cul-ture' (Chodorow, 1989: 89). At the end of the twentieth century, the focus of developmental psychology has shifted from the actions and behaviour of the child to the mother, and more lately the father, serving to regulate and legis-late upon adequate parenting (Burman, 1994: 3–4). The child has remained the primary subject of developmental psychology, in terms of interest directed at its physical, intellectual and moral development, needs and welfare, but the gaze of researchers has moved from investigating the child to investigating the parent.

From the orthodox developmental psychological perspective, the relation-ship that mothers and fathers have with their children is viewed as an individual bond, constituted largely through innate 'instinctive drives' and internal desires and shaped through individual biography and personality development. A dominant belief expounded in the psychological literature since the middle of the century is that mothers should have constant contact with their infants to ensure the infant's 'normal' development. Psychological approaches to parenting have often adopted the ethological or sociobiologi-cal approach based on biological theories of human and primate, mammalian or other animal behaviour. Researchers using this approach have tended to assume that motherhood, in particular, is 'natural' and 'instinctive', 'pro-grammed' by the genes. They have emphasized the important role played by the mother in developing a caring, attentive relationship with her child and meeting her or his biological needs. In these writings, the infant is portrayed as 'close to nature, devoid of the trappings of adult training and (Western) "civilization"' (Burman, 1994: 10).

Writers such as Bowlby (1969) insisted upon the importance of the attach-ment between mother and child in promoting caring behaviour from the mother, protecting the infant from harm and ensuring the development of the child into a 'normal', healthy adult. He took an evolutionary approach, seeing infants as possessing innate signals such as crying and smiling and responses such as sucking which elicited appropriate genetically programmed responses from the mother, ensuring physical closeness. Bowlby and others writing in this vein often drew on primate research involving depriving infant monkeys of their mothers to support their theories about the detrimental effects on human infants of maternal neglect. These biologically based approaches have been used to naturalize the assumption that mothers are the best care-givers for their children and that they, rather than fathers or other family members, should be the ones who take time out from paid employment to care for them. The bonding theory approach became prevalent in the paediatric and obstetric literature in the late 1970s and early 1980s, when textbooks argued that bonding immediately following birth was a 'natural' and 'instinctive' process that was essential in constructing a strong and enduring maternal–infant attachment. This claim was echoed in popular representations of birth in the same period, including those written by proponents of the feminist movement and the natural childbirth lobby, which asserted the importance of bonding as part of the 'good birth' (Crouch and Manderson, 1995: 838).

In such accounts, biology is used as a truth claim, based upon its founding in 'science' and the observation of the behaviour of other primate species. It is accepted, for example, that the 'mother–child' bond, or the strong attachment believed to be characteristic of the maternal–child relationship, is based in fact and in the genes, developed through evolutionary processes as a survival adaptation and enforced through the hormones. The 'bonding' discourse also privileges the mother over the father as the primary care-giver who must establish a bond with the infant as soon as possible after birth. In much of this literature, while it is recognized that other individuals and not only the mother could act as an infant's 'primary carer', writers still tend to insist on the notion that it is better for child development if one person should take on the primary responsibility for the child so that she or he receives adequate attention. Much of this literature has still focused on the mother as primary carer rather than the father, for she is the one who is represented as possessing the hormones that contribute to 'bonding' and 'attachment'. Thus, in an American text entitled *The Nursing Mothers' Companion*, published in 1990, it is argued that 'The nursing mother is thought to produce hormones that promote a physiological bonding between mother and child' (quoted in Crouch and Manderson, 1995: 841). In this writing, therefore, the father has remained a somewhat shadowy figure, an individual who has little to do with meeting the physical and emotional needs of the infant.

Psychologists have, by comparison, undertaken much less research on the nature and development of the paternal–infant relationship. For example, particularly in the 1950s and 1960s, where a major focus of research was attachment and 'bonding' in the maternal–child relationship, very little research was published which addressed attachment between fathers and infants. In the 1940s and 1950s, however, there was a growing interest in the effects of 'father absence', stimulated by the disruptions in family life occasioned by the Second World War, coupled with the supposed pathological effects of 'excessive mothering', on children. The category of the 'war separated child' was constructed as a major problem in expert discourses. Children without fathers were portrayed as being 'at risk' of abnormal physical, sex-role, intellectual and moral development, including lack of independence, passivity, eating and sleeping problems, decreased sociability and so on. There was a particular concern for boys without fathers, who were seen as lacking a 'positive role model' after which they could model their own masculinity. Such boys, it was suggested, were vulnerable to 'abnormal' sexual development, and liable to become homosexual or delinquent (Griswold, 1993: chapter 8).

Since the late 1970s, the number of psychological studies devoted to researching the father–child relationship have grown, although research on motherhood still far outnumbers studies on fatherhood. (In a search of a computer database of psychological articles published between 1984 and late 1996, carried out for the purposes of researching this book, over four times as many articles about mothers as those about fathers were listed.) This type of research burgeoned among American researchers in the 1970s in particular, with study after study conducted into the father–child relationship. The perspective Fein (1978) identified as the 'emergent' perspective, also described by others as 'androgynous fatherhood' or the 'new' father model of fatherhood, was constituted during the 1970s. This perspective incorporates the notion that fathers are psychologically able to participate actively in a range of child care activities and that it is important for both fathers and children that they attempt to do so. As we have shown, however, rather than being a 'new' model, this archetype revisits concerns about fathers' level of interaction and involvement with their children that has emerged at other points in the last few centuries in western societies.

This emphasis on the participative ideal of fatherhood has remained dominant into the late 1990s. Taking this ideal to its most extreme, some psychologists have argued that 'To develop a new kind of father, we must encourage a new kind of man . . . we need to ask, "Why can't a man be more like a woman?"' (Garbarino, 1993: 53). Garbarino goes on to argue that in endeavouring to adopt more 'feminine' qualities, men should become less aggressive, less obsessed with dominating and more aware of their potential for nurturing, humility and patience, so as 'to create the fathers children and society need'. Most writers in this field, however, do not assert that mothers and fathers are capable of exactly the same kinds of response to children. Rather, it is contended that men as fathers should be considered more capable of nurturing than was previously thought, and are equally important to their children's care as are mothers.

Most of the research undertaken by developmental psychologists is very limited in the insights it offers into the ontology of fatherhood for fathers themselves, preoccupied as these researchers are by the ways in which aspects of the child's personality are supposedly influenced by fathers. Empirical studies have set out to measure the effects fathers or their absence have on such aspects as their children's development of a 'sex role' and their moral and intellectual development, focusing on such 'outcome' factors as children's tendency towards delinquency, their intelligence, their school performance, their establishment of peer relationships, self-esteem and self-control (see, for example, the chapters in Lamb, 1981). This research parallels the plethora of psychological studies undertaken into maternal–infant attachment and interaction behaviours, which reiterated the importance of the 'sensitive' mother who was highly responsive to her child's needs (Walkerdine and Lucey, 1989: chapter 3; Burman, 1994). The research that has been published on the paternal–infant relationship has generally replicated maternal–infant research to investigate the interaction of fathers with their infants. A large number of researchers have set out to discern and emphasize different 'interactional styles' in parenting on the part of the father and mother (often in the context of a laboratory so as to have a 'controlled' setting in which to observe fathers and their children). This research includes observing such behaviours on the part of fathers as smiling, looking, talking to and touching the child, and asking fathers about their patterns of time spent with the infant, their feelings towards their children and their thoughts about their children's development (see, for example, Smith and Daglish, 1977; Chibucos and Kail, 1981; Landerholm and Scriven, 1981; Levy-Shiff and Israelashvili, 1988; Cox et al., 1992).

Developmental psychological research has generally concluded that the quality of early father–infant interactions (usually assessed by such indices as 'sensitivity' and 'playfulness' of the father and the intensity of the infant's response to the father) is linked with later father–child attachment. It therefore echoes the findings of maternal–child attachment research. For instance, one researcher argues that 'it is no accident that most fathers as well as mothers express a great attraction to their newborn infants; it is necessary for the survival of a species in which the newborn is totally dependent on others' (Jones, 1985: 92). Phrases such as 'arousal levels' are used to describe both mothers' and fathers' responses to the 'stimuli' such as cries emitted by their infants (for example, Boukydis and Burgess, 1982). While most writers acknowledge that mothers still tend to take the primary responsibility for child care, some have suggested that 'the father can fulfil attachment roles often accorded solely to mothers' (Chibucos and Kail, 1981: 94).

In this research, fathers are said to provide more 'unpredictable, arrhythmic and physical stimulation' to their infants, while mothers' behaviour is more 'rhythmic and containing' (Lamb et al., 1982: 215). Alternatively, it is asserted that fathers' interactions are more 'playful' and 'rough-and-tumble' compared with mothers' 'caretaking' and 'controlling' interactions (for example, Lamb, 1976), or that mothers demonstrate affection such as kissing and smiling more than fathers (for example, Parke and Sawin, 1980). Fathers, it is argued, teach children self-control and how to relate to others' social interactions such as teasing and horseplay, compared to what is described as mothers' 'overly protective' responses. As such, this research tends to construct a model of complementarity that supports traditional gender roles, where the father is positioned as providing certain qualities for the child that complement rather than emulate those provided by the mother (Burman, 1994: 96). The 'masculine', rough-and-tumble father is counterpoised against the 'feminine', nurturing mother. The reliance on 'sex role' models of behaviour serves to present a fixed notion of masculinity and femininity, as 'a kind of laundry list of behavioural characteristics' in which masculine and feminine qualities are portrayed as mutually exclusive dichotomies, viewed as tied to biology and as a set of fixed attributes (Kimmel, 1987: 12; Brittan, 1989: chapter 2).

There is very little psychological research that seeks to demonstrate the ways that men and women have similar experiences of parenting. Although the research undertaken by development psychologists observing fathers' and mothers' interactions with their infants often acknowledges that they are more alike than different in their behaviour, the findings and conclusions are still written around the differences that were observed. In this literature, therefore, a preoccupation remains with emphasizing gender difference in parenting. Often other important aspects of subjectivity related to parenting, such as social class, age, marital status or ethnicity, are obscured by this focus on gender.

Other research, emerging from social psychology, has directed a little more attention at fathers themselves, but generally from an extremely individualistic perspective (one important exception is Lewis, 1986). The 'transition to fatherhood' and 'father role' literature, for example, tends to focus on personality-based differences in men's adaptations to becoming a father and their relationships with other family members. This body of literature conducts empirical research using a battery of scales to measure men's personality traits such as sex role identification, mood, satisfaction and so on (for example, Russell, 1978; Crouter et al., 1987). Again, the emphasis is upon the individual characteristics of the father, described in one article as his 'personal psychological resources' (Levy-Shiff and Israelashvili, 1988: 434); for instance, the level of the father's self-esteem, sensitivity and maturity. In this literature, models of behaviour such as 'internal control beliefs' are frequently used to assess the degree to which fathers can cope with stress. Such contentions are made as: 'It can be assumed that fathers who perceive fatherhood positively and value it as a fulfilling experience and a positive contribution to themselves will be highly motivated and more involved with their infants' (Levy-Shiff and Israelashvili, 1988: 435).

The findings of such research tend towards highly detailed accounts of measures of men's orientations to fatherhood and their marital relationships, with fathers' behaviour with their children portrayed as the dependent variable. The assumptions made about cause and effect in such research are somewhat dubious. It is assumed, for example, that men who register highly on the 'masculine' sex role scale and then display a relative lack of interest in interacting with their children do so because they are more 'masculine' in their role orientation than other men. The findings tend also to be rather banal, with sophisticated statistical analysis used to show 'scientifically', for example, that parents suffer more fatigue after the birth of their first child than before, or that parents who believe that their marriage is a good one seem to suffer less 'strain' when they become parents. The notion of the pre-existing subject who after becoming a father finds himself so distorted and stressed that he can no longer identify his 'real self' and must painfully transform into a 'new self' is dominant in this literature. Individuals are portrayed as taking on roles, such as the 'sex role' or the 'father role', which are merged with their sense of self. This is a fixed, static understanding of subjectivity that tends not to acknowledge the highly contextual nature in which fatherhood is experienced and practised.

The same criticisms that have been made of similar research into motherhood (Woollett and Phoenix, 1991; Burman, 1994) can also be directed at the fatherhood research. It is typically assumed in this literature either that fathering is a 'simple variety of mothering' or that it is complementary to mothering, with little attempt to develop new theoretical and methodological paradigms to explore the ontology of men's experience of fatherhood (Burman, 1994: 97). Such research confines the experience of fatherhood to an individualized, largely asocial context, with little recognition of the 'external world' and relationships beyond the mother–father–infant triad. Little awareness is demonstrated that many parents have more than one child. Further, it is generally assumed that families fit the model of the nuclear family, with the father taking the main responsibility for supporting the family economically and the mother providing most of the child care. While the 'social context' is occasionally acknowledged in this literature, this generally relates to such factors as the nature of the father's marital relationship, his orientation towards his career or his relationship with his own father. Under the rubric of 'social context' there is also a body of psychological research that is directed at identifying the ways in which fathers use 'social networks', or contacts with family members and friends, in seeking advice or support from others (for example, Riley and Cochran, 1985). 'Cultural context' tends to be glossed as issues relating to ethnicity.

This literature therefore tends to position 'the father' as a universal category. It is generally silent on questions of power and knowledge, limited as it is to the father as individual or as member of a particular family 'system' or social network. Just as developmental psychology studies of motherhood tend to represent mothers as 'socializers', carers and providers of stimulating environments for children, rather than as 'having an existence of their own' (Woollett and Phoenix, 1991: 28), so too, similar studies of fatherhood tend to consider fathers as influences, both positive and negative, on their children rather than seeking to explore the men's own perspectives independent of their children's 'needs'. The 'children need their fathers' discourse is reproduced as a taken-for-granted fact, with little interrogation of the political or moral assumptions that underlie this 'fact' (Brittan, 1989: 33–4). Few researchers drawing upon conventional psychology have used indepth interviews with fathers themselves to explore their experiences, preferring to adopt laboratory-based observations of behaviour, quantitative methods and statistical analysis.

The Family Health and Welfare Literature

Developmental and social psychological research has been particularly influential in the family health and welfare literature. Because of this, and because the dominant purpose of this literature is to position 'the family' as an object of professional examination and assistance, many academic publications on fatherhood oriented towards professionals in these fields typically portray fatherhood as an overwhelmingly problematic experience, thus requiring the close attention and help of professionals. The writers tend to apply their findings to explore implications for specific groups of fathers who are deemed to be particularly 'problematic', identified by Robinson and Barret (1986) as single, widowed, divorced or adoptive fathers, stepfathers, gay fathers, teenage fathers and fathers of disabled children.

Research into fatherhood in the nursing and family health literature has predominantly focused on the early stages of fatherhood, taking up many of the concerns and methods of developmental psychology. Nursing research has been directed at such issues as father–infant attachment (Bowen and Miller, 1980; Mercer and Ferketich, 1990), fathers' involvement in the care of their infants (Rustia and Abbott, 1993; Tiedje and Darling-Fisher, 1993), their sensitivity to infant cues (Graham, 1993), men's health status and behaviour during their partner's pregnancy and early fatherhood (Ferketich and Mercer, 1989; Hyssala et al., 1992), the influences of fathers' attitudes about breastfeeding on their female partner's decision to breastfeed (Littman et al., 1994) and the early experiences of new fathers in the context of the 'transition to parenthood' (Jordan, 1990; Henderson and Brouse, 1991).

Like the psychological literature, these texts tend to represent fatherhood as a potentially pathological experience replete with upheavals and the need for major adjustments. Such terms as 'stress', 'strain', 'role transition' and 'psychological disruption' are frequently used in the literature to describe men's experiences of becoming fathers (see, for example, the chapters published in Berman and Pedersen, 1987). Here again, the notion that the prior self must undergo a painful transformation is dominant. Cowan and Cowan (1987: 165) write, for instance, that in the 'transition to parenthood', 'each partner engages in an intrapersonal struggle as he or she attempts to juggle new, competing demands from various aspects of self'. Some research has focused on the stress that men experience as fathers, or fatherhood as a 'stressful life event', related to their lack of readiness for the role, their perceived lack of competence as fathers, a decline in marital quality, demands made of them by their partner, their increased participation in child care accompanying the entry of their partner into the workforce and 'role dissatisfaction' or 'confusion' as a father (for example, McBride, 1989; Terry, 1991; Terry et al., 1991).

One article on expectant and new fatherhood published in a nursing journal, for example, describes men in this situation as 'grappling with the reality of the pregnancy and the child', 'struggling for recognition as a parent', feeling 'excluded from the childbearing experience', lacking models of behaviour and 'labouring for relevance' as a father (Jordan, 1990). Another article refers to the 'acute crisis' or 'emotional disequilibrium' experienced by both men and women during the 'high risk perinatal period' (Brown, 1986). So too, psychiatric accounts of fatherhood often dwell on the feelings of hatred, rage, helplessness, jealousy and so on that men are said to experience during their partner's pregnancy and labour and in early fatherhood. As one author put it, the new father 'is faced with a developmental crisis dealing with intrapsychic conflict' and must 'work through shifts in his dependency needs, feelings of envy, and competitiveness strivings . . . He may experience dislocation, denial, or hostility, distancing himself from the mother/infant dyad psychologically or physically' (Hyman, 1995: 263).

A typical focus in such research, even when it uses more sociological approaches, is upon such phenomena as 'role strain'. For example, Hall (1994) interviewed 10 Canadian fathers in dual-earner families on two occasions; once soon after the birth of their first child, and again approximately a year later. Her comments focus on the difficulties of fatherhood in the context of competing objectives –– work and time with the family. The fathers were said to have 'unmet needs' that were seen to contribute to 'role strain'. They were reported as finding fatherhood demanding, tiring and difficult, and as imposing limitations on their capacity for paid work and leisure activities. The men felt pressure to engage as 'involved' fathers, both from their partners and from society in general. The implications for nursing, argues Hall, is that individual men should be assisted to define 'involved fatherhood' in relation to their own family contexts and, if they wish, to improve their skills as nurturing fathers and to convey their own needs to their partners. As these comments suggest, the difficulties of fatherhood often tend to be represented in this literature as individualistic problems that require individual solutions, often assisted by the appropriate 'experts'.

The articles published in medical and public health journals and books mentioning fathers (again, there are far fewer of these articles than those discussing mothers) frequently address issues of how fathers' education level, socioeconomic status and personal behaviour may adversely affect their children's health, including such activities as smoking, drinking alcohol and their exposure to carcinogens through occupational activities (for example, Hoglund et al., 1992; Schnitzer et al., 1995). The effects of 'paternal deprivation', or fathers' absence or lack of interest in their children, is also a favourite topic, particularly in relation to boys, as is the issue of incest and child abuse perpetuated by fathers. Other articles address how fathers adjust to the illness, death or disability of their children, and the social or psychological problems or mental illness (described in one article as 'the psychosis of fatherhood') that may accompany the experience of fatherhood, particularly for such 'problem' fathers as 'teen fathers' (for example, Benvenuti et al., 1995; Dearden et al., 1995). One recent study (Kurki et al., 1995) even set about measuring the heartbeat of fathers while they were watching their child being born, to determine the level of stress upon the men's cardiovascular system!

A recent focus, drawing on the 'fatherless family' debate (described in the Introduction), has been to investigate the involvement that 'non-resident' fathers have with their older children. Reprising the concern in the post-World War 2 psychological literature about 'father absence', researchers addressing this topic argue that such fathers often have very little interaction with their children and that the children's wellbeing is subsequently negatively affected (Marsiglio, 1993: 491–4). Here again there is a particular concern about the effect that paternal absence may have upon male children: 'The degree of pain and the wounded cry of fatherless young males have only recently been recognized. These boys, desperately awaiting their father's return, finally turn in rage toward other male support systems' (Shapiro et al., 1995: 7). Girls are also believed to suffer from absent fathers, if to a somewhat lesser extent, particularly in relation to fathers 'validating' their daughters' femininity and thus enhancing their self-esteem. As three male psychologists recently argued, women who have been deprived of a paternal presence seek 'inferior' men for their partners and thus are doomed to experience a continuing lack of fulfilment and dissatisfaction with their partners (Shapiro et al., 1995: 8).

The father identified as 'normal' or 'unproblematic' tends to be absent or largely ignored in this body of literature. Not only is fatherhood represented as replete with difficulties and strains for the father himself, but fathers are portrayed primarily as potentially pathogenic variables in relation to their children's health and psychological status. Men are positioned as requiring much in the way of expert help in terms of preparing themselves for fatherhood, getting through pregnancy and birth unscathed. Fatherhood, therefore, is represented as replete with traps for the unprepared and unwary, a profoundly difficult and demanding and potentially emotionally disturbing experience and even a health risk. The primary intention of such literature is to ensure that men conform to the expectations of 'appropriate' fatherhood as they are designated by experts. The focus on the need to counsel men, to allow them to express their feelings, that is evident in this literature is typical of the contemporary importance placed on self-expression and therapeutic practice (Rose, 1996).

Most writers in contemporary family health continue to insist that parenting is profoundly gendered and that the mother and father can each offer different qualities to their children. Little is made of the possibility that men tend to have less opportunity to engage with their children as infants and that this, more than inherent gender differences in parenting, may be a major source of perceived differing styles. Shapiro et al. assert, for instance, that 'A father cannot, nor should he be asked to, parent as his wife does and conversely, a mother should not be expected to parent as her husband does. Children flourish best with *two* parents, each bringing their unique and complementary styles of parenting' (1995: 9). Despite the vehemence of this statement, the authors provide no evidence in its support. In a later chapter in this same book, a male psychiatrist contends that 'Obviously, fathers are not mothers – they never will be and shouldn't try . . . the mother-mimic tactic soon falters. It feels wrong at all levels, because it is. The child does not expect it, and the father cannot do it' (Pruett, 1995: 36). Pruett emphasizes throughout his discussion that fathers respond differently from mothers to their children. He also describes research, however, that shows that as young children boys demonstrate similar nurturing behaviour to girls and that men have demonstrated that they are as capable as women in nurturing and child care, if given the opportunity. Pruett goes on to point to the lack of interaction men have with young children as a possible reason for differing parental styles. Despite this, he fails to recognize the contradictions in his insistence that men cannot (and indeed should not) act in a 'mothering' capacity.

This type of research is generally carried out with the intention of using the findings to develop new or better strategies or 'interventions' for infant care, parenting skills and the support of families. In doing so, it provides a highly normative perspective on fatherhood by advocating appropriate behaviours in men and identifying those who fail to fit the ideal of the involved father. In research articles and books written for nurses, other health care workers and family therapists and counsellors, these professionals are often exhorted to encourage men to participate actively in child care activities. Hanson and Bozett (1987) assert, for example, that in the interests of promoting 'quality fatherhood', nurses and other health care professionals should encourage men to participate in antenatal classes with their female partner, to be present at the birth of their child and to attend health clinics with their partners and children and classes on child growth and development. They argue that if men engaged in such activities they would increase their knowledge and willingness to engage in child care and improve their position as 'role model' for their children.

Despite this primarily individualistic focus that is evident in much of the family health and welfare literature, some writers have begun to move towards an understanding of the social and cultural dimensions of fatherhood. Recent writing in gender studies has made some impact upon the interpretations of both motherhood and fatherhood as sociocultural constructions. In a review of contemporary scholarship on fatherhood, Marsiglio (1993), for instance, makes reference to the 'cultural images of fatherhood'. Bozett and Hanson's edited book *Fatherhood and Families in Cultural Context* (1991) represents one extended attempt to address the cultural aspects of fatherhood. The contributors, from a range of disciplines, explore such aspects as historical perspectives on fatherhood, different ethnic cultures, legal issues for fathers in minority cultures, social class, religion, the experience of fatherhood for urban versus rural men, organizational culture and family cultures. This book is a step towards a recognition that fatherhood is a cultural construct that shifts and changes, that is multiple and contextual. Comparing modes and ideals around fatherhood historically, or across ethnic cultures, can be enlightening in demonstrating the contingent nature of fatherhood and challenging taken-for-granted assumptions about what fatherhood is or should be. Nonetheless, 'culture' still tends to be represented in the chapters as an external influence, shaped predominantly via social structures such as the family, education, ethnicity, economic and workplace issues and so on. Further, there is no chapter that addresses specifically the issue of fatherhood as a cultural construct for the dominant western culture, and none of the chapters explores the role of language, discourse and representation in the cultural construction of fatherhood.

Sociological Research

Sociologists have displayed comparatively much less interest than have psychologists in either motherhood or fatherhood. Until very recently they have demonstrated a general orientation towards more 'weighty' topics such as labour relations and political theory. Sociologists have frequently been accused of neglecting aspects of human society that focus attention on such 'private' and 'banal' matters as marriage, the family, the body and the emotions, and demonstrating a lack of interest in everyday routine activities such as parenting, child care and housework. Few sociologists until the emergence of the second-wave feminist movement were interested in such activities because of their link to women and their menial, unpaid and largely taken-for-granted nature (Oakley, 1974). In the early 1970s, one sociologist dolefully drew attention to the low reputation of the sociology of the family among sociologists: 'Many see it as an academic deadend which contributes little or nothing of importance to the discipline as a whole; as concentrating on trivial and value-laden problems of more concern to journalism or social work' (Anderson, 1971a: 8). More than two decades later, others are still making the same point: 'sociologists have tended to overlook the potential of family study not just as a site for the *application* of sociological theory, but as a site for the *development* of such theory' (Ribbens, 1994: 14; original emphases).

Nonetheless, there was a burst of interest in the sociology of parenting and the family in the 1970s and 1980s in response to issues raised by second-wave feminism and the mass movement of women with young children into the paid workforce. Much research tended to focus on the ways that couples negotiated domestic and child care responsibilities in relation to their paid labour. Sociological research on parenting and the family has addressed such topics as motherhood and fatherhood as learned social roles; the division of domestic labour between women and men in relation to parenting; the social aspects of the transition to parenthood; the impact of parenthood on relationships between marital partners; employment issues for parents; the experiences of divorced or single mothers and fathers and the effects of such issues on parents' relationships with their children. There are far more sociological studies published on motherhood, particularly emerging from feminist perspectives, than exist on fatherhood. We noted above that a search of psychological articles revealed that those on motherhood outnumbered those on fatherhood by over four to one. This discrepancy was even more marked for sociological articles published between 1974 and late 1996 – the sociological database we searched turned up 13 times more articles discussing mothers than those dealing with fathers.

In the 1950s and 1960s, most sociological research directed at parenting and the family explored such issues as kin networks, family 'systems' and conjugal roles from a rather conservative perspective (see, for example, the chapters in Anderson, 1971b). Early sociological writing on parenting and the family was undertaken by the well-known functional structuralist, Talcott Parsons and his co-workers. As the term implies, the functional structuralist approach is interested in the functions that individuals play as part of the working of a society, and how they are socialized into taking up responsibilities and duties as members of the society. Applied to parenthood, this perspective viewed men and women as having defined roles as fathers and mothers related to their gender-differentiated capacities and functions. Parsons put forward the view that mothers and fathers have quite different but equally important roles to play in the nuclear family in western societies. He argued that while the mother mainly performed an expressive or emotive function in caring for her children, the father performed a primarily instrumental function, in terms of engaging in paid work to support the family. Parsons went on to argue that this division of labour itself within an 'isolated' rather than extended family unit functioned in a wider sense to support the needs of the capitalist economic system, including the need for geographical and social mobility and the continuing productive performance of male workers (Parsons and Bales, 1955; Parsons, 1964).

The functionalist approach has been strongly criticized for its overly consensual nature, its ignoring of power differentials and its unproblematic replication of gender stereotypes. Like much developmental psychological research, proponents of this perspective have focused on how men and women's behaviours in relation to parenting are different and complementary, adhering to a conceptualizing of parenting that sees it as related to specific 'sex roles'. As is the case with all academic writings, the work of Parsons and his colleagues in some ways articulates the discourses that are dominant within their own social context (the United States in the 1950s and 1960s), including an emphasis on the importance of women staying in the home to best fulfil their responsibilities as mothers.

Later sociological research, itself influenced by broader social changes (as well as contributing to these changes), has been far more critical of supporting the division of labour between women and men in parenting. The critical structuralist perspective, emerging from Marxist and feminist critiques of social structures and social inequality, has been predominant in exploring the macro-structures shaping family relationships and parenting styles. This perspective has had a particular focus on how the economic system and the labour market, in conjunction with patriarchy, have influenced the way that motherhood and fatherhood are understood and experienced. Rather than supporting functionalist assertions as to the fit between the family unit and the industrialist economic system, critical structuralists have sought to draw attention to the conflicts, inequalities and social costs produced through the competing demands of the family and paid labour.

Like the contemporary developmental psychological literature, most contemporary sociological writers commentating on social policy and family issues call for men to have increased participation with their children. The major reason usually given is the need to protect children against the supposed developmental ill-effects of 'father absence'. Unlike much writing in psychology, however, social policy texts also identify the economic disadvantages suffered by an increasing number of 'mother-only' families, where 'father absence' caused primarily by divorced or separated fathers not providing adequate child support means a reduced income for the family (the so-called 'deadbeat dads' or 'feckless fathers').

Feminism has been particularly influential in these types of analyses, seeking to draw attention to the effects on women. Many feminists have been critical of men's participation in domestic life. They have argued that women's social and economic inequality and their general alienation and unhappiness are perpetuated by men's reluctance to engage in household work and take equal or greater responsibility for child care, and the patriarchal expectations that ideal femininity is equated with marriage and motherhood. In addition, feminist critics have addressed structural factors relating to the organization of work, calling for the better provision of child care and parental leave to support women who choose to engage in paid labour at the same time as mothering. Since the early 1970s, sociological research has focused on the problems and conflicts in parenting around notions of gender equity, adopting a liberal humanist approach and often using the term 'parenthood' to replace the terms 'motherhood' and 'fatherhood' in the attempt to move towards men's equal participation in child care. Child care and other parenting tasks, therefore, are routinely depicted in critical structuralist writing both as reproducing and reflecting gender inequalities and entrenching women's subordinate position to men.

Other feminists, sometimes described as 'difference theorists', responded to the critique of the 'myth of motherhood' by arguing that, rather than women giving up their roles as mothers, the values attributed to motherhood should be supported and promoted. They asserted that many women, feminists included, make a considered decision to be mothers and derive satisfactions as well as frustrations from motherhood. Such 'feminine' attributes as nurturing and sensitivity to others' needs, these feminists contended, should be reassessed and given far greater value than has previously been the case (see, for example, Gilligan and Rogers, 1993; Jordan, 1993; Surrey, 1993). They have called for a 'new relational theory of self' (Jordan, 1993: 138) that recognizes the contextual and intersubjective nature of human experience and privileges mutuality and empathy, pointing in particular to the ways in which women as mothers experience this relatedness with their children. The problematic for this feminist critique, therefore, is not to work towards 'freeing' women from the duties of motherhood but rather to represent motherhood as being just as important as paid work in economic production, if not more so. They in turn have been criticized for promoting certain values and perspectives as 'feminine' rather than 'masculine', thereby perpetuating social and economic inequality between women and men, keeping women in the home as wives and mothers, rather than working towards a society in which both men and women are expected to share in child care and other domestic tasks.

Many feminist academics continue to take an extremely critical approach towards men as fathers. In relation to fatherhood, some feminists have critiqued the figure of power and authority represented by the father. They have sought to demonstrate that the father figure both supports and reproduces patterns of the oppression of women and their subordination to men in embodying wider male authority and supremacy within the family context. Pollack and Sutton, for example, interpret the trend towards men participating in childbirth as an assertion of male dominance over what should remain a female domain: 'Their presence is not a simple expression of support for women who are giving birth, but an assertion of men's rights' (1985: 596). So too, they contend, encouraging men to participate more in child care simply reproduces gender stereotypes and subsequent inequalities, for fathers treat their sons differently from their daughters. They assert that the vast majority of research into fatherhood neither challenges the right of men to be fathers nor addresses the question of patriarchal power embodied by the father. Rather, it is directed at supporting men in their experience of fatherhood. Curiously, Pollack and Sutton do not acknowledge the feminist arguments for encouraging men to be present at birth and to participate more fully in child care, preferring to assert that attempts to do so are 'apolitical', glossing over political relations (1985: 598). They imply that it would be most beneficial for women if they were to bring up their children alone, without any participation of male partners.

Sociological research has found that despite the growing influence of feminism in the 1970s there seems little evidence that men were embracing a more participative model of fatherhood. Even into the 1980s, while more men appeared to articulate and support the ideals of 'new' fatherhood, little change was apparent. Structural features are clearly important in limiting men's participation in parenting. For example, Horna and Lupri (1987) examined fathers' participation in work, family life and leisure in Canada. Their study found that the vast majority of fathers, particularly those with very young children, participated in the main provider role, with many of them working longer hours than childless men or men with older children. Only 50 per cent of fathers with young children and fewer than 30 per cent of fathers with older children in their sample said that they participated in child care often. Horna and Lupri conclude from their data: 'clearly it is seldom the father who puts the children to bed, tells them what chores to do at home, helps them with their schoolwork, teaches them work skills, or disciplines them' (1987: 70). They point to the competing obligations fathers experience between spending time with their children and supporting the family economically. It is still expected that men with young children should work full-time rather than part-time, and should value their careers over domestic duties, whereas the reverse is true for women with young children. Horna and Lupri's call for greater flexibility in attitudes towards work and leave provision is repeated in many critical analyses of fatherhood (for example, Moss and Brannen, 1987; Hochschild, 1989).

While men's lack of participation in child care continues to be documented in study after study focusing on structural aspects, little light is thrown upon reasons other than economic or gender roles for the continued quite marked division of labour in relation to parenting. The questions about why it is that men and women continue to participate in this division of labour and the subsequent implications for their relationship and their subjectivity are only partly answered through such research. Proponents of the phenomenological approach have criticized structuralism for its implicit assumption that family members easily identify and adopt clearly defined norms when they take up their roles as father, as mother, as child, as grandparent and so on (Backett, 1982: 3). They argue that this process is more problematic, that roles are more fluid and open to interpretation and change than structuralism allows. Inquiries adopting a phenomenological or symbolic interactionist methodological approach move from the macro to the micro dimensions of fatherhood. Such approaches are primarily interested in the meanings and features of everyday life, the 'lived experience' of fatherhood, seeing fathers' interactions and negotiations with others, including their partners, children and other family members, as central to individuals' construction of the meanings of fatherhood. They therefore potentially go some way in understanding and theorizing the ontology and sociocultural meanings of fatherhood.

Within the range of broadly phenomenological research about fatherhood, the ways that the empirical data gathered from interviews are theorized varies markedly. Some research is largely descriptive, mostly reporting the interview data with little attempt to place the interviewees' remarks into a wider theoretical context. Others have more overtly critical purposes, incorporating an interest in power relations and the social structural aspects shaping men's experiences of fatherhood, often with feminist concerns. More recently, some researchers have begun to respond to poststructuralist theoretical perspectives, incorporating notions of discourse and subjectivity into a phenomenological approach.

One example of this type of research is a study conducted by Brannen and Moss (1987) who interviewed men and women in two-parent households in the Greater London area. All the women had returned to full-time paid work within nine months of the birth of their first child. As with most sociological research into this area, Brannen and Moss found that the women tended to have primary responsibility for organizing child care and continued to perform most of the household and child care tasks. They move beyond this finding, however, to examine the discursive constructions underlying this familiar division of labour. Brannen and Moss noted that the women's decision to return to work was often discursively described as 'their choice'. Women tend to subscribe to the notion of the 'good' mother as one who does not leave her children when they are young. Most women did not articulate strong criticisms of the failure of their partners to engage in household and child care activities. Brannen and Moss argue that it was affective support, intimacy, romantic love and a companionate marriage that women said they valued above the sharing of domestic labour, even though they may have espoused the ideal of 'equality' in domestic arrangements. There is, therefore, a combination of assumptions and discourses around the notion of the 'good' father and mother, and the 'good' marriage, interlinked with material issues, each of which, while not overtly linked, work to reinforce the other.

As this research suggests, women are not passively shaped by 'patriarchal' sociocultural norms and meanings. Rather, they actively participate in the reproduction of these norms and meanings for their own ends, as well as challenging them. This point is take up by Doucet (1995), who suggests that much of the sociological literature tends to assume that women who choose to opt out of paid employment to engage in mothering are suffering from the 'false consciousness' of the ideology of motherhood. She contends that gender differences are automatically assumed to lead to gender-based disadvantages. Writers tend to devalue household and child care activities as boring, repetitive and unfulfilling, thus reproducing assumptions around the greater importance of paid work for individual fulfilment derived from 'public life' settings. Doucet argues that this approach tends to ignore the complexities, intimacies and rhythms of routine household life, and the importance that caring activities have for most mothers.

The findings of recent empirical research have tended to support the contention that motherhood, as both an embodied and a 'thinking' practice, differs significantly from fatherhood. Drawing on her research involving interviews with Canadian parents, Martha McMahon (1995) argues that the experience of being a mother is typically conceptualized by women as achieving a feminized adult sense of self. She contends that because caring, responsibility, love and affection towards others are understood culturally as more feminine than masculine capacities, the women she interviewed tended to interpret the strong loving feelings they felt towards their children as evidence of femininity. McMahon argues that even those women who work full-time tend to experience motherhood as being the most responsible parent, while fathers are seen to contribute but have a lesser role: 'Men and women may both be parents, I was told, but they *act*, *think*, and *feel* differently as parents' (1995: 234; original emphases). Her female interviewees thought of motherhood as involving far greater participation in domestic work and child care duties, in feelings of responsibility and in a different or special awareness of their children compared with fatherhood:

> Men could potentially learn to *behave* like involved parents, but they didn't *feel* or *think* like mothers, they concluded . . . Indicative of their male partners' different consciousness, several women pointed out, was their ability to compartmentalize and segregate parts of themselves and their lives in ways women felt they did not, or could not, do. (McMahon, 1995: 251; original emphases)

Interestingly enough, a lesbian interviewed for the study who was the biological mother of a child whom she and her partner had planned together pointed to the difference she noted between her own heightened awareness of and alertness to the child's needs compared with that of her partner (McMahon, 1995: 252).

Another interview study involved 50 couples living in upstate New York who had had a child in the previous year (Walzer, 1996). The researcher identified a strong tendency for women to engage in what she calls 'the invisible mental labour' involved in caring for an infant; that is 'aspects of baby care that involve thinking or feeling, managing thoughts or feelings, and that are not necessarily perceived as work by the person performing it' (Walzer, 1996: 219). The mothers in this study tended to talk about mothering as involving worrying about the child, feeling primarily responsible for her or him, seeking and implementing information and advice on child care and feeling that the child's behaviour and welfare were directly attributable to them as 'good' or 'bad' mothers. In contrast, the fathers were less likely to discuss these processes as part of their role, and even argued, for example, that their partners 'worried too much' about the child. Walzer argues that a father may be perceived as a 'good' father in the absence of such mental labour, but the same could not be said of mothers.

Ehrensaft (1995) came to similar conclusions, even though the group of American parents she interviewed included only those who had made a choice to participate equally in child care activities. Mothers, she found, tended to conceptualize their young children as 'part of themselves' and to think and worry about them constantly, while fathers, although equally proficient and experienced in the care of their children, appeared more easily able to create boundaries between self and the child. This was the case even where women had demanding and fulfilling paid employment outside the home and considered their paid work to be important. Ehrensaft argues that 'To be able to maintain a separateness between self and other is the prerequisite for the male element of doing' (1995: 55). She contends that women, almost despite themselves, find this maintenance of individuation between themselves and their child far more difficult.

This type of empirical research tends to support the contentions of feminist object relations theorists, in its focus on the ways that men and women may have different orientations to intimate relationships with others. However, it also highlights the importance of the dominant meanings and discourses circulating in relation to how 'good' motherhood and fatherhood are defined and practised.

The Academic Masculinity Literature

We observed in the Introduction that despite the fact that academic writings on masculinity have burgeoned over the past few years (many of them written by men), little detailed attention has been paid in this literature to fatherhood. When they have discussed fatherhood, several male academics have often echoed the assertions of feminists that men and women's equal participation in child care forms part of a change towards equality of the sexes, without examining or theorizing in any great detail the difficulties and conflicts inherent in such utopian statements (see, for example, Connell, 1987: xii). Other male writers have taken a more personalized approach to addressing issues of fatherhood. David Cohen's *Being a Man* (1990) and David Jackson's *Unmasking Masculinity* (1990) are typical of the spate of books that merge academic theorizing on masculinity with self-help philosophies and autobiographical accounts of the writer's relationship with his own father and with his own children. These books take up the second-wave feminist approach that 'the personal is the political' and adopt the somewhat informal, often confessional style mixed with formal academic references that has characterized much feminist writing of this kind.

While they devote quite a lot of attention to their own fathers, neither Cohen nor Jackson discuss in great detail their own position as fathers. In a chapter entitled 'Being a father', Cohen describes his childhood memories of his (typically) absent father and his experiences as an adult in the 1970s of juggling work demands with the demands of his feminist wife that he participate more actively in child care. He intersperses these musings with academic sources to address the historical, economic and sociological aspects of fatherhood. Cohen argues that men should begin to learn about and acknowledge the importance of fatherhood. He suggests that change is taking place – 'many men are beginning to understand what we lose by not caring for our children' (1990: 188). He then points to the need for 'both personal and political action', including men changing their participation in work and women accepting men as 'equal parents' as well as a political agenda for change which gives women better job opportunities and allows men greater flexibility in the workplace (1990: 189). Jackson, who notes in his book that he was divorced when his son was 11 years old, and thenceforth had very little interaction with him, refers briefly to the distance he feels between himself and his son (now an adult). His own father, Jackson argues, was distant and oppressive of his son's emotional needs, unwilling to acknowledge his achievements and thereby contributing to Jackson's lack of security and self-confidence as an adult man.

Other writers in this area have tended to represent men as victims, subject to attack on all sides. For Horrocks, who was an academic and is now a practising psychotherapist in England, 'masculinity in Western society is in deep crisis' (1994: 1). The reasons he provides for this extreme statement is that men experience feelings of emptiness, impotence and rage and are afflicted by 'emotional autism, emptiness and despair'. Horrocks argues that the power relations men experience under patriarchy serve to encourage self-denial and a 'shrinkage of the self', the destruction of men's vulnerability, their need to present to the self and others a strong face and to dominate others (1994: 25). He contends that men's power is economic and political, while women hold emotional power. Interestingly, in his book Horrocks devotes little attention to fatherhood (only a few pages). His comments on fatherhood contend that 'the absent father', or the father who leaves the family for long hours to work each day, is a primary cause of the emotional emptiness men feel, their lack of a sense of self as men and their inability to relate to women. Horrocks argues that this is because the father was not there to bond with the boy, to demonstrate masculinity and to 'rescue the boy from the female world, so that he can identify himself as male' (1994: 77).

Such writings taking up liberal feminist and therapeutic approaches tend to represent manhood and fatherhood as 'a kind of prison, a set of "roles" with unrealistic expectations that lead men to do bad things and put them out of touch with their "real", more nurturing selves' (Griswold, 1993: 247). In their focus on personal enlightenment and change, they tend to ignore the vested interests that many men have in perpetuating rather than challenging or breaking down the status quo of gender relations, often treating the category of 'men' in an essentialist manner (Cornwall and Lindisfarne, 1994: 34).

Interestingly enough, functionalism has re-emerged recently in sociological writing – often by male academics – on the issue of the 'fatherless family'. For example, in his book *Fatherless America: Confronting Our Most Urgent Social Problem* (1995), the American sociologist David Blankenhorn argues that 'the traditional father' or 'good family man' (that is, the breadwinner and authoritative head of household figure) has been marginalized and denigrated. In the book, which received much media attention in the United States, Blankenhorn contends that fatherlessness is the central cause of a host of contemporary social problems in that country, including poverty and rising crime and violence rates. He calls for the ideal-type 'good family man' to be restored and supported as the solution to these problems. Blankenhorn's thesis, therefore, attempts to position marital breakdown and the absence of fathers as the primary reason for such social problems without considering the possibility that they are associated with, or part of, such problems. Blankenhorn goes so far as to argue that by the year 2000 the presence or absence of a father in a child's family will be more important than such factors as ethnicity or race, social class or gender in shaping that child's future psychological health and socioeconomic status. Other male sociologists have sought to counter what they see as the current valorizing of the 'new' father archetype. Popenoe (1993) has argued, for example, that an 'androgynous' father who attempts to perform a more 'mother-like' role, resulting in a reduction of gender differentiation between parents, may destabilize his children's development and cause marital problems.

Concluding Comments

In this chapter we have reviewed the dominant approaches in the social scientific, family health and welfare and masculinity literature to researching and representing fatherhood. As we have shown, fatherhood is constructed in these forums in certain dominant ways that are related to the purpose and audience to which the writings are directed. The discourses from the 'expert' literature tend to be somewhat 'clinical' or 'distant' in their approach to fatherhood, with the exception of writings on the topic of masculinity, which are often directed to a more general as well as academic audience. These 'expert' discourses, particularly in those writings emerging from developmental and social psychology and the field of family health and welfare, tend to pathologize fatherhood, positioning fathers themselves either as variables having 'effects' upon their children or as troubled fathers, subject to a range of social, psychological and physical difficulties requiring expert assistance.

They take a largely individualistic approach to representing, understanding and dealing with what are identified as the 'problems' associated with fathers and fatherhood. Sociological research has tended to focus either on the structural, politico-economic features of parenting, particularly from within a feminist critique, or upon the phenomenological 'lived experience' of fatherhood from the men's own perspective. This literature also typically seeks to identify and discuss the problematic features of fatherhood.

The emotional, and indeed the pleasurable, dimensions of fatherhood are rather underplayed in the 'expert' literature. When emotions *are* discussed it is often in the context of men's difficulties in adjusting to the fatherly role, relating to conflict with the fathers' partners or their problems in expressing their 'true feelings'. There is still routinely an academic distance maintained between subject (fathers) and researcher, in which issues of domestic relations, men's relationships with their partners and children and so on may be described, but the affective, sensual, intensely embodied dimension of fatherhood tends to get somewhat lost in the interests of 'normalizing' fathers. The next chapter considers how more popular texts, addressed to a somewhat different and more general audience, represent fathers and fatherhood.

3

Fatherhood in the Popular Media

We contended in the previous chapter that academic discourses on father-hood, particularly in the health care and developmental psychological literature, tend either to neglect consideration of the views and experiences of men themselves on fatherhood or to focus mainly on the negative aspects of the fatherhood experience. As we argued, this is because this literature is written for an audience – professionals and researchers working in the field of child and family health and welfare – in which fatherhood (and indeed the family in general) is generally positioned as problematic, requiring the help and advice of experts. Popular media accounts of fatherhood are written for different purposes and for a different audience – the general or 'lay' public, in particular parents themselves. As such, the objectives of popular media accounts generally differ from those of the professional literature. Some mem-bers of the media may set out to inform, but they also commonly seek to entertain in their efforts to gain a wide audience.

Despite the fact that the popular media enjoy a far greater audience than academic or professional texts, there are surprisingly few analyses of con-temporary media representations of fathers and fatherhood. As is the case with most other academic research efforts, the attention of those interested in media analysis has tended to focus on the portrayal of mothers and mother-hood in these forums (and even these analyses are few in number). To address the ways in which fathers and fatherhood are portrayed in the popular media, we look at a number of different genres of media in this chapter, including mainstream television and film, self-help books for men, newspapers, maga-zines, greeting cards, child care and parenting manuals. As in the previous chapter, the aim of this analysis is to identify the dominant discourses on fatherhood that are reproduced in these media, and the consequent role they play in the sociocultural construction of fatherhood.

Television Comedy, Drama and Advertising

In an episode in the 1995 season of the American sitcom *Frasier*, one of the central characters, Niles Crane, aged around 40, is shown agonizing over the decision whether to become a father or not. To help him make up his mind, Frasier, his brother, advises him to engage in an activity used with adolescents to teach them the responsibilities of parenthood: carrying around a bag of flour of the approximate size and weight of an infant for several days. Niles engages in this activity, amusingly becoming quite devoted to his bag of flour, treating and talking about it as if it were, in fact, a real child, including speculating on its future education. After some days, however, the bag of flour becomes rather worn and tattered after meeting a series of misadventures, such as falling into a fire and being attacked by a dog. Niles becomes weary of the task, coming to the realization that fatherhood is replete with difficulties and burdens. The episode ends when he decides that he is 'not ready' to be a father.

Amongst other things, what this episode reveals is a perception that parenthood is an onerous task, one that limits personal autonomy and requires reserves of virtues such as patience, diligence and a well-developed sense of responsibility for men as well as women. Interestingly, Frasier is himself a father of a young boy, Frederick, who is occasionally mentioned, if never seen, in the show. Frasier's role as father, however, is rarely emphasized, because Frederick lives in another city with Frasier's estranged wife and has little contact with his father. Frasier and Niles's own elderly father, Martin, lives with Frasier in a household unusual for prime-time television. Martin Crane, a retired policeman, acts as a gruff counterpoint to the somewhat pretentious Niles and Frasier, both of whom are psychiatrists. A continuing joke is the disappointment both of them, despite their wealth and professional standing, are for their father, who considers them soft and effeminate, not 'real men', because of their occupations, expensive tastes, 'girlish' sensibilities and dislike of such 'masculine' activities as sport. Both of these middle-aged men, therefore, are represented as perennial sons rather than as fathers, successfully avoiding the responsibilities of parenthood.

The characters of Frasier and Niles Crane exemplify an interesting development in recent years in American sitcoms. There are now a number of successful comedy series that feature male and female characters, ranging in age from their late 20s to their early 40s, living a kind of extended adolescence, as in the series *Seinfeld*, *Friends* and *Ellen*. The characters live in city apartments, either alone or with their friends, rather than with marital partners. Much of the action in these series focuses on the characters' continuing searches for appropriate romantic relationships. These relationships are always short-lived for one reason or another, and so questions of marriage, let alone parenthood, rarely arise. These characters' own ageing parents feature from time to time largely as annoyances who nag them about finding an appropriate partner and 'settling down'. The fathers are generally ineffectual buffoons while the mothers are harridans who attempt to dominate both their husbands and their adult children. The implication is that the model of marriage and the nuclear family, as represented by the characters' parents, no longer holds many attractions for younger people. Parenthood is no longer an accepted part of adulthood, and indeed, may be actively avoided.

Mainstream television representations of fictional fathers have tended to cohere around a number of archetypes. There is the 'father as authoritative but wise and caring breadwinner', a mainstay of American television comedy and drama in the 1950s and early 1960s in such family series as *Leave it to Beaver* and *Father Knows Best*. In such series, fathers were represented as participating little in domestic labour or child care, but as frequently available to spend time with their children, show interest in their affairs and provide sage advice to them. Indeed, the fathers in these series were often portrayed as more knowledgeable about the important issues of child rearing and family life than were their wives (Walters, 1992: 82). The father character Mike Brady in the late 1960s and early 1970s family comedy *The Brady Bunch* also predominantly served the role of economic provider, authority figure and source of sensible, rational advice to his wife and blended family of six children. Some father characters in contemporary television comedies continue to conform to this archetype. For instance, the father character in the contemporary *The Nanny* series, Maxwell Sheffield, provides a more sensible foil to his zany nanny Fran Fine. As a wealthy widower left with three children, Maxwell Sheffield is portrayed in many scenes as engaging in work activities to maintain his children in luxury. Few scenes show him interacting with his children – this is left to the nanny and butler who are paid for the task.

Walters (1992: 227) notes that while mother–daughter relationships predominated in American sitcoms in the 1970s in such programmes as *Maude* and *Rhoda*, by the late 1980s the father–child relationship was re-emerging as a focal point. A rash of sitcoms, such as *Who's the Boss, Coach* and *Major Dad*, dealt with families in which the mother was absent (often due to an early death) and the father was left to attempt valiantly to bring up his young children alone. The emphasis in such series was on the difficulties of being a single father but also the nurturing qualities a man could exhibit if he were to find himself in such a situation: mothers seemed no longer to be a necessity. A further example of a prominent father character in the 1980s was that invented by the comedian Bill Cosby in his successful sitcom *The Cosby Show*. In this series, Cosby portrayed Cliff Huxtable, a doctor married to a lawyer. His character blended affection with discipline, in what has been described as a return 'to the father-knows-best world of the 1950s domestic comedy' (Feuer, 1992: 155), albeit revolving around a black rather than a white middle-class family and with the addition of a wife and mother character who was also a high status working professional rather than just a housewife in an apron. In 1996, according to a poll commissioned by the newspaper *USA Today*, Cosby was voted 'the most memorable TV dad' of six father characters listed. Cosby went on to write a popular book on his own experiences as a father, in which his on-screen persona as a lovable, somewhat bemused but attentive father was reproduced (see discussion below).

There has typically been a social class differentiation in the portrayal of fathers in prime-time American comedies, however. While middle-class fathers (almost all of whom were also white) have been frequently represented as wise and affectionate since the 1950s, working-class fathers have commonly been shown to be the butt of other members of the family's derision, as possessing little wisdom in family or other matters and as rarely winning respect from their wives or even their young children. In contemporary television comedies, the cartoon character of Homer Simpson of *The*

Simpsons, the Al Bundy father character in *Married . . . With Children* and Dan Conner, the genial husband of the eponymous *Roseanne*, are portrayed far more as figures of fun than as authority figures. While these men continue to act as breadwinners, they hold little authority over their children. Their role as head of the household is constantly undermined, while the mother figure is shown both as dominating of her husband and as wiser and more successful in matters of household policy. These men are also spectacularly unattractive physically, with flabby, overweight bodies caused by overeating and too much beer.

While television comedy has apparently shied away in the main from featuring characters who conform to the 'new' father archetype, television drama has included some father characters who take their role very seriously. Indeed, from the 1980s, characters who are fathers have often been shown agonizing over their role as father and how best they should fulfil it. One example is the central character of Michael in the late 1980s American 'upscale' drama *thirtysomething*. This series differed from other 'quality' prime-time dramas at the time in focusing specifically on domestic relationships and the characters' articulation of their feelings and problems to each other in great detail. Michael was an advertising executive married to Hope, a journalist. The couple had a young daughter, and many scenes in the series showed Michael engaging in parental activities with her or discussing her welfare with Hope. Indeed, the creators of the series specifically designed it to appeal to educated, middle-class men as well as women by including extended treatment of the male perspective on fatherhood (Bonner and du Gay, 1992: 70).

Despite the emerging appearance of such father characters, television 'quality' dramas, particularly those revolving around the workplace, such as medical, court-room and police drama series, often reveal little about the main characters' private lives (male or female) in favour of devoting attention to their exciting professional activities. In more recent times, however, such dramas have begun to explore the tensions that both men and women may experience between engaging in professional activities and sustaining personal and family relationships. For example, the powerful and successful middle-aged lawyer Ted Hoffman in the 1995 season of the American legal drama *Murder One* was shown as utterly devoted to his young daughter. While the demands of his job, working as the head of the legal defence team on a sensational murder trial, eventually destroyed Hoffman's marriage and kept him from spending much time with his daughter, the lawyer was shown making efforts to deal sensitively and lovingly with her and maintain regular contact. His marital difficulties, caused by his work, and his desire to have contact with his daughter were not enough reason, however, for him to withdraw from his demanding, high-profile job. The middle-aged hero of the English legal drama *Kavanagh QC* is similarly successful in his career as a barrister. Kavanagh's home life, however, receives almost equal attention in the series, including his often difficult relationships with his adolescent son and daughter as well as with his wife.

In many mainstream dramatic representations of fathers on television, fatherhood is portrayed as potentially rewarding but also problematic. The clash between professional objectives and demands in the case of men who are successful doctors and lawyers, and the resulting problems their jobs may cause for their relationships with their partners and children, is emphasized. In very few cases are male characters who are fathers shown to devote a great deal of attention to their children; their work role primarily dominates their characterization.

Television soap opera, in its focus on the intimate lives of its characters, often features father characters interacting with their partners and children. Particularly in 'realist' soap (for example, the British *EastEnders* and *Brookside* and the Australian *Neighbours* and *Home and Away*), the action of this genre typically revolves around social issues and events within the family and domestic context. In their focus on the banal features of everyday domestic life and 'ordinary people', the events of pregnancy and childbirth, single parenthood, marital separation and divorce and minor arguments or clashes between parents and their children provide many of the plots in soap opera. The *Neighbours* or *EastEnders* type of soap opera spends far more time exploring the private realm of domestic life than the realm of paid labour.

Particularly in Australian soap operas, both fathers and mothers tend to be portrayed as espousing middle-class suburban values and decency. The *Neighbours* family is a nuclear family, generally with both parents living reasonably happily together with their adolescent children. Family crises are generally solved through rational discussion among family members, with the parents offering wise guidance (Crofts, 1995). In this idealized, nostalgic scenario, the social changes that have taken place over the past few decades, including the feminist movement, may never have happened. The difficulties experienced by members of dual-career families, for example, in relation to juggling work and parenting, are rarely explored, and nor are single parent families a major feature. Young fathers are generally portrayed as caring and attuned to their partner's feelings; older fathers are stolid and dependable.

British soap operas tend to be somewhat more gritty, with family conflicts less easily resolved and poor or working-class people and 'broken families' featuring in greater numbers. Indeed Geraghty (1995) has observed that single fatherhood has become quite a regular feature in the British soap opera *Brookside* in the 1990s. She contends that this emphasis on single fatherhood indicates a concern with more complex male characters and a challenge to the secure gender positions of traditional soap operas: 'The program's dominant point of view now tends to be that of the father, uneasy in handling personal relationships, somewhat baffled by his children's needs, and confused about how to handle his own role as father' (Geraghty, 1995: 79).

American daytime soap operas differ again in their representation of fathers from both Australian and British prime-time soaps. Mumford (1995) argues that the issue of paternity is a central feature of American daytime soap opera. She contends that the events of unplanned pregnancies, disputes over who is the father and secrets or mistakes over paternity and the importance that characters attach to discovering who is the father of a child are common plot devices in this genre of television. According to Mumford, this obsession is a product of a wider cultural anxiety about the identification of paternity related to the fact that men can never be exactly sure if they are the father of their children: 'Fatherhood is, in this sense, a myth, an ultimately unprovable claim that we agree to accept as fact' (Mumford, 1995: 165). In soap opera, unlike 'real life', this anxiety is always resolved: 'true' paternity is invariably established and proven. Fathers in these soaps, once established as such, are portrayed as having an almost mystical bond with their children: 'A man's discovery that he has fathered a child arouses powerful feelings of love and attachment, frequently drawing him to the child's mother . . . and almost always drawing him to the newly recognized child' (Mumford, 1995: 173–4). In this way, the paternal bond is represented as having a special emotional weight, overcoming other problems or conflicts. Mumford (1995: 174) inter- prets this portrayal as a feminized version of fatherhood, a pleasurable fantasy that privileges love and devotion on the part of the (often previously estranged) father as a bind that brings together couples and their children and maintains family solidarity. The paternal bond tends not to be manifested, however, in representations of men sharing child care tasks or domestic labour.

Stereotypes of the comic, slightly pathetic or else middle-class professional and distant father are also frequently reproduced in television advertisements. One quantitative content analysis of American television commercials (Coltrane and Allan, 1994) compared images of men and women presented in the 1950s with those in the 1980s. The researchers found that in the 1950s commercials, men were six times more likely to be represented as workers in the paid workforce than parents, while women were twice as likely to be por- trayed as parents than as paid workers. By the 1980s, little had changed in the representation of men, but women were shown more frequently as in occu- pational rather than domestic roles; they were now twice as often portrayed as members of the paid workforce than as parents. In both periods, if men and women were shown in a parenting role, they were both likely to display behaviours the researchers categorized as 'nurturing' and 'supportive'. Nonetheless, the most dominant representation of men in the 1980s por- trayed them as displaying qualities of independence, autonomy and forcefulness in a public rather than a domestic setting. Coltrane and Allan conclude that their study revealed little to suggest that the 'new' father image was apparent in mainstream American television advertising in the 1980s: the portrayal of women had changed over the decades far more than had that of men.

Contemporary Australian television advertisements demonstrate a similar conservative portrayal of fatherhood. For instance, advertisements for vita- mins and medicines, especially preparations for coughs and colds, feature a concerned mother caring for her husband and male child by providing them with the medicine, tucking them warmly up in bed, rubbing vaporizing mix- tures on their chests and so on. In such portrayals the husband is infantilized, depicted as equally helpless and needful of loving care as the child, often wearing pyjamas and sniffing or coughing pitifully. Much more rare is the depiction of the mother in bed being cared for by her male partner or her children, or the husband tending to the health needs of his children, or even an ill female (rather than male) child being cared for by her mother. So too, in advertisements for sticking plasters and ointments, it is invariably a dishevelled male child who runs to his mother for help when his daring physical adventures result in a cut or scrape. Female children are rarely depicted as hurting themselves in active play, and fathers are never shown ministering to the needs of their children in this way. The archetype of the loving wife and mother who soldiers on and tends to the needs of others, even if she herself may be feeling ill, is reproduced and championed in these advertisements, as is the archetype of the (temporarily) sick male child or husband requiring care and attention from her.

Similarly, advertisements for food and cleaning products continue overwhelmingly to feature women in the role of mother as the primary provider of meals for the family and the person responsible for domestic tasks such as washing clothes and cleaning. When men are represented as performing domestic tasks, they are often shown to be foolishly incompetent. One Australian television advertisement, for example, portrayed a man coming home with the groceries he had purchased and proceeding to store the washing powder absent-mindedly in the refrigerator. Another television advertisement for McDonald's restaurants featured a father in charge of getting his son (aged about six or seven years) off to school (the mother is absent for some explained reason). The father is a professional, attired in a suit and tie, and is clearly unused to taking on these duties. He does not have the resources or time to organize breakfast for his son, so he hurriedly bustles his son into the car and they go to a McDonald's drive-in where they order breakfast. The father and son are then shown rushing into the father's office, where they settle themselves down contentedly and tuck in to their McDonald's food. All seems well, until the son innocently asks the father, 'Dad, what about school?' The father, who has forgotten this important requirement of the morning, clasps his hand to his head in chagrin, grabs his son's hand, and they rush out of the office. The suggestion of this advertisement, while it is clearly intended to be humorous, is that fathers simply do not know or understand the routines of their young children's day. It is difficult to imagine a similar advertisement which features a mother absent-mindedly forgetting to take her child to school or shows her unable to provide her child with a home-prepared breakfast.

Popular Film

Mainstream cinematic representations of fatherhood have demonstrated some move towards the 'new' father archetype. According to Mellen (1978), until the late 1970s at least, the predominant archetype of masculinity portrayed in the dramatic Hollywood film was that of the dominating, fearless and often violent man, overcoming women and lesser men by his sheer determination and will. These types of screen heroes ranged from Errol Flynn and Douglas Fairbanks to John Wayne, Clint Eastwood, Charles Bronson and Steve McQueen. In the 1990s such action heroes as Sylvester Stallone, Jean-Claude van Damme and Bruce Willis have taken over the 'tough guy' mantle. Marriage, the family or fatherhood rarely feature as dominant aspects of the characters' lives in films starring these actors. Rather, male friendship is represented as more important to men. By contrast, in the 1920s and 1930s and into the 1950s men were quite often shown as loving husbands and fathers, as openly affectionate to children and displaying their emotions. This was particularly the case for characters played by such actors as Spencer Tracy, Clark Gable, Tom Mix and John Barrymore (Mellen, 1978: 19).

It is telling that the genre of contemporary mainstream film that has focused most on men in a fathering role is the comedy. A spate of Hollywood fatherhood comedies were released in the 1980s and early 1990s. As Kaplan notes, 'Fathers are beginning to steal the show in regard to parenting: That they are the new heroes in this role is fascinating just because the narratives of so many traditional maternal melodramas precisely show mothers and daughters *alone*, and the fathers dead, unknown or absent' (1994: 267–8; original emphasis). The implication of many such films is that the spectacle of a grown man taking on the duties of caring for a child is amusing in its incongruity. This was the case of *Mr Mom* (1983), a film featuring the situation of a male executive who loses his job and finds himself having to play the role of 'house husband' and full-time carer of his children while his wife becomes the breadwinner for the family. His utter ineptitude at performing domestic tasks is the main comedic device of the film.

Three Men and a Baby (1987) was constructed around the narrative device of three 'confirmed bachelors', enjoying the carefree life of the young, well-off single man, finding a female infant on their doorstep, left by one of the men's former girlfriends. The men have no previous experience with child care, and the film humorously portrays their incompetence as well as their growing love and affection for the infant. By the end of the film, between them the three men have developed an efficient and affectionate routine for the baby's care and are loath to give her up to her mother, who eventually returns to claim her. Despite this, there is never an indication that the men's lives would be ruined by the loss of the baby. As Kaplan notes, 'Fathering is not seen as part of any identity they *need* to assume. The film shows how understandable it is that the men would want to rid themselves of the baby, but also understandable that some attachment to the baby might develop. In this film, fatherhood is shared and chosen, not demanded' (1994: 264; original emphasis).

The Steve Martin comedy *Parenthood* (1989) provided a series of vignettes of parents and children in one extended family, including the attempts of fathers to encourage their children to be successful in life, going out of their way to entertain their children at birthday parties, worrying about their children's lack of popularity with other children, cuddling babies and so on. None of the fathers, however, was portrayed as taking a predominant role in the everyday care of his children. In contrast, the more recent Robin Williams comedy *Mrs Doubtfire* (1993) tells the story of a man, Daniel Hillard, played by Williams, who takes on child care tasks after his wife divorces him. Daniel is portrayed as finding the loss of his children distressing, and is forced, in his efforts to gain access to them, to dress in drag and masquerade as an elderly Scottish nanny, Mrs Doubtfire. In this guise Daniel is employed by his wife, who is busy with her high-powered career, to look after their children. A major irony of the film is that it is only in the persona of Mrs Doubtfire that Daniel is able to behave responsibly as an authoritative parent figure, bringing order to the household and winning his wife's affections and gratitude. Nonetheless, a dominant theme of *Mrs Doubtfire* is the sheer love and affection that the father character has for his children and the lengths to which he is willing to go to be with them. As Mrs Doubtfire he is simultaneously the ideal mother figure and the ideal father figure, combining love for his children with giving them a stable, orderly environment.

Fewer films have featured a dramatic rather than a comic narrative centring around fatherhood. One popular Hollywood film to depart from the lampooning of the man as primary carer is *Kramer vs Kramer* (1979), a drama which portrayed the travails of a successful advertising executive in his mid-thirties (played by Dustin Hoffman) learning to care for his six-year-old son after his feckless (and lesbian) wife (Meryl Streep) abandons them. The film movingly portrays the warmth and love in the relationship between father and son in the context of a marital breakdown and bitter divorce battle. At first the father, who previously had been preoccupied with his work, knows little about his son – he does not even know what grade he is in at school when he takes his son to school the first time. Over time, however, a strong and loving relationship builds between the two. Hoffman's sensitive characterization contrasts strongly with Streep's character of the preoccupied, distant mother who so 'unfairly' is given custody of the son. As Segal (1990: 29) has commented, this type of film tends to portray fathers as more sensitive and nurturing than their wives, who are characterized as far more self-centred and ambitious by comparison.

This is not the case in the more recent British drama *Jack and Sarah* (1995), where the early scenes of the film show the mother dying in childbirth. Nonetheless, the theme of the father growing to develop a close bond with his child in the absence of the mother is the same. Richard E. Grant plays Jack, a successful London lawyer who is left grieving and bitter after his wife's unexpected death. Jack takes to drink and evinces little interest in his new-born daughter until forced to by his concerned parents and mother-in-law. As is typical of this genre, although Jack is shown in the early scenes of the film being a concerned father-to-be, including attending antenatal classes with his wife, when he is left 'holding the baby' he is at a loss. Jack knows nothing about changing nappies, and is disgusted when he catches his first whiff of his daughter's dirty nappy, rushing to hold her under a tap to clean her up. When Jack first tries to dress the infant, he again has little idea, putting her in a paper bag and using one of his socks as a hat for her.

Very quickly, however, the film shows Jack acquiring a range of maternal skills and becoming besotted with his tiny daughter, whom he names Sarah after his wife. This gives his parents and mother-in-law peace of mind, as they were concerned about how he would manage. Jack takes to carrying Sarah around with him, including in trendy cafés and to work, much to the disapproval of the managing partner of his firm (a single, childless and ambitious woman, who is portrayed, villain-like, as self-centred and as lacking a properly feminine appreciation of infants and their needs). He eventually employs a young American woman as a nanny, and the plot proceeds to explore their relationship, with Jack relinquishing daily care of Sarah to the nanny and becoming a 'quality-time' weekend parent. The suggestion is that this is a more 'normal' mode of relationship for a busy, ambitious male lawyer to have with his child. The film makes clear that without his nanny, Jack would find it very difficult to combine his career with taking care of Sarah.

The gentleness and affection that such male characters demonstrate towards their children is represented as laudable, a sign of good character, in its very opposition with the 'muscular tough-guy' image that remains more dominant in Hollywood films. The 'fatherhood' film replicates the heroic narrative of other films (and popular texts) about men, in that it portrays the (male) heroes undergoing tests, overcoming obstacles and chaos and finally emerging triumphant, restoring order. Unlike most heroic narratives, however, which tend to represent their male protagonists as espousing the principles of absolute individuation and solitude (Sparks, 1996: 353), the men in fatherhood films are portrayed as heroic in their very desire to be good fathers – that is, to seek a closer and better relationship with their children, and in most cases requiring others' help to do so.

A common theme throughout these films is that the men in question are left 'holding the baby' through accident or misfortune rather than by choice, and have little idea about what to do when this happens. In most films this is a source of comedy, in others it is a source of high drama. The implication is that men should not be expected to 'know instinctively' about baby and child care. Rarely are women characters portrayed as lacking this knowledge, for it is assumed that most women would know how to manage an infant, and would certainly not require extra help if their male partner were to disappear or die. In few popular films is the fact of a father taking a predominant role in the care of his child represented as a routine, as an everyday phenomenon. These types of films also overwhelmingly represent the fathers as occupying professional positions. The implication is that 'new age' fathering is a middle-class phenomenon, perhaps because it is expected that middle-class men have the reserves of sensitivity that the working-class male stereotype tends to deny. As in television comedy, in popular film the working-class father is far more often held up as a figure of fun and even contempt, as lacking the skills to relate to his family and win their respect. Middle-class men are far less often portrayed in this role, continuing to maintain their authority by virtue of the status of their employment and the economic benefits associated with it.

Recently popular films have begun to address the issue of men who take up with female partners with children, often highlighting the risks and threats that such men may pose to their stepchildren. For instance, the British film *Hollow Reed* (1996) presented a narrative involving a father whose ex-wife has a relationship with a man who, unbeknown to her, batters her nine-year-old son. One twist in this tale is that the father (played by Martin Donovan) has left his wife (Joely Richardson) for another man. The drama revolves around this gay father seeking to expose his son's abuser and to gain custody of the boy so as to remove him from the stepfather's sphere of influence. In so doing, the boy's mother is portrayed as weak and self-centred. She is overly trusting of and dependent on her new lover, refusing to believe her ex-husband's allegations and deal with the cause of her son's abuse. As such, the mother is shown to be complicit with her son's abuser, even if unwittingly, through her need for her lover. In contrast, the father is portrayed as a heroic, strong and concerned figure, wanting only what is best for his son.

These trends in the representation of fathers and fatherhood may be compared to the portrayals of motherhood and mothers that have appeared in mainstream cinema over the same period. Kaplan (1994) has identified some major changes in the American popular cinematic representation of mothers. She asserts that underlying films appearing in the 1980s and early 1990s there is 'anxiety in relation to white women and cultural changes in sex, family, and work spheres that are emerging in tandem with changes in the technological, economic, and industrial spheres. This anxiety partly has to do with the fact that childbirth and child care are no longer an automatic, "natural" part of the white woman's life cycle' (1994: 258). In earlier decades there was little focus on self-fulfilment for women in childbearing and rearing; mothering was culturally represented as a duty, involving suffering and self-sacrifice. By the 1980s, however, motherhood was often portrayed in Hollywood as a choice from alternatives, particularly for middle-class women in their 30s (for example, the films *The Good Mother* (1988), *Baby Boom* (1988), *Heartburn* (1986), *Raising Arizona* (1988)). It is rarely suggested in such films that women can successfully combine motherhood with a fulfilling career. The suggestion is rather that a woman must choose one over the other to be happy.

Famous Fathers

Portrayals of 'famous fathers' in popular magazines and other media have frequently discussed the value they supposedly place on their family in order to represent their 'human', 'vulnerable' side. This has particularly been the case with rock singers and actors – the likes of Michael Hutchence, Bruce Willis and Sean Penn – who are often reported as making a decision to reform their 'bad boy ways' in the attempt to become a better father. It is also a common way of describing male politicians, who have often used the reason that they wish to spend more time with their families to explain their decision to quit politics.

Detailed 'profiles' of famous men who are also fathers have begun to elicit their experiences and opinions of fatherhood. For instance, in a 1996 feature article published in the colour magazine of the *Weekend Australian* newspaper, Australian actor Bryan Brown, known for his portrayal in film and television drama of the stereotype of the blunt, laconic Australian male, was lauded for his concern for his family and his participation as a father. One part of the article described Brown's response to his children when they visited him on the set of his latest film: 'As soon as their car nudges over the bumpy track, Brown is out of his chair, grinning and loping towards them, the kids squealing happily, running for a hug. He doesn't have to act the family man. "I can put the kids' stuff together when [his wife] Rachel's got the shits with doing it or when she's not around", he says nonchalantly. "Pretty basic."'

The journalist goes on to note approvingly that Brown puts his family ahead of his friends, and stays at home on Saturday nights rather than going out, quoting him as saying: '"Look, I've got three kids and a family. Most of the time is devoted to us being together, doing whatever."' Brown is then described as 'a caring, attentive father' who is interested in environmental issues because, as he is quoted, '"If you've got kids you think about it."' Brown is therefore applauded for his ability to step in on occasions to organize his children and for positioning himself as a 'family man'. The suggestion is that underneath his 'straight-talking', strong, archetypal masculine exterior is a warm, caring individual. Nonetheless, it is clear that Brown's parenting duties are secondary to his career, and that his wife Rachel has the major responsibility for the children: he 'puts the kids' stuff together' almost as a favour when she is fed up or absent, but not as a routine, everyday task.

In some magazine 'profiles' of famous fathers, the sheer status and position of the man in question is acknowledged as precluding very much involvement with his children, however much the man would like to engage as an involved father. This is an interesting tension for high-profile male politicians, who juggle presenting themselves as committed 'family men' with attempting to meet expectations that they should serve their country by devoting virtually all their waking hours to their work. In a profile of the then Labour Party leader and Prime Minister aspirant Tony Blair published in the July 1996 issue of the British *Parents* magazine, photographs of the beaming Blair wearing a dark suit seated at his dark-panelled office desk were juxtaposed with more casual shots of him in a domestic environment with his three young children. The article was headlined with a quotation from Blair – 'Being a dad is harder than being a politician'. Blair then discussed the births of his children, his worries about them and his pleasure at being a father, as well as his efforts in trying to spend time with them: '"It doesn't always work like that, of course, because being Leader of the Opposition can be pretty much a 24-hour-a-day job."'

As noted above, the comedian Bill Cosby built on the success of his Cliff Huxtable character in *The Cosby Show* to write an autobiographical book on fatherhood. In *Fatherhood* (1986) Cosby discusses his personal experiences of fathering his own five children. He presents himself in a comic mode as a somewhat powerless figure under the ultimate control of his wife and out-smarted by his children. At one point he notes that 'I am not the boss of my house . . . My wife is the boss' (Cosby, 1986: 57). Cosby portrays himself and fathers in general as lacking authority, describing 'the father' as hapless and inept, presiding over an anarchic domestic world over which he has little control and where he is no longer allowed to remove himself from household chores: 'Any man today who returns from work, sinks into a chair, and calls for his pipe is a man with an appetite for danger' (1986: 61). Despite this, another central point that Cosby makes throughout the book is that father-hood has more rewards and joys than anything else in life.

Over the past decade or so, a genre of photography has emerged which shows famous men cradling their infants protectively or playing with older children. This image has particular resonance when a man known for his archetypal masculine muscularity and toughness, such as a prize fighter or elite football player, is shown in such a pose. In one such portrayal, an Australian women's magazine featured an article on 'Footy fever and father-hood' (*New Idea*, 28 September 1996), focusing on four burly football players with their infants. Large photographs of the men carefully and proudly hold-ing their babies (one man holds his infant son in one arm and a football in the other) were juxtaposed with shots of the men in action on the football field, displaying their strength, toughness and agility. All the men were quoted as drawing a distinction between their 'footballer' and their 'fatherly' self. The article emphasized the 'softer' emotions that the men demonstrated in talking about their children, as in the following excerpt: 'Paul Harragon is a rugby league giant. He is muscle-bound, battle-scarred and as tough as they come, but there is one person who can bring the big man to his knees – five-month-old daughter Emily . . . "She brings out so many emotions in me", Paul says.' The infants' mothers are not included in the photographs and are hardly mentioned in the article.

These types of images are also more and more commonly found on greet-ing cards, in which again a favourite pose is the tiny naked infant asleep and peaceful in the huge, hairy hands or extremely muscular arms of a bare-chested man. The juxtaposition of the tiny, delicate, pale and smooth-skinned baby in these images with the bulk, hairiness and darker skin of the man hold-ing it serves to convey a masculinity that is both caring and gentle and vastly strong and protective. As Segal notes, 'Today, the hardest of macho male images can combine with the softest portrayals of paternity' (1990: 33). Such images serve to sexualize the male body in conventional ways (emphasizing muscularity and hairiness) at the same time as they represent men as pos-sessing more 'feminine' attributes rivalling those of women, suggesting that the combination of physical, protective power and potential for tenderness is superior to merely 'feminine' nurturing qualities. It is interesting that these types of images on greeting cards are beginning to outnumber those that portray a contemporary mother figure cradling a child.

Self-help Books for Men

As noted in Chapter 2, part of the growing interest in masculinity in the academic literature is an intensification of focus on the relationships between adult men and their fathers. Most popular books on masculinity also seek to address this relationship, positioning it as integral to the way men feel about themselves as adults, including their ability to relate to intimate others and their relationships with their own children. Much of this genre of self-help literature seeks to redress the negative emotions that men harbour about their fathers, including the hurts they remember from their boyhood and the anger and frustration they now feel in relation to their fathers. They draw on one of the dominant themes of the American-based 'men's movement', led by men such as Robert Bly, who have sought to encourage men to identify their feelings and express them to others, particularly to other men, and to defend their masculinity against the threats of feminism. Bly (1990) has called upon men to discover the 'real man' within through engaging in rituals with other men that supposedly re-establish an instinctive 'deep masculinity' to counter the 'feminization' and 'domestication' of western men. A pivotal issue of this literature is that of men's self-esteem, and the enormous influence that fathers are alleged to have upon their sons' view of themselves.

In his self-help book *Wrestling with Love: How Men Struggle with Intimacy with Women, Children, Parents and Each Other* (Osherson, 1992), the American author, a psychologist, addresses the fear of intimacy and dependence that he contends underlies most men's psyche. Osherson provides many case studies of men he has met through his work running encounter groups, as well as describing his own relationships with his father and his young son. He focuses on the pain, distress and emotional vulnerability of the men he has counselled, and underlines the importance for men of having a good relationship with their father. Osherson (1992: 231) argues that fathers are essential to their sons' development of masculinity, by setting limits and helping them learn to express 'healthy male aggression'. Boys, he argues, are continually striving for their father's affection and approval: 'The essence of a boy's dilemma is that it is very hard for him to truly feel what his heart most yearns for: that he is his father's beloved son' (1992: 66). Osherson further contends that many men go through their lives at times wanting a father figure to give them approval, and this in itself can be a source of distress: 'yearning for a strong daddy who will make everything right can feel very humiliating for a grown man' (1992: 78). Osherson seeks not to blame fathers but rather to argue that fathers do not often realize the importance they have for their children's self-esteem. Fathers may themselves feel inadequate, he contends, and unable to express their love and affection. Indeed one of his main arguments is that 'Fatherhood is a continual dance with uncertainty . . . There are few simple, easy answers, and often the uncertainty of being a father can be the hardest part of the experience' (1992: 243).

Steve Biddulph, an Australian psychologist who is well known in that country for his popular books and magazine articles on parenting and masculinity, similarly argues in his *Manhood: a Book about Setting Men Free* (1994) that men are victims, the 'prisoners' of their emotional timidity. Biddulph claims that 'there are very few happy men' (1994: 5) and that 'every man is damaged – limping along, putting a brave face on it' (1994: 6). Part of the problem, for Biddulph and fellow writers like Osherson and Robert Bly, is what they call 'father hunger', or

> the deep biological need for strong, humorous, hairy, wild, tender, sweaty, caring, intelligent masculine output. For long satisfying hours spent learning to be confident and capable in the world, in the pleasure of doing and making, striving together and laughing at adversity, learning the joy of being a man from men who know these things and are willing to share them. (Biddulph, 1994: 25–6)

Biddulph sees 'father hunger' as 'perhaps the most important concept in male psychology' and 'the starting point for most men in their own journey to health'. In his chapter 'You and your father', Biddulph elaborates on the father–son relationship and its implications for 'manhood'. He argues that men's masculinity is based on their fathers, and therefore 'If you are at war with him in your head, you are at war with masculinity itself . . . Unless you come to terms with him *he will haunt you from the inside*, where he symbolically lives forever' (1994: 31; original emphasis). Here again, the major route advised for coming to terms with one's father is to share one's thoughts and feelings with him, whether they are positive or negative. Biddulph contends that honest communication is the key, the solution to unhappiness, feelings of inadequacy and negative emotions between adult sons and fathers.

Biddulph goes on in a later chapter on 'Being a real father' to assert that without fathers, children become 'very screwed up', and indeed 'boys who do not get active fathering – either by their own father or someone who is willing to step in – will never get their lives as men to work' (1994: 94). He contends that the 'under-fathered' boy inevitably results in two (undesirable) archetypes: the overly aggressive boy and the 'Mummy's boy' (1994: 105–6). It is up to fathers, he argues, to ensure that children – particularly boys – are firmly disciplined as well as nurtured, because mothers are so caring that they find such discipline difficult. Fathers are also required to protect their adolescent daughters from dangerous or difficult situations.

Another book to argue against a more 'feminized' model of fathering is the American *Reinventing Fatherhood* (Gould and Gunther, 1993), a joint effort by a male psychologist and a male professional writer. The book addresses the 'men's movement' in developing its theme of the joys and challenges facing fathers today. Gould and Gunther argue that fathers need to learn from their negative experiences with their own fathers. Rather than hiding their feelings, using force to win compliance or simply ignoring their children, as 'fathers of the fifties and sixties' are assumed to have done, the authors suggest that men today should seek to engage in a closer, more 'open' relationship with their children. They argue that fathers should spend more time thinking about how to develop this relationship and learning how to be a better father. Indeed according to Gould and Gunther, fatherhood is more difficult than motherhood, because women 'instinctively' know how to engage in mothering:

> We all know that mothering is tied directly to a woman's biology. It seems to come naturally to her, surging forth from deep inside – wanting to nurture, wanting to care for, wanting to give love and wanting to communicate. But fathering? Where does that come from? It does not seem biological. Therefore, it must be a learned behavior. Where then do we learn to be fathers? (1993: 39)

As a result, Gould and Gunther contend, men require better preparation to be fathers. However, they should avoid becoming a 'feminized man' or 'A gentle, soft soul who has sold his power, his aggression, his unique maleness to the church of complacency. He has surrendered what made men different from women because he now believes that feminism can tell him how to be a better lover, a better husband and a better father' (1993: 41). They argue that to avoid this, men need to go back to 'what it means to be a man' and 'must concentrate on developing a sense of fatherhood that teaches his children that being a father is not being a mother' (1993: 41). As this suggests, Gould and Gunther are very much against the notion of the 'androgynous father' or the 'New Sensitive Male', whom they see as repressing his 'natural' maleness and male instincts. Rather, they claim to 'seek a way to use what is special to us as men and bring that into the family' (1993: 42). They see fatherhood as being unique, stating emphatically that 'Fatherhood is not motherhood' (1993: 43). Fathers, they contend, should use the 'male force' within them, the 'beast of maleness' to act as strong fathers and proper role models for their children (1993: 44).

In such writings, men's alleged inarticulateness, their inability to 'get in touch' with their feelings, the threat they feel from feminism, the supposed emasculinization that has occurred in men since feminism (that is, lack of encouragement to be 'hairy', 'sweaty', 'hard' and 'aggressive') are seen to be a source of powerlessness for men. These books suggest a profound anxiety around 'masculinity' and a need to define its boundaries in a time in which the distinctions between 'femininity' and 'masculinity' are seen to be blurring. In constantly seeking to define masculinity, and to comment upon the emotional lives of men, this literature positions women as Other. Sometimes women are overtly blamed for pushing fathers and sons away from each other, for smothering their sons with their love or as wives for threatening and emasculating men with their newly acquired feminist assertiveness and inner strength of will. Biddulph actually claims in his book, for example, that 'Some women hate all men and will see in male children an avenue of revenge' (1994: 113)! These writers typically contend that men should rediscover their lost power and should stand up to women, refusing to allow women to emasculate them. Men, it is argued, need to find out 'what it means to be a man' before they can know 'what it means to be a father'.

More subtly, the implication of this writing is that as a group, women are happy, emotionally fulfilled individuals by dint of their alleged superior capacity for expressing their feelings. In contrast, it is argued, men are in danger of becoming the lesser sex. Life, it seems, is much more complex for men than for women. Men are constantly needing to prove themselves to their fathers – the implication being that women do not have this need. This literature is addressed to men alone, and focuses on issues of manhood and masculinity, rather than to more universal questions of how people relate to each other. The solutions offered are superficial, with the assumption that revealing one's feelings will solve most problems. Another assumption is that the major cause of a poor father–son relationship is their shared inarticulateness, rather than, for example, a family history of abusive behaviour, violence or alcoholism on the part of the father. The problems that may be created by the potentially damaging secrets which might emerge from encouraging fathers and sons to reveal their feelings to each other is also glossed over. 'Openness', 'honesty' and 'talking things over' are represented unproblematically as universal panaceas.

Newspaper Reports

'Hard' news tends to depend on issues that are considered politically relevant and involves discoveries, conflict, announcements or criminal activities, while 'soft' news includes feature articles, opinion pieces and human interest stories (Bell, 1991: 14). Stories on fatherhood fit both categories. Fathers appear in 'hard' news reports if the stories are about new findings in academic research on fatherhood, social policy and trends analysis relating to fathers and families and fathers who abuse or kill their children. Issues around fatherhood also frequently appear as feature articles about fathers, masculinity and gender relations and as opinion pieces, including personal accounts of men's experiences as fathers and with their own fathers. News stories on fathers and fatherhood draw from a wide range of sources. These include not only the opinions of 'expert' knowledges of psychology, sociology and medical and public health research, but also, in the journalists' attempt to personalize the issues, men themselves in their role as fathers. Non-academic writers on self-help books on masculinity and child care, as well as academics, appear regularly as the voices of expert authority in news accounts and sometimes write feature articles themselves promulgating their perspective on fatherhood.

Like the social science literature, news accounts of fatherhood frequently single out particular groups of fathers as 'unusual'; that is, those who are defined as differing from the norm in some way, and therefore worthy of news attention. This is because the values of news are arranged around such properties as uniqueness, difference and bizarreness (Bell, 1991). Such groups include fathers who are deemed to be unusually young (the 'teen father' archetype) or the older than average or 'late-blooming father'. News articles have also regularly addressed the issue of the divorced father as a contemporary social problem.

As in the academic and popular literature on fatherhood, the 'absent' father has received a high level of attention in the print news media reporting of issues around fatherhood. One example is a feature article published in the *Weekend Australian* newspaper (2–3 September 1995) entitled 'A letter to absent fathers'. In the article, writer Bettina Arndt (known in Australia for her journalism on family relationships and sexuality) considered the issue of what she terms 'disposable dads'. Arndt argues that many men who have divorced their wives have been prevented from gaining familiarity with the basics of their children's lives and will inevitably find themselves isolated and alienated from their children. The article is illustrated with a photograph of a crying infant being held awkwardly by a man in a three-piece business suit. Arndt has continued with this theme, later publishing a controversial piece in the *Sydney Morning Herald* (30 July 1996) on single-mother families, in which she argued that sole motherhood is accepted uncritically, men's participation in family life has become devalued and that paternity is being treated with contempt. Arndt draws attention to the alleged ill-effects the lack of a father may have upon children, including poverty and lack of a nurturing male presence, contending that 'Every day in Australia, women are making decisions that deny children access to their fathers and sometimes even knowledge of who their fathers actually are. And in choosing to raise children in a single-parent family, the sad truth is that many are sentencing their offspring to a lesser life'. While she does not refer specifically to it, Arndt's debt to the 'fatherless families' thesis (see Introduction and Chapter 2) is apparent in her argument.

In another Australian newspaper article, journalist Ali Gripper discussed the phenomenon of '15 minute fathers', or those men who spend 15 minutes or less each day with their adolescent children (*Sydney Morning Herald*, 22 January 1996). The various experts (sociologists and psychologists) quoted in the article make reference to the 'devaluing of fatherhood' and the lack of energy and time that men busy with their careers have to devote to their children. It is contended that this is detrimental to the children's wellbeing. As one family psychologist is quoted as saying: '"If more people realised the enormous influence fathers have over their children, they'd spend far less time in the office."' These articles imply that simply acting as the 'breadwinner' is not enough for contemporary fathers – they must also have a presence within the domestic setting as a participative father.

The discourse of the 'absent' father has also been expressed in news coverage of criminals, particularly mass murderers. Attempting to employ psychological insights and even popular interpretations of psychoanalytic theory, journalists often seek to provide a portrait of a killer that examines his (in such cases the criminal is nearly always a man) motives and psyche, attempting to find clues from the man's early childhood and relationship with his parents to give some sense and meaning to his actions. Both fathers and mothers are implicated in this search for meaning as the source of their child's psychosis. Thus, for example, magazine and newspaper articles about Martin Bryant, the young man responsible for shooting and killing 35 people at Port Arthur, Tasmania in April 1996, made several references to his relationship with his father as the source of his apparently psychotic behaviour.

In a lengthy article published on 4 May 1996, the *Sydney Morning Herald*, for instance, alleged that Bryant was a loner who found it difficult to relate to people but desperately craved attention. It was reported that he was the product of a broken home in which his father regularly beat him: 'Neighbours described his father as a bully.' There were allegations quoted in the article that Bryant may even have been involved in his father's death, which had been classified as a suicide by police: 'He had often threatened to kill his father . . . friction was the main reason the son left home.'

So too, in the British press, profiles of the two 10-year-old boys, Jon Venables and Robert Thompson, who abducted and murdered two-year-old James Bulger near Liverpool, England, in 1993, sought to find explanations for the boys' actions in their family backgrounds. As Young (1996: 89–90) notes, the fathers of both boys were represented as physically or emotionally absent. Jon Venables' father, who was separated from his wife at the time of the murder, was portrayed as weak, ineffectual and soft, while media accounts routinely noted that Robert Thompson's father had left the family for another woman. This case instigated intense discussions in the news media about the problems of 'broken homes', paternal absence or lack of authority and the association of these phenomena with juvenile crime and delinquency.

'Toxic fathers' also regularly appear in the news in relation to sexual abuse of their children (particularly their daughters), violence towards their wives and abduction of their children. The effects that fathers may have upon their children's health are also frequently reported (although less so than news stories about the influence of mothers' behaviour upon their foetuses and children – see Petersen and Lupton, 1996: 75–80). In such articles the journalist usually draws upon medical or public health research as the basis for the story. One example is an article that appeared in the *Sydney Morning Herald* (28 September 1995) with the headline 'Babies smaller if father has a lot of coffee, study shows.' The journalist put forward the contention that if fathers have more than six cups of coffee a day then their infants are more likely to be born underweight and to die in infancy. Another article published that year in the same newspaper looked at the link that had been identified between miscarriages and fathers' exposure to toxic chemicals such as those emanating from oil-based paints and strong glues (4 January 1995).

In contrast to the 'absent' father debate, the 'new' father ideal has emerged over the past few years in news accounts. It is generally contended in stories on the 'new' father that this archetype includes men who are willing to take extra time from the demands of paid work to be nurturing and emotionally demonstrative with their children, as well as perform their fair share of the housework. This archetype is often lampooned in opinion pieces, with reference made to wimpish New Age Men with baby-food-stained trousers and a child hanging from each leg or to an ideal that men find impossible to achieve in 'real life'.

In more serious reports, the difficulties as well as the rewards that men face in attempting to emulate this archetype are explored. Men who have chosen to stay at home and be 'house husbands' or 'Mr Moms' are generally singled out as unusual and therefore worthy of attention. For instance, in an article on the lives of contemporary men, the British *Independent* newspaper (5 July 1996) reported on one man who had decided to switch to part-time work for a while to look after his baby. While it was noted that this man was enjoying having more time to spend with his child, his ambivalence was also discussed: "'I see all the traffic rushing to work; half of me feels elated that I'm doing something pleasurable with [his son] and half of me feels terrified that I'm not rushing to work too.'" This father went on to note that women are quick to offer their advice and criticism to him about his care of his son in ways that they would seldom venture to do with other women. A man interviewed for the Sydney *Sun Herald* newspaper (25 September 1994) similarly noted that staying at home as a full-time father was isolating and that fatherhood is underrated. Nonetheless, he was quoted as saying that "'It's a great opportunity for me as a father to be involved in parenting actively. I get so much from [the] children by doing that.'"

News reports often reproduce the notion that men and women have different styles of parenting. For instance, a *Sydney Morning Herald* article (19 October 1995) quoted the opinion of an Australian psychologist that fathers have an important and unique effect on their children's psyches, with the ability to both harm and enhance their emotional stability, and indeed could 'protect' their children from the negative effects of poor mothering. A lengthy article on 'dads flying solo', published in the March/April 1996 issue of the Australian general interest magazine *HQ*, gave several case studies of fathers who had custody of their children after divorce. The article quotes a child psychiatrist as observing that children are parented differently by fathers than by mothers. According to the psychiatrist, "'Men are more action-oriented; they have a natural inclination to focus on activities and experiences . . . it's a logical, deductive approach, whereas mothers are more intuitive, and tend to think along the lines of fostering relationships.'" Most of the fathers interviewed for the article described the 'steep learning curve' they had to enter after having been given custody of their children, including knowledge about domestic tasks and about the children themselves that they did not previously possess. There is a suggestion in the article that it is more difficult for solo fathers raising daughters than sons. The awkwardness experienced by fathers in talking to their daughters about such things as menstruation and sexuality is highlighted, as are the current sensitivities about fathers and sexual abuse of their daughters.

Several news articles have responded to and documented the development of the 'men's movement', raising the issue of the confusion, fear, frustration and sense of crisis that men in western societies allegedly currently feel about their masculinity and their role in life. As the male writer of one feature article published in the *Weekend Australian*'s feature section (9–10 March 1996) claimed, 'It's an epidemic, a great hollow-eyed army of stunned-mullet men, meandering in aimless circles across the blasted tundra of the industrialised world going, "Is this all?"' Part of men's supposed confusion, it is contended, is their uncertainty about what is expected of them as husband and father.

Writers of popular books on masculinity and fatherhood, such as Robert Bly and Steve Biddulph (see above), are frequently quoted in such articles as authorities on men. As in these books, women are portrayed as possessing certainty about their lives, as having 'found themselves', while men are left to ponder how best to pull together the fragments of their masculinity into some form of coherent whole. It is contended that, armed with feminism, women now have power, while men have become disarmed. As the author of the above article argued, 'while the men were getting soft, the women were getting hard . . . women have become the men of our generation. We have become the women. It is the men who learned to bake cakes, do the washing, care for the kids and unearthed 101 things to do with tofu.'

In an earlier piece, another Australian newspaper, the *Sun Herald* (5 September 1993), quoted the views of American writer Warren Farrell, who suggested that men have become 'disposable' and 'unlovable', and deprived of power: 'Middle-class men in industrialised nations are the most powerless people in the world.' Other pieces in this vein have addressed the concerns that fatherhood is becoming redundant, that men have been emasculated by the feminist movement and that what were seen as previously clear distinctions between fathers and mothers have blurred. One *Sydney Morning Herald* article (2 September 1994), for example, quoted the convenor of the conservative Institute of Men's Studies as saying that 'The father is the authority figure and that gives a sense of security to the family . . . Only a wholesale return to traditional roles will save and preserve the family unit in this country.'

Personal Accounts

It is not only the views of experts on fatherhood that are published in the popular media. A growing number of autobiographical accounts have begun to appear, in which men describe their own experiences of fatherhood. These writers include not only journalists and popular writers but academics writing on masculinity and men working in the 'expert' professions associated with family health and welfare. Thus, for instance, the psychologist Samuel Osherson in another of his books addressed to a popular audience, *The Passions of Fatherhood* (1996), notes in his Prologue that his professional interest and insights in fatherhood and family relations has inevitably stemmed from his personal experience of having a father and being a father: 'I've used my own parenting dilemmas – the father–daughter dance, cooperation and competition with my son, confronting my own childhood ghosts, finding my spirituality as a father – as a spring-board into understanding what it's like to grow up as a boy who becomes a father' (1996: xii). Such admissions, opening acknowledging that the writer's personal experience will inevitably intrude into his or her professional endeavours, is relatively new in writing about fatherhood, at least by male professionals. It is evident not only in books written for a popular readership but also in more academic texts (see Chapter 2). This trend suggests a new emphasis on the importance of acknowledging the emotional (and indeed 'spiritual') dimensions of fatherhood.

Osherson goes on to argue that 'there's a deeper rhythm of passion and hope that unites many parents. There's poetry in the ordinary, daily struggles of mothers and fathers, a High Drama of Over-looked Moments that I hope to capture in this book' (1996: xii). As these words suggest, fatherhood specifically and parenting in general are elevated in such writing to supreme personal achievements. Part of this, however, is the uncertainty that men and women are represented as having over how best to fulfil their roles as parents. Osherson notes that 'Sometimes it feels as if I'm constantly trying to invent my life, improvising as I go along. My life seems so different from that of my parents, less certain, without the security (and oppression) of clear definitions of what it means to be a father and mother' (1996: 6–7). He dwells in the book on the everyday, mundane aspects of fatherhood that invariably present him with existential and emotional dilemmas requiring much thoughtful consideration almost to the point of obsession. These dilemmas mainly revolve around what Osherson sees as the importance of being continually sensitive to his children's and wife's wishes and needs at the same time as not neglecting his own, and of maintaining an authoritative as well as sensitive demeanour as a father.

Further examples of such personal accounts are the chapters published in *Being a Father: Family, Work, and Self* (Pedersen and O'Mara, 1990). This book is a collection of articles that originally appeared in the American child care publication *Mothering Magazine*. The contributors are very much concentrated in the ranks of professionals: doctors, psychologists, therapists, counsellors, writers, graphic artists, photographers, musicians, social workers, academics and journalists. All the accounts are personalized in some way, even those written by 'experts' in the field. Such accounts of fatherhood frequently use not only an 'expert' discourse that draws upon social scientific and medical research on fatherhood, but also often incorporate a far more personalized view of fatherhood that discusses in detail its emotional dimensions. All tend towards a narrative in which a sense of personal discovery and change gradually emerges: the 'hard man' of stereotypical masculinity 'softens' into a more nurturing and sensitive (and often by corollary, 'feminized') individual. The men typically explore the deficiencies they see in the traditional model of the father as economic provider rather than source of emotional support and carer. In doing so, the writers often compare 'the traditional father', or their own father, represented as absent, preoccupied with his work, with the ideal of the 'new' father to which they seek to aspire.

In some cases, the writers recount their own transformation from the 'traditional father' to the 'new' father model. For instance William Sears (1990), the paediatrician father of seven children, recounts his journey from initially being a somewhat absent father, devoted to his job, with his first few children, to a father who by the time his last two children are born is determined to realize the ideal of participant fatherhood: 'I was determined to become a 100 per cent father – the best darn father in the whole wide world! Mindful of the familiar commercial slogan, '"Be all that you can be", I knew that I wanted to be all that I could be as a father' (Sears, 1990: viii). Sears describes how he participated in his sixth child's birth and was the first person to touch his new son as he emerged from his wife's body: 'As his slippery little body slid into my anxious hands, I knew that we were destined for a special relationship' (1990: viii). From that moment on, Sears asserts, he had much physical contact with his infant son, and became 'addicted' to him: 'I felt right when Matthew and I were together and not right when we were apart' (1990: ix). He goes on to argue that his new role as nurturing father provided a 'healthy sex role model' for his children and his activities, therefore, were 'a long-term investment'. Sears has realized, he says, the 'payoff of those early years of nurturing' as his son grows older. He ends by contending that 'Nothing matures a man more than nurturing his children' (1990: xi).

In these accounts, fatherhood is often referred to as 'a challenge', demanding flexibility and emotional sensitivity from men who may not find these easy. In his account, for example, Jack Heinowitz argues that many men 'have realized that imitating the father-as-provider image they grew up with does not satisfy deeper needs for self-expression, creativity, and personal growth or for closer, more meaningful contact with their children, partners, and friends' (1990: 3). He goes on to contend that his own experience of fatherhood and his attempts to 'becom[e] the kind of father I want to be' involved much work upon the self. For him, fatherhood has meant

> looking back, reliving, and analyzing many of my childhood experiences (pleasant and unpleasant); examining the attitudes and values I've learned about being a man, a father, and a partner; *un*learning much of what I've been taught and practicing the lessons I do value; continually redefining my sense of purpose and my ideas about masculinity and relationships; and saying good-bye to my old relationship with my parents while simultaneously establishing a new, more equal 'parent-to-parent' relationship with them as with my wife. (Heinowitz, 1990: 3; original emphasis)

Heinowitz argues that men in western societies are neglected during pregnancy – they do not have rituals to make them feel important or induct them into new fatherhood. Men need to 'bond' with their children during pregnancy and infancy just as women do. He uses the term 'pregnant fathers' and discusses men's responses to 'their pregnancy', including what he identifies as their feelings of neglect, envy or resentfulness as well as excitement at becoming a father, and their inability to express these feelings.

Similarly Ken Druck (1990: 12) emphasizes the emotional dimension of fatherhood. He advocates that men allow themselves to become emotionally expressive at the birth of their child: 'Expressing his feelings at the birthing can begin a process that enriches marriage and parenting, as well as the lives of his children, immensely.' By allowing himself to do this at the birth of his own daughter, Druck argues, 'I paved the way for a fuller emotional life for myself as a man, a husband, and a father' (1990: 13). So too, Robert Millar (1990: 22) describes the intensity of his feelings towards his son: 'I felt committed the instant my son was born. It was truly love at first sight.' He argues that he developed a new approach to life after the birth of his son, becoming far more empathetic and compassionate towards other people: 'Since his arrival, I have learned more about the nature of the human being and the nature of love than I ever suspected existed' (1990: 23). Millar contends that it is because of these feelings that 'parenthood can play a key role in the creation of a civilized society' by creating a brotherhood of love that extends from one's child to all humans, and encouraging men to recognize the importance of the bonds that attach people to each other and put the needs of others before their own (1990: 24).

Bruce Leigh (1990: 141) describes fatherhood as 'a worthy ambition' and 'perhaps the ultimate creative pursuit'. So too, Peter Dorsen writes that 'Marriage and children have made tremendous changes in my life – but, I would say, changes for the better. My wife and daughters symbolize my first real emotional commitment as a man' (1990: 29). Dorsen argues that men have the same capacities as women to be nurturers: 'It is a mistake to believe that only women have the correct genes to nurture, or that they have an exclusive handle on intimacy. That is to say, we, like women, are now allowed to share in nurturing and to be sensitive' (1990: 31). He describes how he himself had changed his profession from doctor to freelance writer so that he could have more time and flexibility to engage in fatherhood.

While many such personalized accounts recount the joyous and pleasurable dimensions of fatherhood, others discuss the negative aspects. For instance, Howard Skeffington writes:

> I am a father who struggles a great deal with how to spend time with my family. Fatherhood has struck me right to the heart. Unfortunately, my job leaves little room for flexibility. Frequent travel, unanticipated overtime, and weekend work occur all too often . . . It really tears at my soul to sit at a meeting away from home, knowing it will be hours before I see my son and daughter again. (1990: 77)

Victor LaCerva describes the 'importance of grief' in the transition to fatherhood, as well as 'the stress, fatigue and intensity of babydom' and the emotional separation from one's partner fatherhood involves: 'I miss my wife, my mate, my best friend, my lover. Where is she? . . . I am hungry to have time alone with her, to share myself fully . . . I feel like a master juggler, practicing and focusing on the art of balance. I toss work, the children, my wife, and myself high into the air each day and trust that life will provide what is necessary to nurture' (1990: 37). He then expands on the difficulties of his relationship with his wife: 'At those difficult times when we are not getting our needs met by our partners, we feel a great loss. If we do not express that loss and sadness, the walls go up, and with time become too strong to tear down' (1990: 38).

In a more extended personal account, Fraser Harrison (1987), a British professional writer, published a book in journal form about his experiences with his young children in a context in which he was undergoing a personal crisis, including a potential marital breakdown. He notes that 'as far as I am concerned the most important and influential experience of my recent life has been the existence of my children' (1987: 3). The book begins with a description of Harrison's first child's birth. Harrison describes it as the beginning of an adventure with his wife Sally: 'We felt like primitive heroes embarking on a mythic adventure into the unknown to be tested by the very gods of life and death themselves' (1987: 15). He describes his own feelings of anxiety and worry about the birth, his feelings of unaccustomed helplessness and impotence: 'I could never be more than an agitated but helpless observer; a hindrance, if anything. I could not bear the thought of Sally suffering, and I was very anxious about fainting, or worse, being sick' (1987: 17). When the infant finally was born, he writes, 'I felt a great onrush of love, which had a force and immediacy I had never known before' (1987: 23).

After discussing these early intense feelings in relation to his first child, Harrison goes on to describe a period in which he felt deeply unhappy, and for a time lost the intensity of love he had felt for his children:

> Their claims on my time and energy began to seem importunate; their little ways ceased to be charming and eccentric, becoming instead infuriatingly self-centred. Their incessant noise was no longer a merry chorus to our household life, but a clamorous and grating din; their clothes and toys seemed to gather in every room, like heaps of trash, turning the place into a slum; their questions no longer interested me; their games bored me; their jokes irritated me; their presence became intrusive and their very existence became a burden. (1987: 90)

What is interesting about this passage is not only its rare frankness in articulating at some length the negative feelings the writer has towards his children, but the emphasis he places on the way in which the children had apparently ceased to entertain him. There is little indication here of a sense of duty of care that he feels towards the children, but rather almost of the responsibility he feels his children have towards him to be 'bundles of joy', to 'charm' and 'interest' him rather than 'bore' him. Harrison further notes the guilt he feels in relation to his children: 'When I am with them, I feel guilty about my lack of patience; when I am not with them, I feel guilty about my negligence' (1987: 91). He goes on to describe the burden and fatigue imposed in the early years by his two young children, the uncertainties and anxieties he and his wife felt, the crumbling of their sense of self-identities as other than parents, the contradictory feelings both of liberation and of loss they experienced when both their children were finally attending school (he had worked at home throughout their early childhood and thus was quite involved with their care).

Despite recounting such difficulties, these personal narratives of fatherhood typically end on an 'upbeat' note, conveying optimism about the future. Overall, therefore, the positive aspects of fatherhood are very much emphasized in such forums. Fatherhood, it is argued, is a source of great personal joy, emotional development, creativity, personal 'growth', a means of discovering and better understanding the self, of better emphasizing and relating to others, learning greater powers of sensitivity, intensifying the positive feelings of love and altruism, forging a closer relationship with one's wife or partner. Few negative aspects of fatherhood are raised or discussed in detail. Those that are discussed tend to revolve around the competing tensions or pressures that men feel in relation to fulfilling the role of fatherhood, the feelings of resentment or envy they may harbour if they feel neglected by their partner's absorption in her pregnancy or infant. The frustration, fear and anxiety that may be caused by childbirth, dealing with a tiny infant for the first time or a diminishing in sexual activity also receive some mention. Such feelings are represented as 'natural' and understandable, able to be 'worked through' and dealt with if both partners are willing to be honest about their feelings and convey them 'openly' to the other.

The dominant discourse underlying the discussions of both the positive and negative aspects of fatherhood is that of fatherhood as an experience of personal growth for the father, a means to improve upon the self, a journey of self-discovery and fulfilment. It is assumed that the experience of fatherhood will lead invariably to a transformed, 'better person'. At the same time, it is considered important that men should not lose a sense of identity as individuals in coping with the demands of work, being a husband and a father and succeeding in all these areas.

Less emphasis is placed in these texts on social structural issues around the father–mother–child relationship; that is, the world of work, financial pressures, the welfare system, child care provision, parental leave and so on. Although the man's employment is often mentioned, it is usually in relation to the demands and pressures of the individual's own career rather than an analysis of the structure of paid work in general and its conflicts with family life. The difficulties and the joys of fatherhood are very much individualized to the man and his partner. Indeed, because nearly all the men writing such popular personalized accounts are engaged in middle-class occupations, with many of them self-employed or in jobs allowing a great deal of personal autonomy (for example as freelance writers, graphic designers or academics), they are able to arrange their working lives to suit their fathering activities better. As such, these men are far more privileged than most other fathers, who lack such autonomy and flexibility.

While some men discuss the comfort and support they gained from their male friends or a men's support group, there is little discussion of the extended family. The impression is given of the atomized dyad of father and mother, who must solve their problems together; seeking to work towards change in wider society is rarely canvassed. This approach echoes that of Parsons (1964), who wrote about the modern family as a self-supporting subsystem, no longer supported by extended family members, in which the father and mother each had a particular, and different, role to play. There is also little emphasis on men undertaking participative fatherhood in order to allow their partners to engage in paid employment, to address inequalities in men's and women's career trajectories and so on. Rather, the male writers refer mostly to their own self-fulfilment and the needs of the child.

Child Care and Parenting Books and Magazines

Popular child-rearing literature represents itself as a source of expert authority in questions of 'proper' child care and parenting, 'replacing kin,
community and parents themselves as sources from which knowledge about
raising children traditionally sprung' (Philipson, 1981: 57). Like many of the
contemporary books on masculinity, child care manuals blur the boundaries
between popular and 'expert' literature, written as they are mostly for a general audience but often by 'experts' who may refer to academic research in
their writings. Such publications are explicitly directed at parenthood as a
project of the self, a task that requires education and monitoring – it does not
necessarily 'come naturally'. As the English paediatrician Hugh Jolly wrote in
his *Book of Child Care*, 'We accept that training and advice are required for
every job a man or woman undertakes. The job of bringing up our children,
the most important we undertake, is no exception' (1981: 1). Jolly goes on to
contend that the product of such a project, the child itself, is the ultimate
reason for parents to undertake their responsibilities with care and awareness
of the most up-to-date knowledge:

> The early years of life are the most vital in laying down an individual's future pat-
> tern, both as regards whether he [*sic*] achieves his full intellectual potential and
> whether he is sufficiently secure and well rounded as a personality. Since these early
> years are so vital is there any need to argue the need for child upbringing to be a
> subject of study, in books and other media, for all parents? (Jolly, 1981: 1)

We noted in Chapter 2 that both child care manuals and magazines for parents have been in existence in the Anglophone world since the early
nineteenth century, and were at first directed at both fathers and mothers. By
the turn of the twentieth century, however, fathers were rarely mentioned in
these texts, while mothers were positioned as having primary responsibility
for raising children. This has remained the case until the last few decades.

Many manuals on child rearing and family relations these days take care to
use the generic term 'parent' so as not to distinguish between fathers and
mothers, and therefore presuming that parenthood is shared equally between
them. For instance, Jolly emphasizes in the introduction to his book that his
remarks are 'addressed to both mothers and fathers and I am thinking of
both when I use the term "you"' (1981: 1). Nonetheless, many of his remarks
are clearly directed at 'you, the mother' rather than 'you, the parent' or 'you,
father'. There are far more references in his book to 'mothering' activities and
difficulties and several indications that Jolly considers the role of the father as
far more secondary than that of the mother. In a section on the death of a
parent, for example, Jolly notes that 'A small child tends to react to the death
of his [*sic*] father with less open sorrow than to the death of his mother; this
is because it leaves less of a gap in his daily life' (1981: 330).

Similarly, in the British writer Penelope Leach's book *Baby and Child*
(revised and updated in 1988), there is little discussion of fathers. When
Leach does refer to fathers, it is very much as an adjunct to the mother.
Leach argues that fathers tend to be prevented from participating as an

infant's primary caregiver because 'mundane matters like jobs prevent them from being ever-present, always-responsive people' (1988: 122). She sees most fathers' primary role as coming later, when the child is older and the father is able to come home from work and play with the child: 'Because he has not spent the day trying to fit a sufficiency of chores and sanity-preserving adult activities around the baby's needs, he may be able to offer more of the social contact the baby craves' (Leach, 1988: 123–4).

The well-known American paediatrician and authority on child care, Dr Benjamin Spock, first published his *Dr Spock's Baby and Child Care* in 1945. The book has been revised and updated five times since then (and is now co-authored with another doctor, Michael Rothenberg). The first edition made little mention of fathers, devoting only nine pages to the father's role and noting that fathers should only have a minor role in child care, to give mothers the occasional rest (Stearns, 1991: 41). In the most recent edition published in 1992, Spock and Rothenberg address their comments to 'parents' rather than specifically to 'mothers' throughout. Nonetheless, the fact that fathers are singled out in several sections almost as a special case demonstrates that the book is still primarily directed at mothers. Similarly, in Spock's book *Parenting* (1989) there is a separate chapter on 'Being a Father Today' but no specific chapter singling out mothers.

In the first chapter of *Baby and Child Care* (Spock and Rothenberg, 1992), entitled 'The Parent's Part', there are sections on 'The supportive father in pregnancy and delivery' and 'The father as parent'. In these sections Spock and Rothenberg discuss the new father's mixed emotions at becoming a father and the need for fathers to provide support for their partners. Spock and Rothenberg emphasize the importance of the father, in particular, in playing a firm, disciplinary role with his children. They also suggest, however, that men should assist their partners in housework and child care: 'a father with a full-time job – even where a mother is staying at home – will do best by his children, his wife, and himself if he takes on half or more of the management of the children (and also participates in the housework) when he gets home from work and on the weekends' (1992: 27). The authors go on to emphasize the importance of fathers considering the care of their children to be as important as their careers, taking the time to share with their children and partners, putting family life as their first priority and letting it be known at their workplaces that they take their parental responsibilities very seriously (1992: 28–9). None of these injunctions is directed at female readers in relation to motherhood. Rather, it is simply assumed that mothers will automatically adopt such priorities and approaches to their role as mothers.

It was not until the late 1980s that most parenting magazines again began to include a substantial number of articles dealing specifically with fatherhood and appealing to fathers as a readership. Even these articles tend to portray fathers in a peripheral role – popular parenting magazines remain directed far more at mothers than at fathers. One British magazine, despite being entitled *Parents*, suggesting an appeal to both fathers and mothers, is subtitled 'Smart solutions for today's *mums*' (emphasis added). The text of feature articles and advice columns and the visual imagery in the front covers, illustrating articles and in the advertising in these 'parenting' magazines similarly betray an almost exclusive focus on motherhood rather than fatherhood. The front covers usually portray either a baby by itself or a smiling young and pretty mother with her baby. Similarly, the visual images inside abound with young women either in a state of advanced pregnancy or cuddling their infant protectively, feeding it, changing its nappy or playing with it. There are far fewer men shown, either with infants, by themselves or even as part of a family unit (mother, father and child or children) together.

The content of the articles published in such magazines also tend to be directed more at mothers than fathers. We reviewed a sample of issues of *Australia's Parents*, an Australian parenting magazine that is published every two months and has a circulation of over 40,000. In the 18 issues of this magazine published between August 1991 and March 1995, we found only four articles directed specifically at men in their role as fathers. One was a humorous account of the role played by fathers at the birth of their child, a second gave advice to fathers on the handling of their infants, the third described the personal experiences of three men at their child's birth and during their child's early years and the fourth discussed the relationship between fathers and sons. An additional article humorously explored the experience of vasectomy 'from a father's point of view', while several others discussed issues dealing with relationships between parents.

Many articles, in contrast, focused specifically on the pregnant woman or mother and her health or relationship with her child, bearing such titles as 'Mothers of all ages: teens, 20, 30 and 40' (December/January 1991) and 'Love, sex and motherhood: what to expect in the bedroom when you have a family' (April/May 1992). The magazine carried regular features on health for pregnant women and mothers, recounting women's stories of the birth of their children and fashion and beauty tips for pregnant women and mothers. So too, the advice and letters columns in the magazine were dominated by letters from women requesting help with their concerns or expressing their experiences in relation to pregnancy, childbirth or raising children.

The rhetoric of parenting magazines and books, thus, in their use of the term 'parent' in their titles, is somewhat contradictory and misleading. The use of the term 'parent' implies a joint endeavour, equally shared between men and women. Nonetheless, the actual content of such magazines and books demonstrates a continuing focus on the dominant role played by the mother in parenting. Women are constructed and interpellated as the predominant readership of the magazines. Marshall (1991) examined best-selling British and American child care and parenting manuals published from 1979 to 1988 for the ways in which they represented motherhood. She found that the manuals suggest that the family with a heterosexual, married couple is the best context within which to bring up a child, and the mother is portrayed as the primary care-giver, a more important figure than the father in providing loving care, if not financial support for the child. It is ultimately the mother's responsibility to produce a 'normal', 'well-adjusted' child. Women, however, are encouraged to share the child care with their partners, taking responsibility for involving them in salient activities such as childbirth.

In this context, using 'parent' rather than the more specific 'mother' or 'father' tends to gloss over the continuing differences in the experiences of men and women as parents, including the burden of responsibility that tends to be placed upon women rather than men in terms of infants and children's physical and emotional wellbeing. Reay (1995) has raised a similar point in her analysis of academic texts on parental involvement in children's education. She notes that most of these texts referred to a gender-neutral parent and were premised on the notion of the unitary subject, even though women carried out the majority of activities. Reay argues that 'Usage of the term "parent" without any qualification as to which parent, acts as an invitation; it leaves open the possibility of paternal involvement. Its consequences are the inclusion of fathers in an area where, in reality, many are absent' (1995: 337).

Concluding Comments

Contemporary popular representations of fatherhood frequently seek to portray men as achieving a more 'feminine' side through their fatherly activities. They often draw upon the discourse of the 'sensitive new age man' as the model for appropriate behaviour by fathers. That is, it is assumed that men should seek to express their emotional states when relating to their children and partners (particularly those emotions that are regarded as highly positive, such as love, affection and caring), that they should 'talk over' with their partners, friends or appropriately trained professionals any problems that might arise in the attempt to deal with problems before they become destructive and they should display empathy towards the feelings and experiences of their children and partners.

Popular representations of fatherhood, therefore, are equally prescriptive in their portrayal of the 'good' and the 'bad' father as are academic writings. Some popular accounts, such as parenting manuals and magazines, are overtly didactic, often using 'experts' in the field as the voices of authority advising parents how they should best behave to achieve a well-socialized and successful child and a stable family unit. Other popular media representations of fathers, particularly those intended to entertain rather than to inform their audiences such as television and cinematic comedy and drama, have a less overtly pedagogic style. Nonetheless, the choices of representation made in these texts, the discourses and images that are privileged over others, more subtlely convey a set of meanings that may be just as important in constructing notions of fatherhood.

There is no guarantee, however, that the audiences to which such popular accounts are directed will take up the dominant meanings on fatherhood they convey. As writers in the field of media and cultural studies have noted, audiences' response to popular media texts may vary enormously. Such factors as gender, sexual identity, age, ethnicity and social class, as well as individuals' life experiences and personal biographies, influence the ways in which they respond to the media (Lewis, 1991; Morley, 1992). For example, while a man may possess a large number of popular parenting books and magazines and may often consult them or discuss them with his partner, it is not necessarily the case that his own parenting practices and attitudes will be strongly influenced by the advice imparted within. In the next two chapters, we go on to discuss some of the findings from our interviews with first-time fathers, looking at how they describe their own experiences and from where they think they have derived their knowledge of the appropriate conduct of fatherhood.

4

Biographies of Fatherhood

In this chapter and the next, we draw upon our empirical research with first-time fathers, involving a series of one-to-one semi-structured interviews. As we noted in the Introduction, the research involved a cohort of 16 couples, with the man and woman interviewed separately. All the participants except for one couple were living in Sydney at the time in which the study took place (the other couple lived in Newcastle, a large metropolitan city close to Sydney). Each participant took part in at least six interviews: just before their first child was born, at approximately a week after the birth, and again at three to six weeks, five to six months, one year and 16–18 months after the birth (see the Appendix for further details about the interview process and the participants).

This longitudinal qualitative method of research produced a mass of rich data. As is inevitable with any reporting of qualitative data, we have had to make difficult decisions about which issues to discuss and whose words we use to illustrate our points. While we recognize the importance of providing the perspective of the female partner in the couple on parenting and her partner's involvement in and response to fatherhood, for example, we simply do not have the space here to explore this aspect (although we plan to do this in our future writing). For the purposes of this book, we decided to focus only on the men's interview data, and to present some of the findings from these data in two ways: first, as a number of individual case studies, allowing the presentation of four men's experiences of early fatherhood in detail, and second, under topical themes. The present chapter outlines the case studies of four men – Richard, Mike, Jim and Tony – chosen because their narratives exemplify men from mixed socioeconomic and ethnic backgrounds with a range of different approaches to and experiences of first-time fatherhood.

Poststructuralist Phenomenology

Our approach melds together the traditional interests of phenomenology – attempting to gain access to the 'lived experience' of our participants through their own words and narratives – with poststructuralist notions of the research procedure and the ways that this procedure itself participates in the construction of data. As with the data collected in quantitative methods, researchers adopting phenomenological approaches often tend to view their participants as unified subjects expressing a single 'truth' of their existence through their words. From a poststructuralist critique, these assumptions are rather naive, failing to recognize that the data produced by such methods are social products that are highly contextual. The interview, therefore, may be seen as 'an interactional and discursive accomplishment' , in which language is viewed not simply as 'a neutral conduit for description' but rather as 'the very action through which local realities are accomplished' (Holstein and Gubrium, 1994: 265).

The people we talk to in interviews will always choose particular narratives as demanded by the situation and their own need to present themselves in certain ways. As Hollway has noted,

> I know from paying close attention to myself giving accounts in a variety of different settings, that I have a stock of ready narratives to draw on which fit particular situations and which will tell me nothing new unless the person I am talking to helps me to produce something new. It can be new to me at the same time as seeming a better account of a previous experience than any previous account. I have realized that there is no context, however private and searching, which could provide the account which tells the whole truth. The number of possible accounts is infinite. (1989: 41)

As this suggests, even research methods that deliberately attempt to gain access using sensitive interviewing techniques to participants' thoughts and experiences are never able to obtain 'the whole truth', but rather are inevitably partial versions. The use of language to convey meaning is always mediated through acculturated norms, conventions and rules about 'ways of talking' and 'what might be said'. The ways in which people in an interview or conversation represent themselves is just as much a constructed text, a particular version of reality, as is a newspaper article or academic text. This perspective entails that researchers adopting qualitative methods such as interviewing do not seek to render their methods more 'scientific', but instead turn their attention towards 'understanding the conditions which produce accounts and how meaning is to be produced from them' (Hollway, 1989: 42).

This is not to argue that people's accounts of events, beliefs and experiences are 'fiction' or 'lies'. Rather, they are articulated in response to a number of contextual factors, including the types of questions asked, the style of the interviewer and their mood at the time. Further, as we noted in Chapter 1, the ways in which people articulate their responses about a particular topic are always the product of the resources they have available to them, including the pre-existing discourses that are circulating within their own sociocultural setting acting in conjunction with people's personal biographies and the unconscious level of meaning. Participants in any research study will take up particular ways of expressing their opinions and recounting their experiences that are inevitably shaped through social and cultural processes and meanings.

Thus, rather than assuming such strategies as depth interviews are getting at the 'truth' in a more profound manner than other research methods, the premise is that such strategies provide a means of eliciting and uncovering patterns in the ways people articulate their feelings, experiences and conscious opinions. The emphasis of the analysis is upon the structure of people's explanations, the words, phrases, concepts and belief systems they use to describe phenomena and beliefs and represent their experiences, and the other texts they draw upon in their explanations. Particularly important is the identification of the ways in which speakers organize their explanations to provide coherence. The focus is therefore not so much on to what extent respondents are conveying an 'objective' reality, but how they express their understandings and experiences of reality incorporating both contradictory and overlapping discourses. Such discourses may be identified and theorized with the understanding that they are ways of positioning subjects and allowing them to make sense of their experiences.

So too, we as researchers are co-producers in the data, by formulating a particular research question and deciding to ask certain questions in certain ways, and then by making choices about how we interpret and use the data. Our own personal and psychic biographies, including such aspects as our age, ethnicity, gender and history of relationships with intimate others, will inevitably shape our participation in constructing the data. We bring to the research various epistemologies and beliefs, and we will have our own investments, desires, phantasies and emotional responses in relation to the issues we raise and explore. Like our research participants, we have recourse to the same sorts of pre-established discourses in expressing and understanding meaning and experience. There is no way of removing our own 'ways of seeing' from the research process, but it is possible to attempt to engage reflexively in the process, so that we can at least attempt to be aware of our vested positions and interpretive frameworks.

Richard

At the time of the first interview, Richard was very much looking forward to the birth of his first child. He was 38, somewhat older than most of the other fathers in the study, and had been married to Prue, ten years younger than he, for six years before she became pregnant. The pregnancy had not been planned, but the couple had been discussing 'trying' for a child just before they discovered that Prue was pregnant. Both Richard and Prue were Australian-born of Anglo-Celtic ethnicity. They were living in a rented older-style house in a southern Sydney suburb when the study began. The couple moved to a suburb on the outskirts of the city a year later to share a large house of their own with other family members. Richard had led a very active life, heavily involved in interests such as martial arts and the scouting movement, before meeting Prue and deciding to settle down. He was adopted, and his adoptive parents had divorced when he was a small boy. He had lived with his mother after the divorce, but remained close to his father and said that he loved and respected him very much. Richard did not have brothers and sisters and had developed a very close relationship with Prue's parents and her siblings.

When he was first interviewed, shortly before the birth of his child, Richard described himself as both excited and overwhelmed by the proximity of the birth and impending fatherhood. When asked what was most important or significant to him about the pregnancy, he said: 'Bringing a new life into the world, I think, was the most significant thing, the joy of having something a part of us . . . the child is just sort of a part of me and a part of Prue, growing up so together. We'll bring this child up to be some sort of a decent citizen, and find that to be a bit of a challenge as well.'

Richard commented that he had owned many dogs throughout his life and thought that his experiences with them as puppies would help him manage the responsibilities of fatherhood. In addition, Richard believed that his experience with children through his participation in the scouting movement and teaching martial arts would help him handle this new experience. He argued that his martial arts work had taught him about stress and handling his temper and lack of patience, all qualities he considered important in undertaking fatherhood. Richard had also done a lot of reading – 'we've got a library full of baby books in this place!' – and said that he had found antenatal classes informative, including being able to meet other parents-to-be. He had also attended all Prue's doctors' appointments with her and said that he felt 'ready' and 'prepared' for the child's arrival. Nonetheless, Richard also noted that he felt quite fearful and apprehensive about how he will handle the birth of his child and deal with a new infant:

> Over the years, when a baby's been handed to me, it's either cried or piddled, or both! And so they're very scary to me . . . they're so little, fragile . . . that scares me a little bit, 'cause I want to look after it [but] I would be scared to pick it up because I might break it . . . I feel a little bit anxious, probably more than frightened. I'm not sure how I'm going to handle it. I think I know how I'm going to handle it, I know how I should handle it, but doing that when the time comes is an entirely different matter!

Richard is a salesman. He said that he enjoyed his job and thought that he did it well, but saw his job as only a means to an end – his first priority was Prue, and then the baby. Richard had negotiated his working life to meet this priority. The responsibilities of providing for both Prue and the baby were very important to him. He said that of the two jobs he held during the first six months in which he participated in the study, he preferred the former, because the boss was a family man who put his wife and children first. However, Richard had changed jobs, moving to a position with a higher salary so that they could manage more comfortably without Prue's wages: she had decided to give up her job as an administrative assistant with a large company to stay at home for a while with the baby. Richard said that he saw himself very much as the provider for both Prue and the baby, although this was not in the sense of future career plans but rather his immediate earning capacity. Richard was apprehensive about how they would manage financially, as Prue was earning more money than he was. He commented, however, that he and Prue felt strongly that the baby needed someone at home with it constantly, and as Prue wanted to be the one to stay at home to care for the child, he was the one who had to work. Richard said that fulfilling Prue's needs was important to him.

Richard's vision of what a father should be was very much shaped by his own (adoptive) father. He said that he saw himself as quite similar to his father, who had done all he could for him financially, including working extra hours to pay for private education at 'the right school'. For Richard, his father was a role model to look up to and emulate. When talking about his father, Richard did not mention love or sharing activities with his father as part of the relationship, and indeed in a later interview he commented that it was his mother who actually cared for and disciplined him. Although Richard still perceived his father as highly influential, he began to see that his mother might have been the most important, formative person in his early life. He said, 'if I can bring my child up half as good as she brought me up, I'll be really happy.'

Richard also saw part of his preparation for his child as emotional. He said that he expected that the baby might be strong willed and determined:

> It's probably going to be a right little terror! I was a little terror when I was a kid, from all accounts. Prue was a little terror too. I was a real rebel when I was a child. Everybody hopes that their child will be nice and easy to handle, so there's not too much disruption to their sleep patterns, and everything else. That is fine, but on the other side of the coin, it may not be that way. I was a stubborn child and I'm still a stubborn adult, just stubborn in different ways now. I am a determined person and I hope my child will be the same. Prue's very similar too. I'm pretty sure we will have a stubborn child – with two stubborn parents there's going to be a lot happening!

Richard also described both Prue and himself as having quick tempers, but thought that they were able to talk about problems openly and easily and were both able to show affection and love openly: 'I don't mind going up and giving somebody a cuddle, or I sit down and watch a movie sometimes and start crying.' He did not imagine he and Prue would have difficulty allowing a child into their relationship. He perceived this openness in expressing emotion as positive and as potentially contributing to a harmonious family life with their future child. Richard thought that the pregnancy had resulted in he and Prue becoming closer as a couple, more affectionate and mature. They had been going without sex, for example, because they wanted what was best for the baby even if that meant a little inconvenience.

Richard felt that the pregnancy had had a maturing effect on his approach to life: 'As I mentioned to the other guys in the [antenatal] class last night, I've just grown up. I've grown up – the responsibility has made me grow up a little bit, and look at life a little bit differently. There is life after me.' He said that he found this sense of social continuity and the notion that each life leads into another important. Richard described the reason that he and Prue had pets was to give them 'something to bond to' while they waited until they were ready to have a child. He had considered that the baby might be born 'handicapped' and had already decided that whatever happened they would give the child a home and care for it.

Richard described the first few days of his new son Daniel's life as 'a great learning experience for me'. While he said that he found fatherhood very enjoyable, he noted that it is not something you can just take on very lightly, so you do have to be prepared for it, with your attitude and your emotions. You've got to prepare yourself, whether that be through books and magazines or watching videos or talking to other people. I think you've just got, you've got to do a bit of research on it to find out what it's like. You've got to either have friends or know people who have friends or go and talk to a professional to find out what it's all about.

After the birth, an uncomplicated and relatively straightforward delivery, and a 'honeymoon' period of a week or so, reality set in. From being optimistic and excited, Richard described several weeks after the birth how his and Prue's positive attitudes have become 'a bit undermined'. The difficulties they experienced were unanticipated by them both. Richard said he knew 'it was not going to be easy', but they did not dream it would be as hard as it was. Daniel cried a lot, and neither he nor Prue knew what to do to stop the crying. He said that they soon learned to recognize a 'feeding cry', which they could easily deal with, but Daniel's other cries were less straightforward: 'It wasn't wet nappies, it wasn't wind, it wasn't cold, he may have been over-tired – we didn't know what it was, and we couldn't help him stop crying. It frustrated me, because we thought we were pretty well on the ball here. Why couldn't we stop him crying? Nothing we did made any difference. We didn't know *what* was wrong with him.'

Richard found this very frustrating and difficult to cope with, and said that he had 'learnt a lot about myself' in dealing with the experience. He described how Daniel's incessant crying tried his patience to a level that actually distressed and angered him, so much so that he had to just leave the house at times to regain some emotional equilibrium:

> I'm not an impatient person, but I do have a limit of how far I can go. I'm usually a great person when I'm in control of things, but when I can't [control things] I get upset with myself. If the baby gets too stroppy, sometimes if he doesn't settle, I get upset. I end up giving him to Prue, or putting him down somewhere, and walking out. I'm not as patient as I thought I was, and I'm not in control as much as I thought I should be.

Richard had to redefine his role to fit with a situation he had not expected. He described himself as becoming 'a pacifier of everything, a pacifier of Prue, a pacifier of Daniel and a pacifier of me!' The couple eventually turned to their early childhood nurse for advice on Daniel's crying and difficulty in settling. They found her help reassuring and it astounded them how simple things could be when understood from a different position. Problems were no longer defined as a mark of their own 'failure' as parents. For example, when Daniel had problems getting to sleep, and the nurse had noted that this was consistent with Prue's own light sleeping behaviour, it seemed less their fault that Daniel was not behaving as expected.

According to Richard, one of their biggest problems in dealing with Daniel was their lack of personal experience with infants prior to having their own. Despite going to classes, reading and undertaking other activities offered by health professionals, Richard noted that he and Prue simply did not know 'what babies were like'. Visiting a family support unit to try to manage

Daniel's crying, and seeing other babies and their behaviour, made them realize that their baby was no different from other babies, and that they were not
handling him 'wrongly'. This was immensely reassuring to them. It was only
when Richard realized that they had to try out different things themselves to
see what suited Daniel and themselves that they began to adjust comfortably
to parenting their baby:

> It's very strange – you read all the books and all the books say some things, and
> then you talk to health workers and they say something else and you talk to
> another health worker and they say something entirely different. [You could] talk
> to another half a dozen [professionals] and they would give a different opinion
> again. We could have managed it a lot better than we did. We were getting frus-
> trated, so he was picking up on our tension and of course he was getting upset.
> They [the health professionals] didn't have any magic answers, but they could say,
> 'You're not doing anything wrong.' This was reassuring because we always thought
> what we were doing was wrong because this baby should not be crying.

As Daniel became older, things got a little easier, and Richard and Prue grew
in confidence and skill in caring for him. Some of the joys of fatherhood now
became evident, and Richard's identification with the baby, including recognizing physical or personality traits in Daniel that reflected his own, became
even stronger. At five weeks of age, Daniel was demonstrating the characteristics that Richard expected: 'He is his own person, he is pretty stubborn,
because we're both very stubborn people, [and] because we've both got tempers.' Richard found that he and Prue needed to 'read Daniel's signals' in the
same way they had learned to 'read each other's signals' over the duration of
their relationship. By the time Daniel was a month old they had begun to
work out some of these signs. Richard started to define a 'good' father differently as time went on. The role of provider became less important as he
began to realize that for him a 'good' father was someone who was able to
learn, take advice from others and eventually be able to make his own judgement. He commented, 'I don't care what anybody says, there's no harder job
in the world than looking after a baby.'

Richard described Daniel at five weeks old as an 'angelic devil'. This phrase
well demonstrates Richard's ambivalent feelings about new fatherhood,
incorporating his intense love for Daniel as well as his disappointment with
an experience that did not live up to his expectations and his own sense of
failure in not coping with this as well as he had hoped. When Daniel was
crying he was exhibiting his 'devil' state. Crying signalled failure for this
father and caused him distress. When Daniel was happy or asleep he was an
'angel'. Richard said that he enjoyed cuddling Daniel when he was happy but
found this distressing if he was fractious or crying.

At the interview held when Daniel was six months old, Richard described
how pleased he was when the baby was weaned, a few months after birth
and how he 'fell in love' with Daniel when he could feed him using the
bottle. Richard gave Daniel his very first bottle after weaning, and commented that was really very important to him. He said that he enjoyed
feeding Daniel, and did it regularly, which allowed him to give more help

with Daniel's care. Indeed Richard felt, in retrospect, that most problems were resolved when Daniel went on the bottle. He claimed that Prue never liked breastfeeding in the first place and only did it because she was told it was better for her and the baby. The issue of loss of spontaneity in, and control over, their lives was a major feature of Richard's early experiences of fatherhood. He commented that their lives were 'now controlled by this little person' in a way that was 'impossible to imagine beforehand'. He and Prue no longer had any outside entertainment and while this was not a big issue for them, it was not possible for them to do what they wanted just when they felt like it. For example, he commented, 'You've got to pack nappy bags and you've got to get organized . . . you can't make love on the lounge room floor anymore!'

This relatively negative portrayal of fatherhood was put into perspective in an interview conducted 16 months after Daniel's birth, when Prue was pregnant with a second child. Richard was asked how he felt about having another small baby in the family. He replied that he felt confident and was looking forward to the experience because he believed it would not be so difficult the next time around. He and Prue now knew how to handle parenting a new baby. Richard described how it was attitude that mattered, and their attitude had now changed because they had learnt from experience: 'before we were floating around in "no man's land", not knowing what we were supposed to do and doing everything by trial and error.' Richard said their anxiety levels would be much less and, as they would be living with his mother-in-law who had had seven of her own children, they would have a lot of help this time. Life was enjoyable again and while they still did not get out much, they enjoyed having friends over, just watching Daniel grow up and enjoying one another's company.

Richard's role as a father at this stage was still very much related to being the economic provider, as Prue had not returned to work. Richard said that there were no arguments over who does the chores for Daniel or the household, as tasks were divided up on the basis of the person for whom it is most convenient at the time. This was usually Prue, because she was the one who spent most time at home, although Richard said that he did his best to engage in such activities as bottle feeding when he was at home. He argued that Prue herself wanted to stay at home:

> I've seen people that go to work and leave their kids in child care and stuff like that. I think the child and the mother miss out on a fair bit. With Prue, I don't think she'd go back. I couldn't tempt her to go back to work for 50 or 60,000 dollars a year. She wouldn't go . . . She thoroughly enjoys staying at home – she likes being a mum. She likes looking after him, likes being with him. She gets her spare time to herself when he's asleep and she gets the housework done – it's a bit hard to do it when he's awake. But yeah, she would prefer to be at home.

Richard said that he eagerly anticipated the time where he could be more involved in activities with Daniel as he gets older: 'I'd take him camping tomorrow if I could!' Even though he worked long hours and was away from home for 12 hours on week days because of travelling for his work as a salesman, he described how he spent the first hour and a half in the morning every day playing with Daniel. Richard said that he was now 'having a ball . . . I don't think I've ever been this happy in my life!' He said that he felt 'complete', emotionally stable, 'comfortable, whole and healthy' as a father. He felt that he had become much more emotionally expressive, able to articulate his feelings better. When asked how he would define a 'good' father now, he said: 'Well, *I* am now. Providing, spending time with my family – every spare minute I spend with him – just doing things as a family and enjoying one another's company, and just watching him grow.'

When asked to look back over the time since Daniel's birth and comment on it, Richard said that he had been surprised by two things. First, that while he and Prue expected it to be difficult with a new baby, they were not expecting it to be '*that* difficult'. Those distressing times, however, were now too far distant to remember: 'that was long ago, that was yesterday, two thousand years ago!' Second, and more profoundly, that it is possible to love two people as deeply as he loves Prue and Daniel: 'as far as the emotions are concerned, I didn't know I would get so deeply involved. I knew I would get involved but I didn't think I'd get to the stage where I'd run out of work 'cause I wanted to come home!' Richard noted that the intensity and depth of love he felt for Daniel began when he started to feed him with the bottle, and the more he cared for Daniel, the stronger his relationship became with Prue as they shared this care.

Richard argued that every man should provide this care to his child: 'I think if they did, they'd never raise a hand to hurt [their children] at all . . . It's falling in love with another person. That's all it is.' He contrasted this intensity of feeling with his father's generation: 'they never spent time watching [their children] grow up. They were too busy working and socializing or doing other things so I just don't think they spent the time with them.' Richard said that if he could work from home, he would do so, to enable him to spend more time with Daniel. He described the joy he felt at arriving home from work and seeing Daniel's response to him: 'I come in the door. If he's down the hallway or something like that and he hears the door close, he comes around and puts his head around the corner and goes, "Ohhh Dad!" and runs up the hall to me. What more could you ask for?'

Mike

Mike and Jenny had been married for a little over three years when she became pregnant with their first child. At the time, Mike was in his early thirties and Jenny was five years younger. Mike, a plumber, grew up in a large Greek working-class family in the inner suburbs of Sydney. Jenny was born and grew up in Wales and worked in a plant nursery before the birth of their daughter Grace. The couple met when Mike was on a working holiday in Europe and married after Jenny decided to visit him in Australia. At the time of the first interview, the couple were living in their own semi-detached house in suburban Sydney, but they moved a year or so afterwards to a house with more room and a larger garden for their child.

At the first interview, Mike said that he was highly delighted about his partner's pregnancy, although it was unplanned and Jenny would have preferred to wait longer before having children. He said that he had wanted to have a child since his early twenties. Now, a decade later, he wanted it to happen before he got any older. Mike described preparing for fatherhood during the pregnancy by changing his priorities, 'getting finances in order', and gradually reducing his time away from home with male friends on sporting activities. He believed that fathers should be providers who 'will steer the kid in the right direction and be there for them'. Mike contrasted this image with his experiences of his own father, describing him as 'a drinker, a gambler who was never home – I don't want to be like this'. He talked about worrying about the baby being healthy and wondered if it would look like either of them.

Mike found preparing for the baby more demanding than he had initially expected. He had attended antenatal classes and the birth centre with Jenny and said that he found the information of good quality and useful, although he had some reservations about the number of choices he felt he and Jenny were required to make in relation to how the birth would be conducted. They had eventually chosen a midwife delivery in a birth centre. During the birth, labour progressed slowly and Jenny became distressed and tired. Mike described much effort over many hours and considerable encouragement from the midwife before Jenny finally delivered their daughter Grace: 'how guys can say, "Oh, the birth of my baby was the most wonderful experience of my life!" beats me, because what Jenny went through, I wouldn't put that on anybody.'

In the interview held a week after the birth, Mike said that things were progressing well, although he remained apprehensive that something would go wrong. He seemed not to have quite conceptualized his child as an individual yet, describing her as 'the baby' and 'it' rather than using her name, as in the following description of Grace: 'it's obviously not playful, it's not playing yet, it's actually wondering what's going on because it doesn't know, most of the time when it's awake it just wants to be fed.' Mike commented that he was finding things easier than expected, although he described Jenny as very 'edgy' and 'nervous'. He thought this was because of her lack of sleep. He said that he himself sleeps heavily and, if woken, he finds it very difficult to get out of bed. Mike related how they had 'no sleep' for about four nights but that it was improving. The first night at home Jenny had got up seven times to change and feed the baby, while he had slept through.

Sleeplessness remained a major issue for Mike and for the couple and their relationship. In the interview held when Grace was four weeks old, Mike described how Jenny was now sleeping in a different room. This was because, as Jenny was breastfeeding, she was the only one who could feed Grace, who was waking every two hours throughout the night. Mike commented that he now did not even hear the baby crying. Mike's daily routine had not changed very much as Jenny was undertaking almost all Grace's care and most household responsibilities: 'I have bathed her a few times. I like bathing her, I don't like changing her, but I don't dislike it, I'll change her when I have to.' In the first few weeks, the couple argued about his contribution to the household and work generated by the baby. This was frequently expressed in disagreements over missed sleep. Mike said that Jenny expected him to initiate or offer to help more than he did and was resentful that he could find it possible to get out of bed early to go fishing on a Sunday morning but not to feed the baby. He was concerned that Jenny was losing sleep but felt that, unlike him, she could catch up on sleep during the day, because she did not have to 'go to work': 'at 11 o'clock at night, Grace's still screaming and Jenny is trying to put her to sleep. I feel guilty because I'm lying in bed trying to sleep because I know if I don't get my sleep I can't get up in the morning and function normally.'

Four weeks after his daughter's birth, Mike was reviewing his new responsibilities as a parent. He was thinking about the importance of protecting Grace from 'the corrupt side of life, drugs and things like that' and helping her lead a useful life: 'I'm there to protect her – I hope she looks back when she's 21 and she says, "What a great dad!"' It surprised him that he was already concerned about Grace's education and future relationships with others, and how he could help her in life: 'I just hope I do everything right, that I don't have any regrets about being a father. I'll do my best to be a good dad, spend as much time with her as I can, that's one of the main concerns.' Mike said that he was getting some of the social rewards he expected and wanted in his changed status as father. For example, he described the pleasure of taking Grace for a walk: 'I wanted to push the pram around, everybody walking past was just looking in the pram. It made me feel good inside.' Nonetheless, when he was asked to describe the nature of his relationship with Grace, he found it difficult to articulate this, and noted that he did not spend very much time with her during the working week.

Five months after Grace's birth, as Mike looked back on the early weeks, he noted how surprised he was that he and Jenny 'fought and argued so much'. According to Mike, the household was more 'under control' and he was not required to help as much. Mike commented that he thought his own role had actually changed very little, apart from the fact that his participation in child care was less than when Grace was smaller. As Jenny was getting more sleep, he felt less guilty about his own need for sleep. It appears that Jenny's perception that he did not do as much as he should to help caused most of the dissension. Mike felt misunderstood and devalued in terms of what he felt he did provide, and that Jenny did not appreciate his dependability or the things he did to help. In addition, he argued, his own emotional needs and work problems were ignored. A few months after Grace's birth, the couple travelled to Wales to visit Jenny's family and show off Grace. The trip provided Mike with more time to be with Grace. Mike said that he enjoyed this and was proud about how much more skilful he became in caring for her. However, a resumption of his more familiar patterns on his return home caused resentment from Jenny, who accused him of 'getting lazy'.

When Mike was asked to whom he turned for help when things were so difficult, he denied that he needed assistance but recognized that Jenny needed help. He explained this was because she was home all day coping with the baby and therefore needed support. Mike described how Jenny read books and depended on friends and her mother to become better informed about mothering, but he relied on what Jenny told him in terms of his parenting activities. He did not look further for information and welcomed Jenny's expertise, advice and teaching. He also described observing her and copying her behaviour. Mike said that he did have some discussions with 'the guys at work' about their experiences of dealing with infants, but thought that because they had had their children 10 or 15 years ago they had little to offer in the way of useful advice.

At times, Mike appeared anxious about his competence in caring for the new baby, linked to his inexperience in dealing with infants. This was revealed, for example, in a description of a day a few months after Grace was born when Jenny was tired and upset and he had tried to help: 'I haven't had experience. Someone hands me a ten-weeks-old baby – I didn't know what to do.' Mike recounted another experience where he felt that he had demonstrated his ignorance of infant care and was shown to be incompetent:

> The other day Grace had a shitty nappy, so I had to go and change it. So I brought her in here and put her on the mat on the floor. And I was changing her on the floor, it's just a lot easier so she doesn't fall. She kicked so much that I was worried about her all the more. And I picked her up, and as soon as I picked her up she started howling – a cry that we'd never heard before. [I thought] 'Jeez, I've busted her arm or something!' I put her back down, she wouldn't stop crying. Jenny came flying in and I had a shitty nappy half off. Crap's going everywhere. [She said], 'What did you do? What did you do?' I told her exactly what I did in case I did some damage. Grace just howled non-stop for about half an hour, with the tears and everything – it was a real deep cry. Jenny got her calmed down, put her to bed and she cried again. This went on for about three hours. I've no idea what I did, no idea. I just, maybe, twisted her arm or something, I don't know.

Some months later, Mike's fear of inadvertently hurting or harming Grace had subsided, but he was still anxious about his competence in baby minding. He was now engaging in more activities looking after Grace, and described his feelings as 'being happy, but I'm not relaxed. If I'm watching TV and the baby is asleep, every sound she makes I think she's going to wake up and I'm not going to be able to keep her quiet or put her back down to sleep. I hope Jenny's not too far away because she seems to be the only one that can do it really well.' Later in the same interview, however, Mike articulated the beginnings of confidence and pride in his development of skills in looking after Grace, including managing to put her back to sleep a few times. Mike described how 'just getting to know her' made a difference, including being able to identify why Grace was crying, something that Jenny was far more competent at doing than he was.

Mike noted that Jenny was very tired for some months after the baby was born and this curtailed their social life. The other factor that inhibited outside activities, Mike noted, was the effort required to go out: 'We can't go anywhere that we used to, without hassles, it's the pram or the bags. We need some more nappies and things, you've got to fill the car up with things that we never used to take before.' Mike less frequently undertook other activities that he enjoyed alone, such as fishing with his friends, because he worried about leaving Jenny and Grace without transport, for Jenny did not drive. Mike recognized that Jenny was not happy and felt isolated at home. She had begun to talk of returning to work to provide her with interest outside the house. While Mike prided himself on the fact that Jenny did not have to go back to work, he was supportive because he thought it would relieve the boredom of staying home. Mike said that one way he could help was to teach Jenny to drive and buy her a car. This would make it easier for her to get to work and Grace to child care. In addition it would be a way of reducing his obligation as the only driver in the family.

Grace was weaned from the breast at three months. Mike described the change to bottle feeding very positively, saying that he thought that breast-feeding was 'wearing out' Jenny, seeming to be 'draining' her. As a result, he said, she was 'emotionally strung out, tired and grumpy'. When Grace began to feed from bottles, Mike argued, he could feed her, allowing Jenny to have more freedom. Nonetheless, Jenny took responsibility for sterilizing the bottles and making up the feeds. Mike said that he was pleased Jenny did this, noting that 'women are better at it than men', although he qualified this by saying that if he were at home and Jenny was in paid employment he could learn to do it quickly and well.

Mike continued to see his role as father as very much tied to being a concerned and generous provider. When describing a 'good' father five months after the birth of Grace, Mike noted that his daughter was 'all mummy's girl' because Jenny provided nearly all her care and 'knew' her better than he did. He went on to say, somewhat defensively: 'I'm still a good father aren't I? I don't do much but there's not that much I can do. I'm still going to work, paying the bills, that's part of it isn't it? Well, that's the only thing I can throw back at Jenny when she gets the shits with me. Yeah, someone's got to do that – be the sort of person who a whole lot of people rely on.'

Mike's expressed desire to be loved and respected by his daughter was accompanied by his disappointment with his own father and experience of being fathered and how this has influenced him. Reflecting on his relationship with his father, Mike said that he saw his own adult behaviour towards his partner and his daughter as originating from his experiences with his father. He was trying to be different by 'being there every weekend and every night', and was planning to share his hobbies, like camping and fishing, with Grace when she was older. Five months after Grace's birth, Mike acknowledged that he could be a better father if he were more supportive, helped more and was less 'tired and lazy'. He said the most important efforts that he made as a father were for Jenny, not for the baby. He used as an example of this how sometimes he helped by encouraging Jenny to go to bed early while he watched the baby, so that she could catch up on lost sleep. Mike recognized that there was more he could do to help and that indeed he would have to help more because Jenny was 'wearing out'. Nonetheless, it was difficult for him to stay up late to mind Grace and to get up during the night, as most mornings he had to be up at 5 or 6 am to go to work, and found it difficult to stay awake at night after a long day of manual labour. When he described the division of labour that they adopted, Mike said this was not discussed beforehand. Because Jenny was with the baby more than he, and 'was good at those sort of things', she took on these responsibilities automatically.

In this interview, Mike said that he was resentful of the 'involved' father image he thought was promoted by women's magazines:

> I don't like it. I think men will do as much as they can when they can, like myself, you know, and I don't think it's a good thing to have women's magazines and/or women in general, just to say, 'Oh, men have got to do their share, women shouldn't have to do it all by themselves.' . . . I mean, we do our best. The baby cries, we get up, we feed it. If we have to look after a baby, we'll look after the baby, we don't need to be told every five minutes. You see it on television, you see it in the papers, see it in women's magazines; I think the women's magazines are the worst things out.

He contended that a similar message was given at the antenatal classes he and Jenny had attended. Mike argued that the men at these classes were demonstrating they were responsible and caring fathers-to-be by their very attendance. Therefore they had no need to be told to help their partners after the baby was born. Mike said that he felt that the push to get men to share child care and domestic tasks caused marital unrest, as women compared with each other how much their husbands helped them. Later in the same interview he returned to the subject of the unfair pressures he thinks are put on men today:

> [It's said that] you've got to do this and men shouldn't be like – men don't do enough. You have a full day, it's constantly on the go and you really find it very hard to find the spare time to do things. I've never been one to listen to women's movements, and I've never worried about it, but now when it concerns me, I get it pushed down my throat all the time, it starts to annoy you.

As Mike looked back on the first five months of fatherhood he was surprised and distressed by the problems having Grace caused between him and Jenny: 'I think we were both stumped when Grace was born.' He believed this was because of the added household work involved, and in particular how this interfered with their sleep. Nonetheless, he noted that 'I never thought we would have as much fun and joy out of the baby.' He said that he now had a much better idea of the nature of the relationship between himself and Grace, describing it as: 'A good relationship, I guess. She knows who I am and she knows I'm her father but she knows, I think she recognizes my face. Like, when I came in this afternoon and Jenny was feeding [her] and Grace instantly turned around and started smiling.' At five months of age, Grace's responsiveness to her father made her enjoyable because she was no longer 'just something wrapped in a sheet that has got to be fed'. Mike said that he enjoyed playing with Grace in the bath. He carried a picture of Grace in his wallet and said that he had become more comfortable in showing this to people. The only criticism he made of fatherhood at this point was his daughter's continuing wakefulness at night.

By the time Grace was 16 months old, Mike was describing how 'I'm always thinking about her. Always talk to all the guys at work about her', and said that he rang home at least once during the day when he was at work to see how she was. He said that he was looking forward to taking Grace into work so that he could show her off to his workmates. At this stage he described a 'good' father as 'doing what's right for your kid, I guess'. He said that even though Jenny still did not think that he was doing enough to help around the house, they had just purchased a larger house which required far more maintenance and repair, and that he would be taking responsibility for this as well as paying the mortgage. Mike still thought that Jenny did not appreciate his contribution, and commented that they were still arguing about these issues. While he resented being told that he was 'not doing enough', he still expressed some ambivalence and doubt: 'At the back of your mind there's always this pressure on . . . the way I'm starting to think now is, am I inadequate? Am I doing the right thing? Can I do more? And you get all these people beating on your bloody head – you're not doing enough . . . men in general really do have their work cut out for them too.'

Jim

Jim is 40 years old and has been with his partner, Megan, who is in her early thirties, for seven years. Both are Anglo-Celtic, and were born in Zimbabwe but had immigrated to Sydney as children, where they met and established their relationship. Jim was married previously but there were no children from this marriage. He has a successful and demanding career as a sports psychologist with elite athletes and sports teams. Megan is interested in his work and often attends sports matches with him. She is a former high school teacher who is enrolled full-time in doctoral studies, begun only a few months after their son Tom was born. They live in a large house in a semi-rural region on the outskirts of Sydney, close to Jim's place of work.

In the first interview Jim shed tears as he described his dreams and expectations of the child soon to be born. Jim believed having a child was the appropriate 'next step', both in his relationship with Megan and in his own life. He said that he would not have been ready for fatherhood earlier as there were too many things he still had to accomplish. He said he felt excited and positive about becoming a father despite the negativity he felt being communicated by other people, mainly friends, about the increased stress, loss of sleep and tasks such as washing dirty nappies associated with caring for tiny infants. When asked to imagine what being a father would be like, Jim described this in terms of 'new experiences' and said he was looking forward, though with some trepidation, to teaching and guiding his child. He found it difficult to describe what a 'good' father is: 'Well, I don't know, it's really hard, I don't think I could identify anything and say "That's what a father's all about."' Nonetheless, he asserted that he wanted to be seen by his child as a 'friend' and for them to do things together.

Jim had been preparing for fatherhood by attending antenatal classes with Megan and most of her appointments with their own midwife. (The couple had decided to employ a midwife and to give birth, with her in attendance, at hospital.) Jim said that he had not read many books about parenting, claiming that he was too tired after work to do so, and that he did not necessarily find such books a very credible source of knowledge. He thought that he had some relevant knowledge from his own university studies in psychology and human development. Jim was discriminating about the information offered by the educator in their antenatal classes, and expressed some scepticism about some of her claims. Nonetheless, he was somewhat ambivalent about whether he knew enough about birth, infants and child care, and noted that he relied heavily on their midwife appointments to feel knowledgeable. Megan and he had recently prepared the room for the baby together and he was beginning to feel ready for the baby to be born.

Jim and Megan's parents and siblings lived overseas. According to Jim, this freed them from pressure to conform to advice older relatives might offer. He anticipated, however, that it may be more difficult ultimately as there would not be help available from their families after the baby was born. He said that the couple did not have many friends having children at the same time, although they had made some new friends from the antenatal classes.

The birth did not go as planned and after a very long and difficult labour Tom was born by caesarean section. Jim sat next to Megan during the operation. When the baby was born, the surgeon gave him straight to Jim as the couple had requested before the operation. Jim accompanied Tom as he was weighed, bathed him and said that he felt 'very involved' in this process and that they had good 'bonding time' together. Jim said that he recognized that Tom was ready for his first feed by the sounds he made, remembering that he had heard these sounds from his younger sister when she was an infant many years earlier. He helped give Tom to Megan for his first feed. After such close involvement with his new son, and being such an important part of the activities, Jim said that he felt excluded when he had to return home from the hospital that night.

This couple noticed and were critical about several facets of the care they received at the hospital. Jim felt the education process at the hospital was 'like a production line' with everyone responsible for a small component of care but no one person seeming constant or very interested in them. Although Jim had been intensely involved at Tom's birth, he noted that it was very different in the postnatal ward where as a father he felt he was 'just standing round looking on'. When he demonstrated his competence in changing Tom's nappy a staff member joked about it in a way that suggested to Jim that fathers were not expected to be helpful or competent.

Megan insisted on returning home from the hospital as soon as possible. It was only then, asserted Jim, that they started to establish their 'own ways' of being parents. In the interview held a few days after Tom's birth, Jim appeared surprised by the differences in the mother–infant and father–infant relationship. For him, feeding exemplified this difference: 'You know, if he is crying and needs feeding, I can't do it. If he needs changing that's OK, but there are six times in the day during the day when I can't do anything to stop him crying. I mean, it is not unexpected, but you feel like, "Gee, I would really like to be able to do something here!"'

Jim found the expectations of fatherhood he held before birth did not match the reality of the first few weeks and was disappointed by this. He realized that the images he held previously were probably those of a slightly older infant, able to be more responsive. The extent of interaction he was able to have with his son was less than he had hoped because of the baby's immaturity and inability to do much more than cry or sleep. He was still unsure of what a 'good' father was at this stage, but felt that it was more about supporting his partner than interacting with the infant: 'I still probably don't know what a good father is and I think, you know, the roles that a good father plays are to support the mother and actually to be involved as much as possible in the things that you can be involved in.' Despite this, Jim was finding the process of being a parent 'fascinating' and was observing his son closely. He noted that he saw characteristics of both himself and Megan in Tom's behaviour and facial expressions. Jim said, for example, that the way Tom slept was just like him.

The most difficult part of this early time for Jim was Tom's frequent inconsolable bursts of crying, which he described as 'the tantrums'. He said that both Megan and he could see these coming on as the baby 'wound himself up' and they knew they would be 'in for between five and thirty minutes of hell'. Tom's extended periods of crying affected Jim on two levels. First, he was frustrated that he could not settle Tom and he consequently felt a sense of failure. Second, tension was created between Megan and him over the distress that Tom's crying caused them both. Jim said that he was frustrated and distressed because he was not able to make things any easier for his partner. At these times, Jim argued, there was nothing that he could do to help. Mostly he was able to ignore it, but a few times he felt himself 'getting a bit short, it's like he is really trying to piss you off'. Jim felt he would eventually develop some 'coping strategies' and could see that Megan had already begun to do so.

Jim's work was particularly busy at this time and sometimes he would leave home early and arrive too late to see Tom awake. This meant that he had little opportunity to become more competent at settling Tom when he was crying. If Jim were home, he said, he would take Tom for a walk in the pram. Eventually he would stop crying but Jim was not sure why. Jim was concerned that Megan was not getting much sleep and he tried to help but felt he was not able to do this as effectively or as much as he would have liked. He described Megan as doing 'a wonderful job' of mothering the baby and said that one of the best ways he could help was to be positive and supportive.

Jim seemed to develop a sense of the baby as an individual very quickly.

When asked to describe his son about six weeks after his birth, Jim described him as a 'robust character' and noted how his son had a definite 'presence' and was 'strong'. He said that he loved to watch him sleep, when he looked 'so peaceful, quite amazing, that total trust and peacefulness of his hands'. He commented that he was looking forward to Tom being able to respond to him more and was disturbed that Tom responded more readily to Megan. Jim contended that his absences at work were responsible for this, and was planning how, when work was quieter, he would spend some more time with Tom. While, six weeks after birth, Tom was still having his 'tantrums', this was now only for 20 minutes or so in the evening, and the couple were therefore finding him more manageable than previously. Tom had begun to develop patterns of behaviour that made their lives more predictable.

At this stage Jim and Megan were also exploring child care options for Tom, so that Megan could return to her doctoral studies. Jim expressed several concerns about choosing child care. He was anxious that people who spent a lot of time as paid carers with Tom should not have a negative influence on him. He also expressed concern that Tom would contract childhood diseases when mixing with other children. Jim favoured a University-run crèche for Tom's care and was already apprehensive about the quality of teaching that Tom will receive when he goes to school.

The plans the couple had made for Jim to be actively involved in parenting, however, had not been achieved at this stage because of the demands of his work. Jim said that this was partly why he still saw a 'good' father as someone in a supportive role, but this understanding was also related, he said, to the fact that his son was breastfed: 'I mean, it's still hard to get that total involvement situation when you can't get involved with the feeding which is what he is predominantly doing. He's either feeding or sleeping and neither of those you can actually do with them.' Jim described how much he was enjoying the contact he was managing to have with his son. Because Tom slept in their bed for the first few months, Jim said, he felt that he had developed an intimacy with his son that he would otherwise have missed: 'it's nice, having him sleeping next to you and waking up with him there. He pulls the hairs on my chest even though he doesn't know it. Those are the things I find really nice. You know, being close to him.' Because Jim cannot breastfeed, however, he felt that he missed out on the rewarding times and frequent contact that Megan had with Tom. The couple were considering whether Megan could express breast milk so Jim could feed Tom with a bottle.

Jim commented that he had difficulty imagining how the athletes and sports players with whom he worked would respond if he excused himself from an important commitment because he wanted to be with Tom or was needed to care for him. He said that these people saw their needs for his assistance as paramount, and Jim had not yet worked out how to deal with this. He was disappointed with himself for being so susceptible to work obligations when he perceived these demands as often unreasonable. He still intended to make time to be with Tom but was becoming anxious that this would not eventuate. He said that his male colleagues had expressed interest in Tom, but their questions and interest were non-specific, though generally perceived as supportive by Jim. Female colleagues, however, asked far more detailed questions and Jim found himself providing much more detailed answers and entering into precise discussions with them. Jim contended that men used a bantering type of humour to prevent discussion of the new baby being anything other than fairly superficial.

Four to five months after Tom's birth, Jim had still not managed to extract himself from a 60-hour or so week. He remained concerned that 'the guys' with whom he worked would not understand if he put Tom before their own needs to have his help in their training routines. Yet he perceived it was not fair to his partner to continue as he was doing. More important even than this, he felt he was missing out on time he wanted to spend with Tom. Jim found this somewhat paradoxical, claiming that his industry recognized the important role families played in supporting and assisting elite athletes. Children were welcome at sporting events and Jim claimed the negative male stereotypes attached to the men in sport did not hold up. Nevertheless, he found it difficult to extract himself from an excessive workload to give time to his own son. The few hours here and there that he was snatching from work were insufficient: 'the time never seems as much as you want and think it will be. I mean, three hours on paper looks like a lot, but then, you know, sort of half an hour is sort of settling down and after three quarters of an hour for lunch and the time has gone.'

After 16 months, Jim found fatherhood much more rewarding. He noted that Tom had developed favourite activities that he liked to do with each parent, and Jim could already identify personality traits in Tom that he saw in himself: 'his personality is a lot like mine in some ways, in that he's not very good one-on-one with people, but you know, if you have a crowd there, he's quite happy to stand up and be a performer.' Jim felt very positively about his new role as a father and acknowledged that Tom had improved his tolerance levels and made him calmer. More importantly, Jim contended, Tom's birth had changed his priorities in life. He said that Tom preoccupied his thoughts even when they were not together, and that he had become emotionally involved with Tom in a way he did not imagine would happen. Jim was taking Tom to baby gym classes and said that he enjoyed seeing Tom's physical and cognitive development take place:

> At the end of the gym class a coloured parachute is floated up and down and all the babies lie underneath. A lot of babies don't like it because it's at the end of the class, they look pretty tired, but Tom's absolutely besotted. He can hardly control himself with excitement with the colours going around and changing and that sort of thing. And so even when he's really tired and scratchy he just lies there and laughs so much.

Jim believed it was important for him to stimulate Tom's development. He felt that after these sessions, Tom demonstrated his enjoyment to his father in return by 'singing and clapping all the way home in the car'.

Sixteen months after Tom's birth, Jim was quite clear about the relation-ship he wanted with his son in the long term, returning to many of the concepts he raised prior to his birth. He saw the ultimate expression of good fathering expressed through a very close and unique friendship rather than a typical authoritarian parent–child relationship. Jim said that he found his relationship with Tom 'very relaxing, very sort of comfortable, very natural'. His love for and involvement with his child, he said, had changed his perspective on his work:

> You know, where there's people who aren't doing the things in the work situation, where I ask someone to do something and they don't do it, [I think], 'Why am I wasting my time with you? I could be doing something I really enjoy, like being at home with Tom!' Or, you know, being down the playground with him or being out doing something with him or even just being around him.

He was attempting to foster this relationship in the activities he shared with Tom such as baby gym. Tom and Megan accompanied Jim to sporting activities and the baby had become an important part of their social relationships with colleagues. Jim was now taking one day off during the week to be with Tom and relieved Megan more often so she could get on with her own work. He was still disappointed about how difficult it was to achieve time with Tom but was using the close proximity of home to his work to get more frequent time with his son: 'I'm doing more feeding now. He's on solids now too, and I try and feed him at least one of the two times a day, either morning or night.'

Jim had restructured his working hours and was in the process of appointing more staff to lighten his load and make reasonable working hours attainable. He said that he had become less sensitive about his responsibilities as a father and how these related to his work, but the pressures of a demanding career had not gone away. Some of the athletes and players, he said, appeared 'put out' when he told them that he was not available to see them on demand, and he had started to use the phrase 'my time is fully committed' to turn more of their requests down.

Asked to reflect over his experiences in the past year and a half, Jim admitted that he had found the process of becoming a father much more difficult than he expected, particularly the first couple of months. He said that it was not Tom's crying and the associated lack of sleep that were most difficult, for he knew both these problems would pass in time. Rather, it was the lack of interaction with his son that he found most difficult, and the immaturity which prevented Tom responding emotionally to him. Jim found not being able to be at home as much as he had intended frustrating, but even when he was home, he was not able to do as much as he had hoped because Megan was breastfeeding and was more skilled at caring for Tom than he was.

Despite frustration, uncertainty and some disappointments in the early weeks and months, Jim said that he was enjoying fatherhood very much by the time Tom was 16 months old. He noted that his love for his partner had been strengthened by having their child, as it had 'brought us together' and made them into 'a tight little unit'. Jim reflected on how different his own experience of fatherhood was from that of his own father. He contended that this was unique to his generation of men:

Our experiences now are much wider than our fathers and our expectations are probably much, much more. My father didn't have a choice in the matter. He had a choice in getting married but not in most things. He got a trade, he got married, he had a house and he had children. His role was to provide for the children and, and no matter who you were talking to, that was always what it was. There wasn't the outside experience, not even through television, to give them [men of that generation] concepts that other worlds existed. You know, for reading there was *Popular Mechanics* and *Reader's Digest* and that sort of thing, and perhaps *National Geographic*. There's a lot more opportunity to pick and choose the style of fatherhood that you want these days.

Tony

Tony and Louise, both in their mid-thirties, had been together for over 12 years at the time of the first interview. Both of them are Anglo-Celtic and Australian-born and had always lived in Sydney. Tony is a carpenter, and for the past seven years or so had worked for himself, doing home extensions, renovations and similar work. Louise had held a variety of bookkeeping and clerical jobs since leaving school, and was preparing to give up work for a time after the birth of her infant. Both have an interest in art (she in ceramics, he in photography), and had completed certificates in these fields at technical college. During the research Tony was rebuilding and renovating the family house, a small single-storey terrace in a newly fashionable, inner suburb of Sydney. Renovations had been accelerated to ensure that the house was ready prior to the birth of the baby but had not quite been completed when James was born. Because of this, some early interviews were conducted at the houses of family and friends where Tony, Louise and James stayed while work on their house progressed.

Interviewed just before James's birth, Tony said that both he and Louise felt ready for parenthood and were looking forward to the baby's arrival. Many of their friends had young children, so they felt reasonably well prepared and supported as they embarked on this new venture. Tony described how he always assumed he would become a father. He described fatherhood as 'a normal part of life' and implied that he made no active choice about parenting, but rather had simply 'let it happen'. For Tony, pregnancy was seen as a time of preparation for the different role he believed was now required of fathers. He felt he would be treated differently and have different sorts of interactions with people because of fatherhood. He welcomed this change and had a sense that it was the proper thing to do for him as an adult male.

Tony suggested that there were gender differences in parenting, even though both parents shared a common core of concern about, and focus on, the baby. He described mothers as 'very caring and loving'. It was more difficult for Tony to articulate the father's role. Like many of the other men we interviewed, Tony found it difficult to envision what 'being a father' would actually be like once the baby was born: 'I keep trying to imagine myself but yeah, you can't. I don't know, I just really can't imagine what it's like to have a human being you're looking after, who's always going to be there, you can't just move on when you get sick of them . . . it's very confusing when I think about any of that stuff.'

When Tony was asked to identify his reference point for fathering, he talked about his own father. Tony used his father as an exemplar not because he wanted to emulate him but because he wanted to improve on the deficiencies he perceived in his father's approach. Tony said that he felt he had missed out on contact with his father as a child and emphasized that he did not wish to repeat this with his own child: 'Well I guess for me it's a straight reaction to my old man because, you know, I didn't see him as much, so I'm thinking I want to make sure I didn't do that.' Returning to his own experience as a child, Tony said fathers need to 'just be there' for their children. When pushed to become more specific, he described fatherhood as involving playing with the child, taking it to sport and an expectation of being involved in housework and child care. Unlike many of the other men we interviewed, Tony talked very little about money or his responsibility as breadwinner in relation to the notion of the 'good' father.

Tony noted that he wanted to be closely and actively involved with caring for the baby, not just doing the domestic chores. He believed that his responsibility for the child extended well beyond the roles of domestic support or breadwinner. Tony said that he wanted close, physical contact with his baby and had planned how he could achieve this. He described, for example, how he might get into the bath with the baby after work to enjoy time together. As Tony grappled with developing his view of appropriate fatherhood, he was taking practical steps to be well organized and prepared. He said that he had observed how other fathers and mothers related to their children and imagined what it would be like for him. Tony described installing the baby capsule (cradle for transporting infants in cars) in the car to bring the baby home and referred to his activities renovating the house as all part of his preparation.

Interviewed two days after James's arrival, Tony said that he had had an 'ecstatic' experience of birth. The birth was conducted by a midwife, whom the couple had come to know personally, in a birthing centre. Tony said that he appreciated the attempts by the staff at the birthing centre to encourage his active participation in the birth: 'I think they made an effort to make sure I was included, so I never for one moment felt left out or alienated.' He had been alerted to the fact that this may happen to men in the antenatal classes he had attended with Louise, and did not want this to happen to him. The birth was a very sensory experience for him and he described a 'gushing out of love' immediately his son was born:

> Well, I mean I was just really happy he's here . . . he's staring at every crevice in your face, and he hasn't got any crevices but he's just staring at you, you know, like just checking out every little detail, and just being able to touch him and hold him and sort of try and let him know that you're there for him – 'This is your dad' . . . Yeah, I just can't leave him alone. I'm holding him.

The positive and deeply felt emotions generated by the birth persisted after he returned home alone that night, leaving Louise and his new son in the hospital:

'[I was] just so ecstatic about it. The day he was born I came home and put a lasagne in the oven to be heated up, and the next thing I'm crying my eyes out and laughing my guts out and it was just fantastic!' As well as an emotional peak experience, James's birth also brought Tony confirmation of changed social status and a changed subjectivity. He said,

> Well, this is a high point in my life, [it has] brought a whole new meaning into everything. I have never been this happy. Just having this little baby, that's a bit of each of you to carry on. To me, it's a whole new focus on life really. 'Cause, you know, when you're not a great career-oriented person and not an Olympic sportsman or anything and so, I don't know – to me he's the biggest thing that can come along.

Tony and Louise continued to enjoy contact with their wide-ranging social network after James's birth and he accompanied them to many a café, friend's house or squash court during his first months of life. James's sleeping pattern was not well established by six months, however, and the couple became anxious to settle him into a routine. At this time it was discovered that Tony's mother was dying of cancer, and the couple moved to his parents' house to provide support.

After James was born, Tony took some weeks off work so that he and Louise could have some time together to get to know their new son. Tony continued to describe the great delight he experienced in touching and holding James. In an interview a week or so after the birth Tony reiterated that their couple status had been relinquished and they had become a 'real' family. The emphasis evident in his words before the birth, about the changes he expected to occur in him as he became a father, resurfaced as the social recognition of the importance of fatherhood was confirmed for him by his family and friends. Tony demonstrated a very significant sense of reorientation of his world. He articulated, even more strongly, the perception he identified before his child was born that he now had a focus for the rest of his life. Despite this strong sense of purpose provided for his own life by baby James, Tony was concerned to avoid objectifying him or seeing him in terms of a possession: 'While he is ours, he is a little human. He's not plasticine that we can go squishing to whatever shape we want.'

Tony was very involved in the early physical needs of his son and found this very rewarding. While he initially expressed some apprehension at handling James early on, this quickly subsided as he discovered what 'gets through' to James and found that he was able to soothe James when he cried. By about a month after the birth, Tony said, he was engaging closely in his care: 'I do his bath and I'm around when he gets upset. I get him changed or just hold his hands or whatever or pat him on the head and let him know everything is all right. He actually calms down a bit.' In the same interview he reflected on the day-to-day issues that arose as he grappled with understanding the baby's and Louise's needs. Tony described 'testing' out various activities as he learnt what worked best. He contended that James was also 'training' him and Louise to be good parents, as he let them know by crying or responding positively how effective they were being.

In the interviews, Tony provided unusually intimate and detailed observations of his baby. Tony said that because he had been able to have extensive early interaction with his son, he had became 'tuned in' to what the baby wanted. For example, when the baby was about five weeks old, he described how he spent time 'just trying to figure out what the little bloke wants. He's got a whole bunch of different cries depending on how stressed out he is'. At this time, despite having returned to work, Tony was still very involved in providing physical care for James. The couple had negotiated a division of child care and domestic tasks around what suited them. For example, at weekends Tony got up at night, changed James and gave him to Louise to feed. He did not get up on week nights because Louise worried about him getting overtired, not concentrating and then getting hurt at work. During the week, Tony said, he tried to 'take the load off her' when he got home from work. If he was home all day on weekends, he helped with everything he could.

When asked about his interactions with the baby five weeks after the birth, Tony expressed some amusement at how quickly he responded to his son and how much this little baby controlled him: 'He makes a squeak and I jump, so we're communicating pretty well! I'm learning. It's funny, you know, even your partner can't get you to move that quick. He [cries], and you think, "Oh well, what's wrong with you, poor little fella? We'll have a look." And now he's started smiling, just in the last week. It's like a huge revelation, finally getting a bit of feedback.'

Tony presented a vivid case of the potential satisfaction available to men who care for their infants as they learn about their child's needs and develop competence in meeting them. He described the rewards of physical closeness resulting from providing care for his son: 'Just seeing him and make sure he's happy, just the physical process of looking after him, dressing him, talking to him and just sort of looking at him, his behaviour and that of different stages. And trying to take it all in, 'cause, you know, it's going to change so quick.' The more emotionally close Tony came to James through caring for him, the more he enjoyed fatherhood. As a result, he found it rewarding carrying out tasks that many other of the fathers we interviewed avoided. For example, he said,

> I enjoy nappy changing, 'cause they are fairly frequent. A chance for him to be out of those bloody nappies and have a kick. I guess you're doing something for him. So you get a chance [to interact with him], he sits there and looks at me sometimes and you know if you're not doing a bad job. Bath times are good. Because he's a winter baby, he's always rugged up, and 'Poor little bugger', you sometimes think. They like to be in the duff [naked] but because they lose their heat so quick you just can't let them, unless they're sitting in their nice and warm bath.

Tony also noted that he liked rocking James to sleep because 'it's quite bizarre – you never watch anyone fall asleep, not even your partner'. Tony discussed the close nature of this relationship with his son and the power James had over him: how, on occasions, James would look deeply at Tony and 'just latch on to your eyeballs and I feel like he's boring into my soul'.

Tony talked positively about the professional help he and Louise had received during pregnancy, labour and delivery and postnatally. The couple were unusual in our group of interviewees in that they required very little reassurance from health professionals that the baby was progressing well and that they were doing a good job as parents. Tony said that his primary information sources for his new role was rarely a health professional but rather friends and others with babies. He noted that he learnt about parenting and child care by 'just watching what other people do'. While Tony was somewhat apprehensive about his ability to cope in the early weeks, he said that he always found fatherhood highly emotionally satisfying: 'I just get such joy. I was a bit worried because I thought the magic might wear off.' Tony described the 'negatives' he experienced in the first weeks of James's life as occasional sleepless nights and difficulty in settling James at times. He had no difficulty in balancing these with the 'positives' of parenting. Tony commented how he and Louise had become more skilful and better organized. He acknowledged the hard work required, but said that the rewards outweighed this. He described a new baby as like 'having a house guest who demands 24-hour attention, except when he's asleep, and even then he has supersonic hearing!'

When Tony was interviewed five months after James's birth, work pressures had prevented him having his usual contact with the baby. He said that he felt badly about missing out on time with James, and commented that he was concerned he had lost some of his competence in caring for his son – Louise had moved ahead of him in parenting as he had reverted to being 'a learner'. Even more distressing, Tony noted that he had became self-conscious in his interactions with the baby. For example,

> Well you get to bath time, and I'd run out of conversation after a while. You know, I'd be talking to him and looking at him and, then I'd find myself just sort of bathing him in silence. And Louise would pop in, she'd say, 'Oh, talk to him!' It didn't seem to come naturally. You know for three or four weeks, I used to bathe him and then for three or four weeks I hardly bathed him at all. For a while I only changed his nappy about once a week or something like that. I'd been working seven days straight, so I really felt like I was a bloody stranger around the place.

This feeling of 'being a stranger' upset Tony. It was as if he lost his connection to the baby and that his identity as a father, including the great pleasure he had experienced in interacting with his son, was jeopardized. He was not only disappointed for himself but he sensed rejection from his son: 'He didn't want to know me there for a while.' Tony felt like an outsider and thought that his son saw him as such as well: 'You're supposed to be Dad, and [instead] you're just like a visitor.' He resented the demands that work made on him and how this removed him, for a time, from his son and his role as father. Indeed, he had let Louise know that he would be happy to stay at home as a 'house husband' if she wanted to go back to work. Tony said that he thought about his son often when he was at work: 'I just sort of think about him, how cute he is and what a little darling he is and all that sort of stuff, I wonder about the future . . . And just any story, like any news story, where a child's killed or anything like that, reduces you to jelly.'

When work became less onerous and Tony's opportunity to provide care increased, his sense of enjoyment and wellbeing as a father improved again. Tony felt that he had successfully negotiated the real threat he felt existed, that he would replicate the 'absent' father model he was trying to avoid in his own life with his son. Tony defined himself as a 'pioneer' of a new type of father. He claimed that 'no-one really knows what today's father is like', for there are no traditions being handed down to men. He actively rejected what he saw as an outdated stereotype of fatherhood demonstrated by previous generations:

> Back then, you'd have to be a bit of a shirt-lifter [gay man] to change a nappy if you're a guy. Like my dad apparently boasted, and so did Louise's dad, that they never changed a nappy. I've got a mate in my squash team who is the same today. But you look at your father and see areas where all that handling in the early days might make a difference. You know, my dad and I have never talked about anything deep or meaningful.

When asked to look back on how he imagined it would be as a first-time father, Tony said:

> I used to really bust my brain to try to imagine it, and I just couldn't for the life of me. I just couldn't really get my head around it, and now it seems so much a natural part of life it's hard to imagine the times before. It's a real evolutionary process because it didn't change overnight. I don't know if I had many expectations really 'cause I didn't know what to expect. I've changed. I didn't imagine that you could have such a whirlwind in your heart. It's an unlimited mother lode of love in there which [I feel] gushing out every now and then.

5

Negotiating Fatherhood:
Discourses and Experiences

The accounts outlined in the previous chapter described the thoughts and experiences of four men in relation to first-time fatherhood. By presenting some of the interview data in this format, we were able to give an account positioned in the context of each of these men's biographies, and explore how they made sense of the experience of new fatherhood over time in more depth than is generally the case when reporting such data. The present chapter has a wider focus, also drawing on the interviews of the other men who participated in our study, and looking at themes across the participants' accounts. The chapter is arranged under three major topics relating to new fatherhood: anticipating fatherhood, negotiating domestic and caring labour and men's relationship with their children.

Anticipating Fatherhood

Fatherhood, for the men who participated in the study, was rarely represented by them as a 'choice'. Rather, they described it as an inevitable and logical step for them in their relationships with their partners and part of their own development as an adult man. Some men described this as being 'emotionally settled down', 'financially prepared' or simply as 'ready for fatherhood'. Having children was 'a normal thing to do', according to Simon, or as Ewan commented, 'it's just a natural progression'. Steve argued that: 'I guess I've never really thought that I wouldn't have a child, I really haven't had any doubts about it. I've always thought that I would have a child at some point. But no, it's not been something really that I've thought a lot about. I don't know if it was really based on anything more than just, you know, like a gut feeling.'

There is a sense of social continuity and contribution evident in many men's perceptions of this step. They claimed they always imagined that one day they would become fathers, and that the only uncertainty was *when* this would happen rather than *if* it would occur. For two men we interviewed, their partner's pregnancy had happened earlier than they had intended, but 'non-fatherhood' was not described as an option by any of our participants. Despite this dominant discourse representing fatherhood as a 'natural' thing, several men talked about the importance of gaining as much knowledge as possible so that they would be prepared. Dominic, for example, said before the birth of his child that: 'You try and have as much input as you can and hopefully read up on a lot of information and try and get some information of how to rear your children properly, like education-wise and behavioural-wise. And get as much information as you can even from experts or whatever, 'cause this is our first time, like I mean, we don't know.'

The men in the study varied greatly in how they saw their role as father, but most spent considerable time and energy thinking about it during their part-ner's pregnancy. For several men, their planning for new fatherhood primarily revolved around issues of economic responsibility. As Peter put it: 'You try to plan a few years ahead if possible – try to get into an area where there are good schools and day-care centres and where the jobs are secure. You have got to think about things, like "Am I going to lose my job?", and what things the kids will need later on so you have enough money put by.'

The men were also very conscious of their role as protector of the child, not just in the immediate future but in the long term (cf. Lewis, 1986). Many were already expressing concerns in late pregnancy about their child's future career options and how issues such as drugs and unemployment would affect their child as a young adult. It was common for them to share with the interviewer plans they were making (often privately, without discussing these with their partner) for schooling and their thinking about whether the child might attend university. The male protector role was expressed very differently according to the values held by the men themselves. It ranged from having enough money to buy everything the child needed, and seeing this as a crite-rion for measuring their performance as father, to making sure the child knows right from wrong and grows up as a responsible member of the com-munity.

One central dimension of the 'father as protector' discourse for most men was the representation of the child as vulnerable and utterly dependent, and the consequent responsibility upon parents. Brad, for example, described how fatherhood would mean that 'there is another person relying on you completely 24 hours a day for the next 20 years', while David said that 'To me a father is bringing up a little child, and just a father is someone that, you know, just looks after it and just helps the child grow up and looks after it.' Men such as Steve saw their role as combining a deep emotional connection with the baby with an authority or guardian role. Steve's conceptualization of being a 'guardian' as a father included notions of firm discipline: 'If you love [your children], you are going to stop them from doing some things, and you will use just about every method to do this if you have to. You need to have love but if you let the child get away with everything and do everything, that's the easy way out.'

Only one man in our study (Mike, described in the previous chapter) openly expressed his resentment and rejected the discourse of the 'involved' father. Most men indicated that they had very much embraced this concept as the most appropriate model of contemporary fatherhood. All the partici-pants said that they wanted very much to be involved with the child, and the majority of those who made mention of their own father said that they regretted the lack of time he spent with them as children. The notion of the 'absent' father who was obsessed with work to the detriment of family life was frequently used by the men to denote both their perceptions of their fathers and how they wished to be different from their fathers. As Steve said,

> probably the first thing you sort of think about is what you've been through as a child, like, with your parents. Well, particularly the father because I'm going to be one. I guess I'm wanting to try and be the sort of father that I would have liked when I was a boy. I think just spending time with your child is probably just about one of the most important things . . . I don't want to make the same mistakes that I saw in my father.

Similar findings were noted by Kerry Daly (1993), who interviewed 32 Canadian fathers of children aged less than six years old, seeking to identify the paternal role models they had found important to them in their fathering. Daly found that the men tended to compare themselves against their own fathers as points of reference for how they were 'different', rather than using their fathers as a positive role model. Indeed most of the men said that they had no specific role models to follow in relation to fathering, but had developed notions of desirable behaviour from a range of fathers. As Daly notes, 'From this perspective, learning to be a father is somewhat akin to the thoughtful consumer who stands before the shelves making a careful selection of products that are to be added to the cart' (1993: 522). So too, in her research involving interviews with 14 Australian men, White (1994) found that all the men described their fathers as having little involvement with them when they were children and talked about the 'lack of closeness' in their relationship with their father. They often positioned themselves as attempting to achieve a different and 'better' relationship with their own children.

Most of the men in our study tended to be unsure how this 'differentness' from their own fathers should be played out in the way they organized and experienced their own lives. They appeared to find it particularly difficult to articulate what they perceived the role of a father to be when their child was an infant, as their expectations appeared to revolve around a vision of a son or daughter as an older child. The imagery of their child that almost all participants had created before birth was of a responsive child who appreciated their efforts and could be involved in activities they enjoyed. They expected to be involved with the child as a friend, playmate or guide. They also expected that this involvement with the child would be reciprocal, and that they would gain considerable emotional satisfaction and rewards from the child in return. When these men found themselves dealing with an infant, their expectations were somewhat confounded, because they did not expect such an immature, relatively non-social and demanding baby. Confusion resulted as they tried to understand a situation they did not expect and where they found it difficult to insert themselves actively. Simon, for example, commented in relation to his infant daughter that 'There is not much I can do. You can't really get her on a bike and go for a ride at this stage of her life.'

Many fathers used the phrase 'being there' in their interviews to describe a 'good' father (see also White, 1994). 'Being there' appeared to be a term that has entered the popular vernacular. It is used to convey the ultimate performance as a father as it is measured by one's child, one's partner and others. It is a powerful phrase, which is somewhat amorphous, open to a wide range of interpretations. 'Being there' characterizes what men see makes them different, as 'new' fathers, from the generation of fathers before them. Some said that they would not go out as much because they wanted to 'be there' for the child. As Juan said, 'well, my concept I feel of a father's love is to be able to give his life for that child . . . to be able to give up my life, my wants, my sports or whatever for the benefit of the child and that's the way it is.' Many men saw 'being there' in terms of the future activities that they could share with their children, for example playing soccer together, taking them camping, going fishing together and engaging in other sporting and recreational pursuits. Only one man saw 'being there' in terms of helping the child with homework when she or he started school, and none described engaging in domestic tasks such as cooking and shopping with the child. None reported 'being there' in relation to tasks attached to infancy such as settling a baby for sleep, assisting with bathing or changing nappies.

For most men, however, 'being there' appeared to be centrally about developing a close and loving relationship with their child through shared activities. As Steve put it:

> I guess I – and this is something you can't force – but I'd like to have a relationship where we both want to spend time together, where we both enjoy being together. So in that sort of loving way it can't be a forced sort of love, you know. It's got to be a natural thing where the child will want to spend time with you and you want to spend time with the child so it won't be a burden and it won't be a hassle.

When asked how they envisage fatherhood for themselves, several men noted that there were few rules or guidelines they could follow in their first-time fathering of a tiny infant. This is despite the fact that all of the participants had attended a minimum of eight weeks of antenatal classes designed to prepare them for birth and early fatherhood. One notable exception was Simon, who came from a large family and had younger brothers and sisters, and was also a health worker who had some experience with infants and small children. He therefore thought that he had a better idea than most men about the demands of babies and breastfeeding, as well as more experience in caring for infants. In the first interview, Simon noted that he looked forward to being able to put his baby to sleep and comfort his child when she or he cried.

Some men discussed the importance of observing other men's interactions with their children in developing notions of the appropriate way to practise fatherhood. Tony contended that contemporary 'role models' were increasing in number: 'We go and visit friends and there'll be the guys doing a lot of the caring as well as the women. So the influence is coming there from your peers.' Juan noted that he did not have a happy relationship with his own father as he felt it was 'based on fear'. He also commented that observing his two brothers and their relationship with their children has shown him a better way to be a father than he remembered experiencing himself as a child. Juan said that he had watched his nieces and nephews 'running to their parents and wanting to interact with them'. His brothers' interactions with their young children had demonstrated to him a different sort of discipline from the model they had grown up with in their family of origin. This model, he said, was 'less punishing but more teaching and encouraging them to do right'. However, when asked if he had discussed fatherhood, parenting or his own recent experiences with his brothers, Juan said, 'No, we just don't discuss these things.' He had to rely on observation alone to develop his notions of how best to conduct fatherhood.

A number of men in the study were thinking during their partners' pregnancy about the impact having a baby would have on the relationship with their partner. Some were negotiating in their heads how the relative nature of their contribution to the family would have to change. For example, Peter had worked out that his contribution to the household income would become far greater but the amount of time he could expect with his partner would decrease. The couple were already talking about things that they anticipated might become problems later on, and trying to find solutions. Peter was a light sleeper and had already been disturbed by the baby kicking through the uterus at night, so much so that he had begun sleeping in another room. This had upset his partner, so he had started to establish a sleeping pattern that involved two bursts of deep sleep with a period of wakefulness in the middle. He hoped this would fit into the baby's needs after birth too.

Lewis's (1986) report of his interviews with British men about fatherhood noted the emotional dependency that many men appeared to have on their wives, and the subsequent anxiety the men felt about pregnancy and having a child, in terms of the changes they noted in their wives and their fears about the birth itself and its aftermath. So too, we found in our study that several men demonstrated deep apprehension before the baby was born. Juan described himself as 'petrified' when his partner Trisha discovered she was pregnant and how he hoped that the tests would prove negative. While Juan had always planned on becoming a father, he was unhappy that pregnancy had occurred relatively early in his marriage, and was ambivalent about becoming a father 'so soon', even though he was in his thirties. This feeling of apprehension was diffuse at first and quite poorly articulated. For several men, their fear became focused on their partner closer to delivery and how she would cope with labour, pain and the demands of motherhood. This fear was compounded by their uncertainty about whether they would be able to give her adequate emotional support or not.

The men were also worried about their own capacity to manage parenting and to care for the baby. Some men were anxious about their own emotional vulnerability and saw their partner's ability to deal with difficult situations as greater than their own. For example, in an interview held before the birth of his child, Simon expressed a concern that with a crying baby keeping him awake in a few weeks' time he might get a form of postnatal depression. The session in antenatal classes in which this phenomenon was discussed had not only made him anxious that this could happen to his partner but also for himself. In the same interview, he described the '"horror" stories that you hear about how parents suffocate their children' when suffering from post-natal depression, and how, as a health worker, he had recently had to deal with the cases of two infants who had died of cot death (Sudden Infant Death Syndrome), and how much this had upset him.

As the case studies described in Chapter 4 revealed, however, the over-whelming emotion expressed by nearly all the men in relation to the impending birth of their first child was that of excitement and pleasurable anticipation, a feeling that something momentous and wonderful was about to take place. While the men may also have harboured some apprehension and anxieties about the delivery and the responsibilities that their new child would entail, the notions of 'bringing a new child into the world', having cre-ated something that was 'part' of themselves and their partner and being able to watch the child grow and develop were important and positive for them in their anticipation of fatherhood. As Dominic commented, 'actually thinking about a baby, you know, having a baby and then progressing through life, changing through all its different stages and watching it grow. I mean it's got to be the most exciting thing in my life!'

The communication that occurs between foetus and father during preg-nancy is far more limited than can occur with the mother. As a result, the emotional connection and relationship between father and foetus is often more tenuous and experienced as more 'unreal'. Some men find the kicking of the foetus, particularly at night when their partner is asleep, is rewarding as it begins to link them to the foetus and render it more 'real' to them. As noted above, however, one man found his son's kicking in pregnancy so disruptive to his own sleep that he moved out of the shared bed to try to improve his rest. For many men, viewing the ultrasound of the foetus was a significant moment for them, again making the experience seem more 'real'. Dominic went on to describe how

> sometimes I put my hand on [his partner's] tummy and then a foot goes past or something like that and that's really, really exciting. Like I mean, it shows, you know, it shows there's something alive in there. I mean, now you can see [his part-ner] growing and that sort of stuff but actually feeling the baby move – and we saw it on an ultrasound, and they showed us an image of its lips and its nose and that was quite exciting as well. I mean, I was very, very happy about seeing that . . . I mean, that's what I probably feel, a lot of love for it and [I] just can't wait to see it.

Negotiating Domestic and Caring Labour

The entry of a first child into the family inevitably brings with it an increased burden of domestic labour and upheavals in the couple's usual routine. As was evident in the case studies described in the previous chapter, despite the generally positive expectations reported by the participants in the first inter-view, held just before the birth of their child, most of them found the early weeks and months of fatherhood difficult. The men constantly drew on dis-courses of personal transformation and adjustment when describing their experiences. Becoming a father, they argued, changed their relationships with their partners, the meaning and place of paid work in their lives and their sense of self as competent adults. The trajectory of emotional responses recounted by our participants when describing the birth and ensuing weeks and months was similar to that identified by Hall (1995) in an interview study of three Danish fathers' experiences. She found that the men tended to describe a sense of 'fun and excitement' when describing fatherhood before the birth of their child, a 'love at first sight' response to their child soon after the birth, changing to what she describes as an 'awakening' to the 'reality' of the constant work and responsibility involved once the child and mother returned home, and finally to seeing fatherhood as a mixture of 'joy and trouble' some three months later.

The majority of the men in our study at first found fatherhood much more difficult and distressing than they expected. Their language resonated with words such as 'cope' and they talked of 'struggling', often 'failing', at tasks they thought would be straightforward. One example, referred to by many men, was the task of settling a crying baby, which many of them found difficult to do, even finding themselves at a loss to know what to do. The men expressed being 'stumped' or 'stuck' in such situations, and described the frustration they felt at themselves in finding themselves in a situation they could not manage competently. When his daughter was five months old, Ewan described this vividly: 'A few times it's really like, I sort of get frustrated when Rachael gets hysterical and it's hard to sort of stop yourself from it sort of getting to you. And I've just, there's a couple of times I've had to just keep quiet, but you just learn to sort of to control it and think, "Well, I'm the one who's in charge here, I've got to be the calm one."'

This frustration became played out in the men's relationship with their partners. Instead of being mutually supportive, this relationship was often tense and strained, with men feeling inadequate, reluctant to let their partners know this and feeling guilty that they could not or did not help to the extent that was needed. While these men still tended to support the notion of the 'involved' father, they found that putting into practice the ideal was far more difficult than they had anticipated. The degree of tension that the birth of the baby subsequently caused in the relationship surprised most of the men greatly, particularly after many couples had achieved an emotional high point at the delivery. It appeared that things began to become difficult into the second or third week for most of the couples, after the father had returned to paid employment and when the mother was left alone all day to undertake most of the household tasks as well as care for the infant. As Mike noted: 'The first week was great, then after that things started to get worse. We never thought things would get that bad. Me personally, I never thought that Jenny and I would have fought so much, argue about it as much.' It was not until their child was six months old that this father started really to enjoy fatherhood and the tensions between the couple lessened somewhat as the physical demands on his partner lessened.

In her recent book *No Man's Land: Men's Changing Commitments to*

Family and Work, sociologist Kathleen Gerson (1993) reported the findings of her interviews with 138 men living in New York City from a range of ethnic backgrounds and socioeconomic status. What emerges strongly from Gerson's study is the extreme diversity of response, even among a relatively small group of men, and the conflicts and ambivalences that the men as individuals experienced in attempting to juggle work and intimate life. Gerson found that approximately a third of the men she interviewed defined their family and work commitments in terms of being the primary breadwinner. Another third had eschewed parenthood or significant parental involvement following divorce, while a final third, described by Gerson as 'involved' fathers, had developed a view of parenthood that included active care-taking of children as well as economically supporting the family. There were no clear ethnic, age or social class groupings among these categories. Within the category of 'involved' fathers, many of these men found difficulties in living up to their own ideals about fathering. While they believed in the importance of contributing to parenting, these men tended to be secondary rather than primary carers. They felt torn between the importance they perceived in providing economic support for their family and between the ideal of 'involved' fathering.

Reporting on her empirical research with British heterosexual couples, Doucet (1995) found it difficult to place them neatly into the categories that are often used in the sociological literature (such as 'traditional' or 'egalitarian' relationships and so on), largely because her participants themselves were confused and ambivalent about the issue of gender equality and gender differences, and about what 'egalitarianism' or 'inequality' actually meant to them in practice. She suggests that 'it is important to consider women's and men's varied and constantly changing experiences of parenthood and how the identities and activities associated with parenting actually intersect with other identities and how these alter in relation to the uneven effects of one's personal biography' (1995: 280).

While nearly all of the men in our study could be described as wanting to adhere to the 'involved' father model, we found quite a diversity among them in relation to how they defined what kinds of tasks they thought it appropriate to engage in around the home. For some couples, the negotiation of domestic labour and child care became conflictual and distressing for both partners, while others were more easily able to come to a mutually agreed arrangement that suited each partner's needs and wants. Others recognized and attempted to deal with external factors that influenced parenting arrangements, such as the conditions and demands of paid employment, although not always to their satisfaction. Couples who previously had relied upon the female partner undertaking most of the household tasks often had difficulties managing, as following the birth of their child the woman could no longer undertake the same amount of domestic labour as before. This could be compensated for by other sources of domestic help, such as paid house-cleaners or obliging relatives, but most couples lacked this help. If there was some fluidity between the couple in terms of negotiating how chores were done, most particularly if the male partner was already competent and had been undertaking these tasks before the arrival of the child, the couple appeared to have fewer episodes of conflict.

Juan was surprised how his preferred routine was changed by having a baby and how much 'looking after' he required. There was no opportunity for him and his partner to do the things they used to even on weekends as they had to care for the baby. Juan said that he was astonished at how things such as the volume of washing increased and how his own freedom was curtailed. He found this adjustment very difficult. As discussed in Chapter 4, disrupted sleep patterns following the birth of their child were a difficulty for many men even though it was generally their partners who bore the brunt of this. If the man defined 'work' as 'paid employment', he was also likely to see loss of sleep as his partner's responsibility. He saw her days as free of 'work', and that therefore she could sleep at other times. Mike, for example, was clear that 'work' was 'paid employment'. Although his partner Jenny was waking up and attending to their daughter up to seven times in one night, he argued that she could 'catch up' on her sleep during the day because she was 'not working'. Men who share Mike's position justify their contribution to the family in other ways. Mike noted, for example, that 'I'm still going to work and paying the bills, that's part of it isn't it?' Mike used the word 'guilty' a number of times in interviews as he recognized some legitimacy in his partner's complaints that he was 'lazy', but also resented the expectation that he should help because he went out to 'work' (see a fuller description of this issue in Mike's case study in the previous chapter).

Several men noted that they lacked skills in household tasks they had not attempted before. Some argued that they were not permitted by their partners to undertake some chores in the house because of their incompetence. Brad laughed as he described how: 'I'm not allowed to do the washing because I mess things up. I can do my own work clothes, but not anything else – I've been banned!' Incompetence, in such cases, provides an excuse for avoiding certain tasks. Other men, however, exhibited much more competence and efficiency in their approach to domestic labour and did not see this as divided on lines of gender or paid employment. The division of tasks in such households was not on the basis of status but who had time to do what was needed. These men saw fathers as involved in the whole business of looking after children, including taking responsibility for doing more household work. Ewan described how one of his jobs was cleaning the dirty nappies every two days, by 'hosing them down', putting them to soak and then in the washing machine, a job he found distasteful but saw as something that he should do to help. Even before birth, men such as Simon were more aware of the physical demands that would be placed on their female partner and were planning how to assist: 'If Jane is home 24 hours a day with the baby, she is going to need a break. I think the best thing I can do is that when I get home I relieve her of any chores that need to be done so that she can get a rest . . . Jane will have done at least as much work as I have, and that work is likely to be very draining.'

In his third interview, with his baby about five weeks old, Peter described at length the adjustments he and his partner Donna had made so that he could help. He was assisting with both routine household tasks and also spending time with the baby. According to Peter, the ease with which this occurred related to the fact that he had always been equally involved in domestic work. Peter noted that he and Donna had always tried to talk problems through before and were continuing to be 'open' and deal with issues without 'sitting there and letting it brew'. They were managing to maintain time together. In part this appeared to be because this couple's combined approach to domestic work and parenting gave them time to do things together without the sense of exhaustion or being overwhelmed that was described by other couples.

The families where men had participated equally in domestic labour before the birth of their first child were practically advantaged in their early weeks of parenting. Not only were the men more efficient, given that they were already competent at getting jobs done, but they did not resent this or feel put upon by their partner. For example, as Peter said,

> I don't feel as though I'm expected to do a lot of things. We have been together for a long while. Even before the baby came along, Donna and I would get everything done. We had a routine set up and we would swap round. I've been used to helping for ages. If most blokes can get in and do these things when they are younger, it is not such a shock when they get married or have a kid. They won't have to ask, 'How do I put on the washing machine?' A lot of my friends would not even know one vacuum cleaner from another, because their mother, sister or another woman did all the work.

Peter made little distinction between types of work or who should do it. He believed that his partner was required to feed and spend more time with the baby, and therefore he had taken on far more of the domestic tasks than he had done previously. He interpreted this as a way of getting 'involved' and as 'contributing'. Peter saw this involvement as largely unproblematic if it was taken-for-granted and absorbed into an everyday routine. As he said: 'I just get into it, a routine that is. You come home and you go do the washing and while the machine is filling, you can do the dishes. You can get it all done.' Peter's job required him to do a lot of bending and lifting of equipment. Rather than seeing this a focus for complaints about tiredness when he came home, he adjusted his own patterns and that of the baby to bring their needs together while simultaneously helping out his partner. Peter generally had a shower on his return home from work, and decided to make a habit of taking his son Josh into the shower with him. He said that everyone found this a highly satisfactory and enjoyable arrangement.

Whether they chose to involve themselves in domestic and caring labour, were allowed to by their partner, were prevented from doing so by the requirements of paid employment, or believed it was 'proper' for men to be involved varied considerably across the men in our study and their partners. The men who chose to become closely involved, and had jobs that allowed them to do so, found the emotional rewards were significant (see Tony's case study in the previous chapter). Some men achieved a great deal at times but did so tenuously and reverted to a less involved role when circumstances changed. For example, as discussed in the previous chapter, Mike played a much more involved role in his daughter's care when the family was travelling overseas. When they returned home and he went back to paid employment, his partner accused him of laziness because he returned to having little participation in the infant's care. This father boasted about how good he had become at preparing the bottles and settling his daughter to sleep while on holidays. For him, however, this was not part of everyday behaviour for men who 'worked', and he was quite happy to allow these skills to decline once the holiday was over.

Other men, while espousing an extremely strong commitment to 'involved' fatherhood, experienced difficulties once their child was born, finding that their idealized notions were unachievable. Juan, for example, had clearly accepted a definition of fatherhood that meant he was 'involved' with his son's care but noted in the early weeks and months that: 'I don't think my role as father has begun yet. I think at the moment I am just a protector that keeps him safe and clean. The role as father has not begun yet.' Juan expressed his disappointment that his partner Trisha was the only one who seemed to be able to meet their son Nathan's needs effectively. He said that he was waiting for things to 'balance out a bit' when she stopped breastfeeding and he could feed the baby and become more involved in care. This response was also evident in the study of Australian fathers carried out by White. One of her participants commented that 'The majority of fathers don't have the closeness to their children that mothers do. It's like looking inside the window of the family unit; you want to be there and you can't. It becomes frustrating but you have to accept it' (quoted in White, 1994: 128).

Most of the men in our study noted that they often welcomed their partners teaching them to do things for the infant, as they recognized the superior skills mothers developed over the longer period of time spent caring for the baby. Fathers watched and copied their partners and learned from this. Even those men who, through previous experience with younger brothers and sisters or with nieces or nephews, may have originally been more competent than their partners rapidly fell behind in competence when they returned to paid employment. Men who developed confidence and familiarity with their infant lost this easily when employment or other pressures took them away from providing care and close frequent contact. Tony's case, as described in the previous chapter, showed how tenuous this hold on competence could be and how reliant it is on regular participation. His narrative also demonstrated how the emotional gains he had made disappeared and were only recaptured after he was able to find more time to spend with his son.

As in Lewis's (1986) study, many of our participants expressed some ambivalence about undertaking elements of the care required by a very tiny infant. Sometimes the initial physical incapacity of the female partner, due to surgery or complications at the birth, provided the impetus for men to begin engaging in the care of their infant from the early days onwards. For most men, however, this involvement otherwise did not occur or was substantially delayed. Steve demonstrated this well in a quotation from an interview shortly after his son was born, when his partner Kerry was still in hospital:

> I've been the one wrapping him in the blanket. Kerry can't do a lot because of all the tubes she has coming out of her. I'm looking forward to doing more. Her Mum was there and copped a dirty nappy yesterday so she got to change him. But hopefully I'll get the chance today. You know, I'm not really waiting on a dirty nappy – but to change it and I suppose there will be plenty more to come and I'll be dreading it, but I'd like to be a bit more involved in that way now.

When Steve was interviewed about six weeks later, Kerry had made a full recovery and taken over the care of their son. His attitude to participating in child care appeared somewhat different. He described his growing sense of not wanting to engage in care and his lack of competence: 'I had a feeling of not being able to do it properly – this was dressing him, putting on nappies and bathing. Kerry would put one on and mine would be half falling off. I just got the feeling I didn't want to do it any more.'

Men like Steve differed in their enjoyment of early fatherhood from fathers such as Tony, who continued to engage extensively in child care and found profound satisfaction in fatherhood much sooner. The former group kept looking to a time in the future when the child would be more responsive to them. Many of these men, when interviewed six months after their child's birth, said that they did not yet have the ultimate relationship they wanted with their child, where they could adopt the role of father they wanted. Juan said, for example: 'I don't think I have much of an effect now but will in the future . . . I guess on the one hand I can't wait until he gets to a point where he can run around and do things and play soccer. I can't wait for that.'

Some men, despite determined attempts to become competent over the first weeks of their child's life, became frustrated. They lost heart in trying, and any confidence they had won was tenuous, because their attempts at providing care always seemed to be deficient. Simon, for example, said that he wanted very much to be an 'involved' father. He said that he 'fell in love' with his baby very quickly, and while he was anxious about performing well as a parent he was very keen to provide as much care as his job would allow. It appeared, however, that he was actively excluded from the role he wanted with his daughter, due in part, it seemed, to his partner Jane's difficulties and anxieties about her role. Simon noted that because Jane was feeling fragile about her role and capacity as a mother, his attempts to care for their daughter Sally were more often rejected than welcomed by her.

A few days after the birth of his daughter, despite Simon having to work long hours that week, he had managed to change Sally's nappy a few times, and said that he was looking forward to bathing her. By five weeks after birth, however, the situation appeared to be nightmarish for both parents. Jane had experienced great difficulties with breastfeeding, but nonetheless was persisting. Simon expressed his sadness at the continual exclusion he felt from providing any care at all for Sally. He had wanted to help but felt actively prevented by his partner from doing so:

I'd like to have a go at settling Sally down, but Jane says it's not a good idea to pass her backwards and forwards. And it is probably not, but I begin to think, 'Just bite your tongue and just let her do it.' She is the one who really spends the most time with Sally. When you want to help it has not necessarily been wanted or welcome. I think I can rock a baby as well as anyone else but I'm not allowed to do that. Obviously no better than Jane, but I think the way I've been brought up and the experiences I've had would help. That probably annoys me most, because Jane says, 'No, let me keep trying.' . . . she sort of says, 'No, I don't want you to, put her down.' There are times when you go to help or offer to help and she says 'No!' This is a bit rejecting, I suppose.

Jane had turned to multiple agencies and health workers for advice over the first few months of mothering about both feeding and settling the infant. Simon said that he had found it very difficult to remain patient and support-ive all those months and not dismiss Jane's concerns. She would not allow him to reassure her about the baby's behaviour, even though he himself was a trained nurse. Simon commented that he found this hurtful but that he was conscious of how important it was for him to try not to interfere but to stay patient and not intrude as Jane struggled to feel confident about her moth-ering abilities.

Other researchers have noted that while couples may articulate a desire to share child care tasks, some women may find it difficult to relinquish these tasks to their partners. Everingham (1994) found in her study of Australian parents that even those fathers who participated extensively in child care tended to adopt the routines their female partners had already established with the child, and relied upon their partners to inform them about the child's care when they 'took over' from their partners for short or longer intervals. She suggests that it is because mothers generally engage as the primary carer from the start that this is how they come to 'know' what the child 'needs' and, indeed, position themselves as the individual who 'should know' what the infant 'needs' (Everingham, 1994: 65–6). This attitude, she argues, is sup-ported by contemporary approaches to child care, which emphasize a child-centred approach using empathy, responding to the infant's needs 'intu-itively' and gratifying them immediately.

Cathy Urwin (1985) conducted interviews with 40 young mothers in Cambridge. She too found that many of her interviewees emphasized the importance of their infants' emotional needs in explaining why they had chosen to leave paid employment after the birth. The women were adamant that they would feel guilty giving over the care of their child to another person, as it would not be 'doing the right thing by them'. At a less overt level, Urwin discerned that several of the women feared that another care-taker would pose a threat by competing for their child's affections. The mothers' determination to enjoy their children was expressed in such phrases as 'I feel I want to enjoy them when they're young', 'They grow up so quickly' and 'I quite liked my job, but I'm not a career woman' (Urwin, 1985: 171). Urwin suggests that her participants generally were quite satis-fied to take the major responsibility for parenting: 'there were indications that they have found or sensed that the positive gains which they had

expected to accompany being mothers could be undermined if their husbands took too much responsibility' (1985: 172). This is also noted by
Jordan (1995) in her study of American couples. The mothers she interviewed tended to want to take control of their partners' activities in child
care and to position themselves as the primary parent at the same time as
they asserted that they wanted help from the fathers.

As discussed in Chapter 2, the cultural imperative on women to be 'good
mothers' may mean that women may wish to involve their partners more but
find this difficult. To be shown to be overly willing to hand over more responsibility to one's partner or someone else for child care, however much a
woman may want to, may seem too cavalier an approach to one's responsibilities as a mother. Men's subject position as a 'good' father appears not to
depend to quite the same extent upon demonstrating expertise in, and dedi-
cation to, the care of one's children. As Walzer contends, 'A father can be
perceived as a "good" father without thinking about his baby; in fact, his
baby may pose a distraction to his doing what he is expected to do' (1996:
231). As a result, women are far more likely than are men to express guilt and
uncertainty about leaving their young children in paid child care, even if they
are working in full-time paid employment and find their job rewarding
(Walzer, 1996: 228).

No matter how a man defined work, or how willing or able he was to share
the work of the household, his paid employment profoundly influenced the
amount of time he was able to commit to child care. Men such as Jim had
underestimated the amount of time it took to be involved in a worthwhile way
with their children. For him, an hour or two snatched from work turned out
to be unsatisfying because it was not long enough. Richard was very open
with his employer about the priority his family played in his life. He chose his
employer, in part, because he also put a high value on his own family. Despite
this, the demands of his job meant that he was away from the house for 10 to
12 hours a day during the week. Steve rarely saw his son Luke awake for most
of his early life, as he was still asleep when Steve left home for work and had
gone to bed when he returned. Steve's paid employment was as a systems
designer for a large computer company. He said that his job was demanding
and required a high level of commitment. While Steve accepted this, he did
articulate some regrets about how the demands of his job meant that he saw
little of Luke: 'I hope I'm around in those times when Luke is learning to play.
There are a couple of hours each day when he wants to play and try and talk
and stuff. Because I'm at work I hope I don't miss out on that too much. I can
make the most of him on weekends but I don't want to come home all the
time and find him to be asleep.'

The couples who described the least tension and fewest arguments seemed
to fall into two types. One type was demonstrated by the very few couples
who felt that they shared a strong and clear framework of 'rules' for behaviour within which they operated. Steve and Kerry were the most obvious
example of this. Both held strong Christian beliefs and espoused quite conservative and traditional views on parenting that distinguished between men

and women and what they could each bring to parenting. For example, Steve believed that the mother's major role was to be 'practical', providing caring and feeding. His partner Kerry was positioned as the leader in the provision of care for their son Luke, and in household management. Steve argued, however, that this did not mean that he saw motherhood as less valuable than his economic contribution, or as easier. The other type, at the other extreme, were those couples who appeared able to deal with less certain 'rules', and who appeared comfortable with ambiguity and uncertainty. Tony and Louise fall into this category. Tony appeared able to tolerate, indeed welcome, the freedom and opportunity that his view of parenthood offered. His partner Louise appeared to appreciate his deep engagement with their child and seemed not to feel threatened by this.

Men's Relationships with their Children

In Chapter 2 we described recent research that has suggested that despite some discourses suggesting that parenting is becoming more androgynous, with differences between men and women breaking down, there is still evidence of gender-differentiated parenthood, not only in terms of 'who does what' but for attitudes. This is particularly the case, it has been argued, for the 'invisible' or 'mental' labour in which mothers tend to engage to a greater extent than fathers. The feminist philosopher Sara Ruddick (1989, 1994) has developed a concept that she describes as 'maternal thinking', approaching the question of 'How might a mother, a person who thinks regularly and intently about children, think about "the world"?' (1994: 29). Ruddick (1994: 33) refers to the notion of 'mothering as a kind of work or practice'. She argues that 'To be a "mother" means to "see" children as demanding protection, nurturance, and training, and then to commit oneself to the work of trying to meet these demands' (1994: 33). Mothering, therefore, is relational work 'in which others' responses serve as an intrinsic and primary measure of achievement' (1994: 34).

It is important to emphasize, however, that these 'ways of thinking' or of seeing the world are not themselves 'inherent' or 'natural' but are the results of interactions with the child and drawing upon one's own experiences as both a child and an adult. As Walzer has put it in relation to child care, 'doing becomes a kind of knowing' (1996: 227). 'Mothering', therefore, may be understood primarily as a process of interpretation of the child's responses and expression of subjectivity as 'needs' in a particular social setting. As this suggests, despite its title, 'maternal thinking' need not be limited to women. In her most recent discussions on this point, Ruddick is careful to point out that mothering need not be a distinctly female activity, but can be undertaken by both men and women: 'A child is mothered by whoever protects, nurtures, and trains her. Although it is a material, social, and cultural fact that most mothers are now women, there is no difficulty in imagining men taking up mothering as easily as women – or conversely, women as easily declining to mother' (1994: 350). Ruddick argues, thus, that giving birth may be separated from the act of mothering, and that doing so provides more support for the promotion of men in taking up 'mothering' activities. The bodily interactions that both men and women may have with infants and children leads, she contends, to 'maternal thinking' for carers of both sexes. As Ruddick points out, the acts of giving birth and mothering need not be, and indeed currently sometimes are not, connected (in cases of surrogacy and adoption, for example).

Research with men who extensively engage in child care on an everyday basis (still a small minority of fathers) has also suggested that men are as capable as women of taking on a nurturing role and do so in ways that are not distinctively different from the archetypal 'maternal' role. For instance, Grbich's (1995) research into Australian men who had taken on the primary care-giving role of their young children while their female partners worked full-time noted that the men's interactions with their children were affectionate and sensitive to their children's needs, in ways similar to the type of behaviour expected of mothers. Grbich observed that the children were frequently cuddled and that the children's demands were responded to with patience, attentiveness and immediate response. She gives as one example: 'During a particularly long interview (2.5 hours), Andrew kept his three-month-old baby, who was restless, in a state of constant motion. He would cuddle him, hold him close to his face, murmur soft words; kissing him, he would then stand up, cross his arms across the baby's chest, and gently swing him to and fro between his legs for long periods of time' (Grbich, 1995: 123).

We found from our own interview study that developing skill in caring for their infants required men to invest time and energy in becoming familiar with the infant's requirements. The integral feature relating to whether or not men developed a 'maternal thinking' response to their children was the nature and regularity of their interactions with the child. There is no doubt that some men had accomplished this and, as a result, demonstrated an extremely close and intense, emotionally rewarding relationship with their children from early on. Such men showed a strong awareness of their child's needs and wants, having learnt how to 'read' the child from engaging in regular caring activities with them. They articulated distress and anxiety about being prevented by the demands of their jobs from spending time with their children, and some had set out to change their work patterns to deal with this.

As we discussed above, the men in our study typically found that their relationship to their infant was difficult to imagine during pregnancy. When asked to describe the baby before birth, most men did so in terms of personality characteristics that they expected the baby to exhibit, based on their own traits and those of their partner. After the birth, the emphasis in interviews changed as the participants attempted to describe physical manifestations of the infant. Time and time again in the interviews held in the first few weeks after the birth, the men manifested a need to recognize the infant as their own through their physical characteristics. Richard, for example, said that he was immediately looking for points of physical resemblance between the infant and himself, his partner or her family. He was so surprised at the physical appearance of his son, that if he had not been present he said he would not have believed that he was their baby. Another father, Jim, identified facial expressions and behaviours, such as how baby Tom placed his hands when he slept, that resembled both him and his partner. For these men, it is as if the ownership of the child by the family has to be established in a way that links the infant irrevocably and unmistakably to their own genetic and social inheritance.

After the birth, several men spoke about how important it was to them that they could look upon the child as 'part of themselves' and how protective they felt. These discourses resonate with the 'father as protector' discourse that many men expressed in the interviews held in late pregnancy. As Ewan said of his five-week-old daughter:

> I like the feeling that she's actually part of Naomi and I, and now sort of a permanent member of our family and one that we have to sort of provide everything for and she totally depends on us for everything. And we can give her everything that she needs, like, and watch her and guide her and sort of provide whatever she needs. She'll sort of give us all this love back. That's really nice, that's really good.

The point at which a close relationship with their infant began varied across the group of participants. As noted above, some had attended a caesarean delivery, and this gave them an opportunity to be intimately involved with the infant immediately, and indeed far more so than the partner, who needed to recover from the surgery. Peter described the emotions he felt having watched his son born by caesarean section: 'Everyone says it takes time to get a relationship between you. But because he was a "caesar" I had him from the moment he was born for about two hours before Donna got to see him in recovery. I think straight away I was protective and I wanted to hold him and they let me hold him and there was no one else around. I think that was really good.' Similarly, Dominic described how he had engaged in caring for his new daughter Jessica in the first few days while she and his partner Stella were still in hospital: 'I've changed nappies and then settled her and found that some techniques work with the baby, and I've cuddled her and put her up against my chest and she'd fall asleep. And obviously changed her nappy and wiped her poo off her bum and then cleaned her up and all that sort of stuff.' These comments suggest the importance of men having intimate and private time with their newborn babies, something that was very difficult for them to attain in normal circumstances.

Many men, such as Juan, were surprised that the 'bonding' they expected was not achieved immediately, even though it may have happened quite soon after the birth. They also did not expect to feel the sheer intensity and depth of emotion they experienced when their child arrived. As Juan said:

> I thought as a father there would be a bond there straight away with the child. I thought it would just come naturally. I thought because he was mine I was going to be immediately attracted to this child and love would just come naturally. I was surprised I wasn't overcome with feelings for him straight away. But that came very

soon afterwards. By the next day I didn't want to leave him at all. Then that surprised me a bit, 'cause I didn't know I could feel like that.

A common discourse articulated by the men was of being 'overwhelmed' by strong feelings in relation to their child. Dominic described the strong feelings of joy and love he had experienced as soon as Jessica was born:

I was stroking her, just calming her down, she was quite calm, but, you know, she was obviously stressed by what happened [during the birth]. I held her hand and she just looked helpless there by herself, so I tried to help her along, you know, to make her realize that everything will be fine and I talked to her . . . I mean, I felt very, very happy that this new life is being brought to this world and we were the key to it all and you know, we're parents. I mean there's a lot of things that go through your mind at that time. It's just – it's very overwhelming.

After the birth of their children, there was a strong sense in many men's accounts that their notion of a 'good' father included displaying expertise in dealing with their child and knowledge of their child to do so successfully. Being a 'good' father was about learning, including reading the appropriate material, attending antenatal classes, seeking the advice of 'experts', watching others in their interactions with their children, but perhaps more profoundly, developing a relationship with the child and learning about how to handle her or him from 'trial and error'. As several men pointed out, experts often give conflicting advice. They argued that the best way to deal with problems was to use one's own judgement, based on the child's individual characteristics. As Ewan said, 'You try little things and see what works with [the infant] and you judge it on her reactions, on how it feels, what you are doing, on how it sort of feels for you.'

We noted above that when they were interviewed before the birth of their child, several men articulated a sense of apprehension about the responsibil-ities involved in becoming a parent. Apprehension became transformed into fear for many men as they began to assist with the care of the child. The main concern seemed to be that somehow the men's lack of manual dexterity and skill would become translated into physical activity that actually damaged the baby, who was seen as immensely fragile and vulnerable. Steve, when talking about handling his new son Luke, noted that:

I carry him like he is a China doll – I always worry that I'll drop him or something. Initially I didn't like the baby near me. I was scared in case I dropped him or hurt him or something. At one stage he nearly dropped out of my hands when I was bathing him. If he had slipped he would have fallen about two and a half feet, so he would have injured himself.

Despite Steve taking one month off work to be home, in part to have time to get to know his son and become competent in caring for him, he remained highly anxious and cautious about handling Luke. This fear seemed to sub-side the more experienced fathers became. For several participants, however, a level of anxiety remained for some months, related to what they saw as their lack of ability to cope with the practicalities of baby care and capacity to read and respond to their child's signals. Steve described this anxiety: 'I've always been anxious because I'm not sure how I'll go with the baby. I just want to make sure I can carry him, feed him and change him and look after him and recognize when things go wrong without having to rely on anyone else.'

As discussed above, the men's learning skills in caring for the infant appeared to be a crucial step in them becoming closer to the child. Even those fathers who saw their participation as limited and gave very little time to child care activities started to feel satisfaction in their achievements when they felt they had 'succeeded' in a task. As Mike said of his daughter, 'a few times I've put her back to sleep and gave myself a pat on the back because I don't know how I've done it.' The limited time that most men had with their children reduced their opportunities to learn and develop competence in providing care. As a consequence, they argued, their enjoyment and satisfaction with the role were diminished. The disappointment appears to have arisen, at least in part, from the men's unrealistic expectations of the involvement and rewards that were possible to achieve. Most men found that their role in paid work, combined with the immaturity of their infant, made the rewards they expected unattainable. This resulted in many of them feeling disappointed in early fathering and distant from their very young infants. As the infant grew older, and they were able to provide more care for a more responsive older child, the disappointment appeared to diminish and the men seemed to enjoy their role more.

Those men who did not enter into close, care-providing relationships in the early weeks and months of their child's life took longer to gain rewards from their children. They found this difficult in the early weeks and months. For example, when his baby was about six weeks old, Peter commented that: 'I know I want that bonding. I want to get that feeling that we both know each other and get along. I don't know how long that will take.' Most fathers, however, indicated that they had managed to achieve a satisfying and enjoyable relationship with their infant by the time she or he was six months old. This process appeared to be closely linked to the infant's capacity to be responsive to them.

Even Mike, the father who was probably least involved in caring for his child during the first six months of her life, attempted to articulate the special emotional links that he felt for his child at six months of age. He described, for example, how his daughter 'will be crying in her bed and you go in to try to hush her down and she will turn her head around and see me, and just start smiling. That really gets to me'. The child's recognition of him as father and the response that only he could elicit made him feel very important. This aroused a very strong emotional response in him that he found unexpected. Other fathers, such as Peter, proudly described similar responses from their infants that were perceived to be directed at them alone: 'When I get home [from work], if there is someone else here or [his son] is playing with Donna, he will just stop what he is doing. He hears my voice and he knows that I'm home and he gets really happy.' It was the recognition of the special relationship that they had with their child that satisfied and provided fathers with the emotional rewards they needed. Several men remained preoccupied with thinking about their infants when they were apart. This became more pronounced as the child grew older and they looked forward to getting home to see and play with her or him.

Feeding the infant appears to be of immense symbolic as well as practical significance to men and their partners. Breastfeeding, in particular, proved to be a very important issue for the men we interviewed, as it had enormous implications for the kinds of relationships that mothers developed with their infants compared with those that fathers were able to achieve. Breastfeeding is a powerful metaphor for the unique love only a mother could provide, as well as a biological link between the mother and infant that of necessity excludes the father. All the mothers in our study began by breastfeeding their infants. This provided them with a symbiotic connection that for many re-established the intimacy the women felt had begun when the infant was *in utero*. The intimacy of mother and infant manifested in breastfeeding requires, at least in the early weeks, considerable effort and loss of sleep. Nonetheless, it also brings rewards that may help compensate for the negative side of infant care. Similar compensations are not so evident for men, most of whom found the loss of sleep caused by the infant's crying a highly negative experience of early fatherhood.

The type of physically intimate relationship that the mother was able to develop with the infant through breastfeeding was not at first available to the male partner and resulted in some men feeling more 'detached' from their child than they expected or wanted to be. As Jim said, 'It is hard to get that total involvement when you can't feed him, and this, apart from sleeping, is what he is predominantly doing.' A number of men had mixed feelings about the privileged position of their female partner. Some men were aware of the powerful advantage that breastfeeding the infant gave the mother in requiring her to establish intimate and frequent contact with the child. They did not choose to become involved in other intimate activities they could find equally involving and rewarding.

Many of the men were astounded at how time-consuming breastfeeding the infant proved to be. For those who wanted a greater emotional involvement with the child themselves in the early weeks of parenting, breastfeeding tended to exclude and disenfranchise them in a way that was unexpected. The fathers quickly learned that breastfeeding was 'mother's territory'. Those who expected that their contribution to the child's care was going to be one of immediate closeness and emotional reciprocation had to rethink and were disappointed. For example, Juan thought that perhaps he was slower to 'bond' with his son after birth because his partner Trisha had already known him for nine months of his life (that is, during pregnancy). Juan said, however, that he was not giving up that easily. He had found bottle feeding his son with expressed breast milk was a 'fantastic experience' and said that he 'wanted more of it'. Juan was consequently encouraging his partner to obtain a breast pump so he could feed his son often and easily. He had even developed a plan whereby when he was home, he would always feed Nathan with expressed milk, but when he was at work, his partner Trisha would take over again, breastfeeding him. When asked how Trisha had responded to this plan, Juan admitted that they had not actually discussed it, but he was sure that she would like to 'hand him over'.

The one man who most comfortably transcended the nexus of breastfeeding and privileged closeness to the infant was Tony. Unlike some other men in the research, Tony articulated little disillusionment, discomfort or resentment in relation to his partner breastfeeding, and appeared to have established a very close, care-providing relationship with his infant early on (see his case study in the previous chapter). Tony was able to develop sensory and emotional contact with his son James through taking responsibility for nappy changes and bathing, and he welcomed the opportunities these occasions provided for him to get physically close to his son. Tony appeared not to be inhibited by lack of confidence or skill as he welcomed learning how to do things he had never done before. Nor did he see his role only as caring for the baby, but was actively involved in all the other household work as well.

It is interesting to contrast Tony with Mike. Mike's participation in parenting appeared to conform to the archetype of the 'old' rather than the 'new' father, despite his often expressed desire to be different from his own distant and 'uninvolved' father. His partner Jenny did not share his view of how fathers should behave and resented Mike's lack of participation in domestic and child care tasks. Mike found little joy in the first six months of fatherhood and quite quickly reverted to his day-long absences on weekend fishing trips. While he did gain satisfaction from others' changed response to him now he was a father, including being able to 'show off' his daughter when taking her out in the pram, it was not until he began to bottle feed his daughter that they developed the closeness he needed and the recognition he wanted from her was forthcoming.

We found that among our group of participants it was unusual for men not to express interest in feeding the baby. Mostly this interest was expressed prior to them actually doing so, when feeding was seen as a chore the men should share with their partners rather than experienced as an opportunity for emotional engagement with the infant. As Steve said, 'I don't think [bottle feeding] is hard but I've never fed him, so I'll have to learn how to do it with a bottle, 'cause there will probably be a time when I'll need to do that.' Once they had engaged in the experience, however, the men found that feeding the infant brought emotional rewards and allowed them a closeness and sense of satisfaction in their role that they thought had been missing. It also brought some practical benefits for families where breastfeeding had been difficult or where the female partner found feeding onerous and time-consuming. The father's participation allowed his partner some respite from the demands of feeding.

Some fathers described vividly how the intimacy engendered by bottle feeding their child helped them to 'fall in love' with her or him. This was an experience that appeared to transcend the difficulties posed by the infant's immaturity we discussed above. For some fathers, bottle feeding seemed to be an effective vehicle for the communication and engagement they sought but had not yet managed to achieve with their child. For instance, Richard, when asked when he began to feel the intensity of love for his son that he was now describing said: 'It was the first bottle feed. He wasn't quite capable of smiling in those days, but you could see it in his eyes.' What Richard means by 'it' appears to be the responsiveness that men need to feel engaged and emotionally rewarded and recognized by their children when they are tiny infants. Jim quickly accepted the benefits breastfeeding provided for the baby as well as his partner. Megan fed their baby without problems and very much enjoyed the feeding relationship with her son. Jim readily adjusted to his initial disappointment at being less involved than he had hoped and took great satisfaction in feeding baby Tom his solid food as he got older.

Concluding Comments

It was evident from the interviews that many couples are working towards a notion of parenthood that incorporates joint participation in child care and domestic labour. The men in our study, with only a few exceptions, tended not to adhere to 'traditional' notions of gender-defined child care. Further, there was little recourse in the men's accounts to the notion that women are 'naturally' better at caring for children than are men. It would appear that most of the men felt both that they should participate more actively in domestic labour and child care and that their partner expected them to do so. Our sample of couples was relatively small, and our findings cannot be generalized to a larger population. However, the men who took part were relatively heterogeneous, with a wide range of occupational backgrounds and included a number of men from non-Anglo-Celtic ethnic origins. Our findings are supported by other research undertaken in western societies, which is suggesting that in recent years there has been evidence of gradual change in terms of how men are approaching fatherhood and domestic involvement (for example, Gerson, 1993; White, 1994; Doucet, 1995; Hall, 1995; Benjamin and Sullivan, 1996).

Most men in our study found that their expectations of engaging as an 'involved' father were difficult to achieve in practice. The time available for men to interact with their children was regulated by many factors, which were sometimes within but often outside their control. These factors ranged from the demands of employment through to the right retained by some men to alter their own lives very little. Even the men who sought a more 'traditional' role for themselves, focusing on their provider role as the most important, were disappointed with their experience and the limited nature of the relationship they had managed to achieve with their child in the first few months of her or his life. They were surprised how much additional tension existed between themselves and their female partners. The men tended to have nothing but praise for their female partner's skills in caring for their child, developed through her frequent handling of the infant, but at times resented the closeness and rewards the women obtained from the baby in return, particularly in relation to breastfeeding.

The issue of fathers wanting the emotional reward of feeding their infants and the implications of this for the early stages of development in their relationship with their children is worth considerable further exploration. Men's taking up of feeding has the potential to disrupt the mother's breastfeeding experience, potentially exclude her from an intimate and exclusive relationship with the infant and reduce the benefits the infant might receive from ingesting human milk (if formula is used rather than expressed breast milk). On the other hand, some mothers might relinquish this role with some relief, as not all women enjoy breastfeeding – many find it painful, uncomfortable, inconvenient and even disgusting (see, for example, the women interviewed by Murcott, 1993).

One major limitation of our study was that we were focusing on the earliest stage of first-time parenting, when the demands of the child are at their highest and when most infants are breastfed, reducing the opportunities that men may have to interact with their children at a similar level to their partner. We would emphasize the importance of acknowledging how conditions change over time, particularly in relation to the child's growing maturity and independence, but also including changing paid employment conditions for both parents and the entry of other children into the family. This requires consideration and further research. Nonetheless, it is highly likely that the relationship men and women establish with their children in early infancy and childhood remains important for their future relationships, particularly in relation to parents' ability to identify the needs of their children and to 'know' and 'feel close' to them.

Conclusion

In Chapter 1, we reviewed a range of theoretical perspectives that we suggested were insightful in addressing the ontology of fatherhood. We discussed how parenthood is now dominantly conceptualized as a considered enterprise, part of the project of the self. Children are viewed and treated both as 'sacred' and as 'planning objects', requiring much investment of time, thought and the seeking out of information on the part of their parents so that their quality is maximized. The child is often considered as an opportunity for parents to fulfil their unrealized dreams and hopes, to produce a better version of themselves. As we showed in Chapters 2 and 3, in both 'expert' and popular forums it is typically argued that the 'normal' and 'successful' development and maturation of children into adulthood is dependent upon the kind of care and attention given them by their parents. Further, it is believed that it is via careful and successful parenting, amongst other influences such as formal education, that children come to learn to engage in self-regulation and work upon the self: that is, to become 'civilized'. The construction of parenting as problematic has provided a spring-board for mothers and fathers to engage in continual self-reflection and questioning of their activities as parents, to work towards the ideal of the 'good' mother and the 'good' father.

This approach to parenting might be described as the 'rational' level of human action, which is largely produced and represented through discourse. At the 'extra-rational' level of meaning and action, we have suggested, the affective, embodied, sensual dimensions of parenting also need to be considered, for they are also vital to the meanings of contemporary parenthood. Caring for a child involves heightened physical and emotional sensations that go beyond 'rational' action and originate from individuals' earliest experiences with their primary care-givers. The parent–child relationship is endowed with high emotion from even before a child is born. The physical contact that infants have with their care-givers is the basis of their earliest diffuse sensations of pleasure and emotional states, including the smell and feel of the care-givers' skin, the sound and rhythm of their voices, breathing and heartbeat, the warmth and taste of the milk they feed the infant. The meanings of these sensations go beyond the discursive, constituted as they are before the acquisition of language. Emotion, therefore, is a central component of the parent–child relationship, as is the interplay between unconscious phantasy and a consciously perceived 'reality'. As Chodorow argues, 'our experiences as men and women come from deep within, both within our pasts and, relatedly, within the deepest structures of unconscious meaning and the most emotionally moving relationships that help constitute our daily lives' (1989: 2).

Unlike in previous centuries, children are not valued for their working capacity but solely for affective needs – providing their parents with self-ful-filment, giving their lives a new meaning, a sense of purpose and responsibility, allowing them to express unconditional love and so on. In a world which is considered to be characterized by superficial, self-serving and uncertain relationships with others (including one's marital partner), a child offers a loving relationship that will be stable: 'Where other aims seem arbi-trary and interchangeable, belief in the afterlife vanishes and hopes in this world prove evanescent, a child provides one with a chance to find a firm footing and a home' (Beck and Beck-Gernsheim, 1995: 107).

These contentions are supported by our research with fathers. As demon-strated in Chapters 4 and 5, a number of dominant discourses about fathers and fatherhood emerged in the men's accounts. These include the following: fatherhood as logical step, a 'natural' part of adult masculinity; fatherhood as a revelation, an opening up to intense feeling; fatherhood as overwhelming; fatherhood as an enterprise, something that needs to be worked at, requiring continued devotion and time; fatherhood as a major responsibility; father as protector; father as provider; fatherhood as transformative of the self, an integral life experience that causes the father to reassess and change his sense of self; fatherhood as demanding, a source of stress and strain; 'good' father-hood as close involvement with one's child; 'good' fatherhood as 'being there'; fatherhood as an opportunity to guide and shape another's life; father-hood as a source of fulfilment, joy and wellspring of love; fatherhood as an opportunity for intimacy with another (the child). As we noted in previous chapters, many of these discourses may also be identified in a range of media, including both 'expert' and more popular texts.

All of our interviewees drew upon most of these discourses at some point or another when describing their experiences and feelings related to first-time fatherhood, and many articulated them constantly as a means of making sense of their experience and presenting themselves as fathers. Some of these discourses were more dominant at different points of the men's experience, while others competed for prominence simultaneously. While, for example, the men seemed to see fatherhood as something that was 'natural' or 'just happened' when describing it before the birth of their child, the notion that fatherhood was 'an enterprise' and 'something that needs to be worked at' was also commonly espoused at this time. Fatherhood was said to involve much preparation, thinking about appropriate behaviour and financial arrangements, as well as 'talking things over' with one's partner in relation to the management of domestic labour and child care tasks. This discourse intensified in men's accounts in the first few weeks after the birth of their child. The men also appeared to have tended to take up the notion of the 'sacred child', seeing other people and demands as secondary to the priority of meeting what they perceived to be the child's needs. There appeared to be a continual tension, according to the men's accounts, between their desire to maintain a 'rational', controlled approach to parenting, involving preparation, the seeking after and acquisition of knowledge and negotiation with their partner about respective responsibilities and methods of dealing with the infant, and the representation of the child as an anarchic phenomenon, causing continual disruption, provoking 'irrational' or 'overwhelming' responses and emotional states (including intense love as well as frustration, anger and despair) and generally confounding the parents' attempts to maintain order.

It appeared to be very important to most of the men in our study that they could develop an emotionally close relationship with their child from early infancy onwards, that they could 'get to know' the child. They articulated a longing, a desire for closeness with their children, and they felt frustrated and anxious if they found this relationship not developing as they hoped. The men appeared to see this 'close' and 'involved' relationship as important for the child's development as well as for themselves in providing them with a fulfilling parenting experience. The men often described their loving and protective feelings towards their children as different from those they had ever experienced with others, and they sometimes found it difficult to put into words their strong feelings. These men did not conform to the archetype of the 'emotionally inexpressive male' (Duncombe and Marsden, 1993). Rather, they were quite open in expressing the strong feelings of love they felt for their children, and their distress at not being able to spend much time with them. Several used the term 'falling in love' when describing how their feelings for their children began to emerge. Many men also talked in detail about intimate features of their relationship with their female partners, including the strains on the marriage as well as the greater feelings of love they had for their partners after their child was born.

Further, the men drew on a discourse privileging the expression of affection and love in describing their relationships with their fathers and their idealized notions of how they would like to father their own children. Nearly all the men positioned their own fathers as 'absent', as perhaps doing their best to provide economically for the family but as 'emotionally distant'. Whether or not this was in fact the case, the dominant discourse circulating in contemporary forums labelling the last generation of fathers as 'absent' has proved powerful in this generation's tendency to identify 'absence' as a problem. As we have suggested, for many men the solution to this problematic absence is the discourse of 'being there', a rather amorphous term that suggests, above all, some kind of presence rather than absence. This typical juxtaposition of the negative 'absent' father versus the positive 'involved' father who is 'there' denotes the men's desire for intimate closeness with their own fathers that is projected onto their children. Appropriate masculinity, in this sense, is related to the ability to express and engage in fatherly love for one's child as well as to provide material resources for the family. The men not only wanted their children to love them as they themselves wanted to love their own fathers, but also wished to be able to invest their own love freely in their children, in a reciprocal, mutually loving relationship which was not 'forced'.

There was little indication in most of these men's accounts that 'nurturance' and 'caring' are non-masculine attributes. This would suggest that the ways that attitudes to intimacy are articulated are very much phrased through contemporary discourses on subjectivity and gender. Just as in the eighteenth and early nineteenth centuries, many bourgeois men were quite capable of, and comfortable in, expressing their deep feelings of love for each other, including kissing each other fraternally (Yacavone, 1990), and found the public display of weeping an appropriate expression of fine sensitivity (Vincent-Buffault, 1991), the ability to express affection for one's children openly is championed as part of a masculine demeanour in the late twentieth century.

Fatherhood, for most of the men in our study, did challenge their sense of being 'in control'. This loss of control was associated with distress and frustration, as well as anxieties about dealing physically with a tiny infant. At the same time, however, they found much pleasure in being part of 'the family unit' and taking on responsibility for a child. They commonly described their position as fathers as involving seeing the child as 'a part of me', and as having their futures inextricably linked to that of the child, involving constant responsibility for her or him. Unlike men's relationships with their female partners, the love they can offer to and receive from a child is regarded as more permanent: they will always be their fathers and ideally will always be positioned, in some way, as the guardian and guide for their children. The men's positioning of themselves in this way provides them with a sense of strength and mastery. The infant's response to its father – its recognition of him as 'the father' through such embodied responses as smiling and head-turning as well as its manifestation of physical or personality traits that the father can recognize as 'inherited' from himself – provide an important means for men of connecting emotionally with their child. These responses also give men a sense of potency that they may otherwise lack in dealing with their young children, partly because they have not been able to develop a sense of expertise and control in interacting with them to the same extent as they observe in their female partners.

We found, then, that despite the fact that most of the men in the study described their family of origin as conforming to the archetypal gendered division of labour, with the mother providing most of the child care and the father as generally 'absent' from the home, undertaking paid employment to support the family, they were also able to articulate a desire for closeness and intimacy with their children. This challenges the contentions from feminist theorists using object relations theory that men are not able to develop a 'relatedness' to others – including their children – unless they themselves have been parented by both men and women. Nonetheless, there was still evidence that at least some of the men were struggling with the privileged discourse of emotional 'involvement' with their children. The men's tendency to draw on notions of 'protector' and 'provider', the person who ideally is 'strong' and 'controlled' when describing how best to deal with fatherhood, suggests a discourse of fatherhood that continues to be phrased through gendered assumptions.

This supports Hollway's (1995: 94) argument that as part of their defence against the unconscious anxieties first produced in infancy in the process of individuation from the mother, both men and women may seek recourse in taking up the gender-differentiated discourses available to them. The prevailing sociocultural meanings constructed around femininities and masculinities, therefore, will tend to shape the ways that individuals deal with these anxieties. In the interests of performing 'good' motherhood and presenting themselves as 'good' mothers, for example, women rather than men may have much more invested in worrying about their children, and in describing this concern to an interviewer. As Walzer (1996: 221) has noted, worrying is culturally understood as 'something that mothers do', and the absence of this may challenge the definition of a 'good' mother for a mother herself or her partner. Similarly, the dominant discourse that privileges the notion of fathers acting as economic providers may mean that men are more likely to emphasize this role when describing their experiences of fatherhood. Because the prevailing discourses around fatherhood privilege both the 'father as provider and protector' and 'father as emotionally involved' discourses, men are articulating both as a means of dealing with this challenging new relationship.

The infant, in its state of unpredictable behaviour, its 'uncivilized' lack of control over its body, is a problematic source of love. Infants constantly threaten rationality and order by the grotesqueness of their uncontained bodies, with all the associated work, lack of sleep, noise and 'dirt' (the various bodily fluids they constantly emit) this entails (Murcott, 1993). We suggested in Chapter 1 that because of the sociocultural meanings privileging the contained body/self, and bestowing a masculine rather than feminine gender upon this ideal notion of subjectivity and embodiment, and because men lack some of the physical capacities for merging the body/self with another that women possess (such as pregnancy and breastfeeding), men are more likely than women to find the uncontained liquidities and physical excesses of the infant body confronting. Alan Brien, an English novelist and father of now adult children, has written vividly of the dread and revulsion inspired in men by some of the odours and textures produced by the infant body:

> There seems to be something about that cheesy, beany, cassoulet smell of the infant shit, the ammoniac whiff of infant piss somewhere between a very sour white wine and a concentrated paint stripper, that is too overwhelmingly intimate for the virgin nose of the pre-paternal male. Some fathers never get over this and make sure they will remain forever a stranger to the slopping potty, the warm rubber blanket, the caked sick down the back of the jacket. (1993: 17)

Infants' perceived state of innocence and vulnerability may evoke feelings of affection and the desire to protect them, but their incessant demands may be experienced as excessive, calling into question a man's ability to regulate his life as he was used to.

Men's desires for intimacy with their children are developed and expressed in a sociocultural setting in which men are still expected to work to support their families and where the 'stay-at-home husband' continues to be regarded as an oddity (Russell, 1987; Grbich, 1995). Men's interactions with their children are constrained by the demands of their paid employment. They may also be constrained by women's own desires and anxieties about their role as mothers, the meanings of which are themselves inflected through dominant discourses on the 'good' mother. While some men may want to be the one who stays at home to engage in the kind of personalized, attentive child care that is considered essential for a child's optimal development, the fact that they earn more money than their female partner, or that their partner prefers to be the one to stay home, confounds this. Interestingly enough, we found in our research that an anatomical difference between men and women – women's capacity for breastfeeding – combined with a currently hegemonic discourse that insists upon the importance of breastfeeding infants both for health reasons and for maternal–child 'bonding' often served to shut men out of experiencing a close embodied relationship with their child to the extent they would have liked. We found in the interview data from the women in our study that several of them ascribed so strongly to this discourse of 'breastfeeding is best' that they struggled to continue to breastfeed their child despite experiencing continuing pain or severe discomfort.

The cultural expectations and assumptions around gendered bodies explains why it is that women, as more embodied and emotional subjects, are expected to 'know what to do' with infants and small children, not only through their 'maternal instincts' but because they have a bodily or intuitive/emotional sense of the child's needs and feelings, which men, as more disembodied and rational subjects, are generally assumed to lack. It is assumed, therefore, that women require somewhat less guidance, less reflection upon parenting than do men. There is little that is regarded as 'instinctive' about fatherhood, particularly in relation to the expression of nurturing and emotional sensitivity that is regarded as essential to the practice of 'new' or 'involved' fatherhood. That is, while writers commonly argue that men have a certain *capacity* for nurturance that lies within, fatherhood itself is portrayed as something that is essentially learnt and requires practice and work to allow this nurturance to emerge in appropriate ways. Successful fatherhood is portrayed as the product of acquired knowledge and mastery of action. Motherhood, in contrast, still tends to be represented as having an instinctive core. While women are also encouraged to seek out information about pregnancy, childbirth and parenting, motherhood is still commonly seen as more essentially a part of femininity, not as split from womanhood as fatherhood may sometimes be split from manhood. Men and women, therefore, are negotiating parenting arrangements in a context in which it is still considered that the mother is more important to her child's welfare than the father and 'instinctively' possesses a greater capacity for nurturance.

Counter to these taken-for-granted assumptions, we suggest that men and women should be viewed as possessing equally the capacity for developing a close, intimate relationship with their children through regular caring activities. It is often the female partner who becomes knowledgeable about the child because she is the one engaging in regular, everyday caring. As we found in our study, it is all too easy for men to lag behind their female partner in developing the skills of caring for their children, even when the men may strongly wish to do so, and it can be difficult for them to make up for lost ground. Once it becomes established that one parent 'knows' more about the child and her or his needs and is more competent in dealing with the child, then it is difficult for the other to acquire equivalent knowledge and expertise. It then tends to be assumed that the more expert parent will take major responsibility for child care – it seems 'easier' that way. This defining of the 'more expert' and 'less expert' parent is generally based in early activities such as feeding and soothing the infant. The pleasure that the 'more expert' parent may derive from his or her greater knowledge and ability in dealing with the child may also prove a barrier to allowing the other parent to participate.

If men do not have the opportunity to engage in these activities, they cannot develop a sense of the child's needs to respond to them in ways that their female partners would see as adequate. Barbara Katz Rothman (1994) discusses the importance of practising embodied care for intimate relationships in describing the ways that her own and her husband's approach to caring for others changed after they had had children. Rothman recalls her own awkwardness in having to touch her mother's body in caring for her during an illness, and that of her husband towards herself when he attended the birth of their first child. After caring for the child over a period of years, Rothman notes, her husband had reoriented his approach:

> Nursing me through my first labour, he was infinitely well-meaning. Nursing me through my second, he knew what he was doing. He had been nurturing for seven years of nursing earaches, bellyaches, changing diapers, calming night terrors, holding pans for vomit, taking out splinters, washing bloody wounds. He had grown accustomed to the sheer physicality of the body, the sights and sounds and smells. More essentially, what I showed him in my pain and my fear was not foreign – he saw the baby, the child in me, not the one I was birthing, but the one I myself am, and he nursed it. Now *that* is a man to enter old age with. (Rothman, 1994: 156; original emphasis)

As Rothman's remarks would suggest, the regular embodied caring of a child may overcome the disgust or dislike of the 'dirty' bodily fluids it emits or its other uncontained bodily activities such as prolonged crying. Thus, although men cannot experience pregnancy, childbirth or lactation, their bodies have other potentialities for merging with another. Fatherhood is commonly experienced as a diversification of the body/self from autonomous, single body/self to a joint body/self. This may occur experientially through a man's realization after the birth of his child that he is now responsible for another, vulnerable person's wellbeing and that this other person is (genetically or emotionally or both) 'part of him'. While he is unable physically to experience pregnancy or breastfeeding, a father may engage in a series of other embodied activities with his child that may blur the boundaries between his body and that of his child, such as cuddling or sleeping with the child or bathing together.

This caring may engender intimacy and deep affection through such close physical contact with the child's body. It is the basis for the 'maternal thinking' we discussed in Chapter 5, and for the kind of abiding loving relationship with one's small child for which men are expressing such a strong desire. One man interviewed in our study quite explicitly discussed how his experiences in caring for his child had led him to see the world differently – he could not understand how people could hit their children, for example. He also described how he became emotionally distressed at hearing news reports of children being killed, his responses intensified because of his own position as a father with a much-loved child. Even those men who were not participating to a great extent in child care often reported spending time thinking about their child while at work, including planning the child's future, and ringing home during the day to check on her or him. As we noted above, some men – typically those who had gained much pleasure from their interactions with their children – were even wishing that they were at home engaging with the child rather than at work, and had discussed with their partner the possibility of staying at home while she went back to paid employment.

To some extent, an insistence upon differences between feminine and masculine positions can become somewhat static and reductionist. This may particularly be the case if other sources of shaping and experiencing subjectivity are not acknowledged, for 'gender forms only one axis of a complex, heterogeneous construction, constantly interpenetrating, in historically specific ways, with multiple other axes of identity' (Bordo, 1993: 222). In discussing the subject positions of father and mother, we need also to recognize the importance of acknowledging these positions as other than gendered subjects. That is, the ways in which men's and women's experiences of parenting are similar as well as different should be acknowledged. For both men and women, for example, becoming a parent involves a potential transformation in viewing the self that draws upon both their early experiences as an infant and small child of being cared for by their parents and later experiences with or perceptions of infants and children.

It is generally assumed that women's 'private' or 'domestic' roles as wives or partners, mothers and their other family roles (daughter, sister, grandmother) are integral to their sense of self and their manner of conducting everyday life. Much sociological and psychological research directed at this issue has supported this assumption. In contrast, it is assumed that men's roles as husband or partner, father and so on are less important to their subjectivity, with their 'public' work role providing the most significant definition of the self. To what extent does this assumed difference in the way men and women define their subjectivity exist? Is the oft-made division between the 'male-dominated public sphere' and the 'female-dominated private sphere' valid (if it ever was) as the twentieth century draws to its close?

We would suggest that continuing to draw a distinction between the 'private' and the 'public' spheres in relation to both fatherhood and motherhood is somewhat arbitrary and a false dichotomy. The family and parenthood are by no means separate from the 'outside world'. The body of 'expert' and popular literature that provides advice and norms to parents for the raising of their children we described in Chapters 2 and 3, the legislation around children (for example, in relation to the registering of births, children's schooling and parental neglect) and the power held by the social welfare system to remove children from their parents, are all examples of the ways in which childbirth and child rearing are constantly monitored and regulated by state and other bodies. Further, both women and men are now confronted with dealing with competing imperatives between paid labour and the family. Market economies tend to position their workers as having no demands outside the workplace, expecting them to be flexible, single-minded and ambitious (Beck and Beck-Gernsheim, 1995: 144). As we have shown, however, men often tend to approach their work lives differently once they have become fathers and feel themselves responsible for supporting their children and sometimes their female partners. Fatherhood may provide a point of mutual interest with work colleagues, both male and female, who also have children, allowing men to participate at work in a social network of parents in ways that men without children cannot. The role of fatherhood may also lend a certain gravitas to men in the work context, a sign to their colleagues of their greater 'maturity' and sense of responsibility.

In the contemporary context in which women are called upon to present themselves as masculinized, highly regulated and autonomous subjects in the paid workplace to achieve professional success, motherhood now may confront women (particularly those who have enjoyed success in high status, traditionally male occupations) with similar anxieties and frustrations (see the remarks made about professional women who become mothers in Nippert-Eng, 1996: 219–20). Just as the ambivalence that many women feel around motherhood is linked to their concerns about their own individuality and their role as mothers, including how to balance paid work, other interests and relationships with others with the responsibilities, anxieties and pleasures of child raising, men are confronted with similar concerns.

Continuing to define parenting roles in terms of, on the one hand, notions of 'patriarchy' or, on the other hand, the different 'functions' that fathers and mothers fulfil in response to inherent dispositions or gender norms and expectations, fails to recognize the complexity and constantly changing and negotiated nature of contemporary parenthood. Gender differences in the way men and women approach and experience parenthood remain evident. We have argued, however, that these differences are not simply the result of one gender being 'naturally' or 'instinctively' better at some tasks than others, or the outcome of men setting out to oppress their passive female partners, imposing the burden of child care upon them. Rather, there is a complex intertwining of acculturation and personal biography at work. This involves an interplay of aspects peculiar to couples' immediate situations, such as the nature of their paid work, their infant's behaviour and disposition, the availability of support from family or friends and individuals' experiences with, and observations of, their own parents, with broader sociocultural trends, such as the range of dominant discourses circulating on how a 'good' father and 'good' mother should approach and conduct parenting.

Appendix: Details of the Interview Study and Participants

Recruitment in the study took place progressively over 18 months, between late 1994 and mid-1996. Most of the 16 couples recruited into the study were attending antenatal classes at a Sydney hospital. Members of the class were given information about the study at their second-last session by the class facilitator, including an information sheet to take home and read, and were asked to consider participating. Between one and three couples from any one class eventually decided that they would join the study. Limited snowball sampling was also used, with three couples recruited in this way.

Men and women in each couple were interviewed separately each time, but often simultaneously. Thirteen of the men were interviewed by one of two male interviewers, while the other three were interviewed by a female interviewer (all the women were interviewed by a female interviewer). While all the first interviews were held in the participants' homes, subsequent interviews took place in a variety of locations; for example, hospital wards, coffee shops and work places. Each interview was generally between 30 minutes and one hour in length, and all interviews were audiotaped and fully transcribed for analysis. The interview schedule was semi-structured, involving a number of set questions but allowing the participants to raise other issues. The set questions asked each time differed slightly according to which interview in the series was being conducted. The questions were quite general, allowing the participants to expand upon their answers and diverge if appropriate, but were designed to elicit the participants' experiences and feelings in relation to first-time pregnancy and parenting, how they conceptualized parenthood, their notions of a 'good' mother and father, how they made decisions about aspects of infant care such as feeding and sleeping, and from where they sought help or advice in relation to child care and parenting. The male and female participants were asked the same questions, with some adjustments when relevant (for example, the women but not the men were asked about their experiences of giving birth and breastfeeding).

At the first interview, held in late pregnancy, the male participants were asked the following: What were your first thoughts when you found out that your partner was pregnant? Had you always imagined or expected to be a father? Have your thoughts about being a father changed during the pregnancy? How would you describe your baby? What is it like for you having your partner pregnant? What sort of relationship do you think you will have with your baby? What sort of future would you like for your child? What picture [image or thoughts] do you have of fatherhood? How would you describe a 'good' mother? How would you describe a 'good' father? What sorts of information have you been drawing on or found helpful and why? What are your plans for the birth? Have you planned how you will feed the baby? What has influenced your decision? Do you feel ready for the baby?

The second interview, held between two and ten days after the birth of the child, was designed to be shorter than the others, given that we expected the participants to have their hands full dealing with their new infants. Participants were asked the following questions: Describe your baby to me? Describe the birth? What was it like for you? Describe your response to the baby in the first few hours after the birth? What is it like providing care for your baby? How would you describe your interactions with the health workers [were they helpful or not]?

The set questions asked at the third interview (three to six weeks after the birth) included: How are things going [with the baby]? What was it like when you came home from hospital? How is it different from being in hospital? Tell me about the baby? Your partner is breast [bottle] feeding the baby – how did you make this decision? How do you feel about this decision? There are a wide range of beliefs and practices about a baby's sleeping habits; for example how a baby is settled for sleep and where a baby sleeps. What decisions have you made about your baby's sleep? Cast your mind back to what you imagined it would be like at home with a new baby. Is this what it is like? Describe your relationships with family and friends since the baby arrived home?

At the fourth interview (five to six months after the birth), participants were asked: How are things going [with the baby]? Describe your baby to me? What is it like providing care for your baby? Are there things that you really enjoy doing and things that you really don't like doing? Last time we spoke you told me about the decisions that you had made in relation to feeding your baby and your baby's sleeping habits. Are you still going by these decisions or has this changed? How has this changed? Who do you go to if you need help or advice? What else [if anything] do you find helpful? Describe your interactions with health workers? Describe your interactions with family and friends? How would you now describe a 'good' mother? How would you now describe a 'good' father? Describe the way in which you and the baby communicate? What sort of relationship do you want with your child as she or he gets older? The first time that we spoke together, you described the picture [image, thoughts] that you had of fatherhood. How do these images compare with your experiences now?

The set questions asked at the fifth and sixth interviews (held at approximately one year and 16–18 months after the birth respectively) included: How are things going [with the baby]? Tell me about the baby. Describe any particular time or times that you really felt like a father? Describe how you and the baby communicate [or can you describe the relationship that you have with your baby]? What sort of relationship do you want to have with her or him as she or he gets older? Does your paid employment have an impact on the way that you father? In earlier discussions you described a 'good' mother as [use participant's views from previous interviews]. Can you tell me any more about your ideas about a 'good' mother? In earlier discussions you described a 'good' father as [use participant's views from previous interviews]. Can you tell me any more about your ideas about a 'good' father? Today, there is an expectation that men will be involved in the care of the baby. With your experience, how does this work in your life? In earlier interviews, you described the picture or image that you had of fatherhood as [use views from previous interviews]. Can you compare this picture or image with what it is like for you now?

The Participants

All names used below are pseudonyms.

Ewan and Naomi had been married for five years before Rachael was born, and were living in their own small, semi-detached cottage in a Sydney suburb. Ewan was 32 years old at the time of the first interview, and he is a plumber by trade. He was born and raised in South Africa by his Scottish parents. Naomi, also aged 32, is Australian-born of Anglo-Celtic parents. She is a physiotherapist, and was looking forward to returning to work when the baby was six months old.

Richard and Prue had been married for six years before Daniel was born. They were living in a rented house in a Sydney suburb when the study began, but moved to a suburb on the outskirts of the city a year later to share a larger house with another family. Richard was 38 at the time, while Prue is ten years younger. Prue became pregnant with their second child 18 months after Daniel's birth. Richard was born in Australia and adopted when a baby by his parents, who were Anglo-Celtic in origin, and Prue is also Australian-born of Anglo-Celtic parents. Richard worked in sales and Prue had worked as an administrative officer with a large firm until the later months of pregnancy, and did not want to return to work until their children were older.

David and Anna had been married for three years before Sam was born. They lived in rented accommodation in a Sydney suburb. David was 25 years old, a storeman who was born in Australia of Anglo-Celtic parents. Anna was one year younger and had worked as a clerk before Sam's birth. She is of Anglo-Celtic origin and Australian-born. This couple moved to another state to be closer to Anna's family when Sam was five months old, and did not take part in further interviews.

Mike and Jenny had been married for four years before Grace was born.

They were living in their own semi-detached house in Sydney at the time of the first interview, but moved afterwards to a house with more room and a larger garden for Grace. Mike, a plumber, was born in Australia of Greek parents. Jenny was raised in Wales and met Mike on a working holiday to Australia. She worked in a plant nursery before the baby was born, and was trying to return to work six months after Grace was born. Mike was 33 years old at the time of the first interview, while Jenny was 28.

Jim and Megan had lived together for seven years before the birth of Tom. Both are Anglo-Celtic, and were born in Zimbabwe but had met in Sydney when they met and established their relationship. At the time of the first interview, Jim and Megan were living in their own house in a semi-rural area on the outskirts of Sydney. Jim, aged 40, is a sports psychologist. Megan, 34, is a former high school teacher who enrolled in doctoral studies shortly after Tom's birth.

Juan, aged 36, and Trisha, 26, were living together in a rented home unit in Sydney. They had been married only a short time when Trisha became pregnant. Juan is a researcher who works in the plastics industry. He was born in Chile but has lived a major part of his life in Australia. Trisha was also born overseas, in Scotland. Both have some family in Australia but most of their family live overseas. Trisha is a legal secretary and returned to work five months after their son Nathan was born. Their second child, a daughter, was born 18 months after Nathan.

Tony and Louise had lived together for 12 years before James was born. The couple were renovating their own house in Sydney. Tony owned his own business renovating houses and Louise had worked in an office before James's birth. She had returned to work on a casual basis when James was a year old. Both are Australian-born of Anglo-Celtic parents and both were aged 34 at the time of the first interview.

Simon and Jane had been together for six years and purchased a small house in Sydney shortly before the birth of their first child Sally. Simon was a nurse and Jane had worked as an administrative officer in a busy office before Sally's birth. Both were in their early thirties at the time of the first interview, and are Australian-born of Anglo-Celtic parents. Jane had returned to part-time work by the time Sally was a year old. The couple planned to have another baby before she returned to work full-time.

Peter and Donna had been married for nine years before Josh was born, and were living in a rented house in a Sydney suburb. Peter, who was 27 when first interviewed, runs a sporting facility. Donna was two years younger and had worked in an insurance office. She had returned to part-time work by the time Josh was one year old. Both Peter and Donna are Australian-born of Anglo-Celtic parents.

Steve and Kerry were both in their late twenties when first interviewed. They had been married for nine years before their son Luke was born, and were living in their own three-bedroom home unit in a Sydney suburb. Steve worked in computing as a systems analyst, while Kerry was a registered nurse who returned to work on a casual basis for two shifts a week one year after Luke was born. Both are Australian-born of Anglo-Celtic parents.

Dominic, aged 28 years, and Stella, 26, had been married for eight years before the birth of Jessica, and were living in their own house in a Sydney suburb. Dominic was born in Australia, though his parents were originally from Greece. Stella had lived in Australia for twenty years, but was born in Brazil. Dominic ran his own small business and Stella, formerly a clerical worker, had not worked during her pregnancy. She began helping in the business as Jessica approached her first birthday.

Cameron, aged 29 years, and Helen, 24, had been married for three years when their daughter Katherine was born, and were living in their own house in a middle-class suburb in Newcastle. Cameron worked as a sales representative for a large international machinery and construction company, while Helen had worked as a secretary, but planned to stay at home for a while to care for her child. Both Cameron and Helen are Australian-born of Anglo-Celtic parents.

Joe and Petra were in their early thirties, and had lived together for ten years before the birth of Hannah. At the time of the first interview, they were sharing a small, older-style house in a Sydney suburb with Susan's mother, and were paying off the mortgage on a larger house in a more secluded suburb. Joe was a government-employed manager who also lectured part-time in his field. Petra has undertaken higher degree studies and worked as a university lecturer. Joe's parents were born in Italy but he is Australian-born, while Petra was born in Germany, of German parents, and has lived in Australia for 15 years.

Ray and Cecily, both 24 years of age, had been married for more than four years when Martin was born. Ray is Australian-born of Anglo-Celtic parentage while Cecily was born in South Africa, again of Anglo-Celtic origin, but has grown up in Australia. They have both worked in private enterprise, Ray as a financial analyst and Cecily as an adviser. Cecily did not return to work after Martin's birth, and the couple were planning to have a second child quite soon. They were living in a rented home unit in a Sydney suburb when first interviewed.

Paul and Christine were married and had had nearly ten years of infertility treatment before Christine became pregnant with Edward (having left the infertility programme). They were living in a house they had built themselves in the semi-rural fringes of Sydney at the time of the first interview. Paul had been a police officer but is now working in his family's business. Christine had worked in an office before Edward was born but has not worked since then. Both were in their early 30s at the time of the first interview and are Australian-born of Anglo-Celtic origin.

Brad, 32 years, and Lyn, 31, had lived together for almost two years before the birth of Dylan. They bought their planned wedding forward when Lyn found she was pregnant earlier than they had intended. They were living in an outer Sydney suburb in a rented home unit when first interviewed. Brad and Lyn are both Australian-born of Anglo-Celtic parentage. Brad is employed as a supervisor in a large factory and Lyn worked as a clerk prior to Dylan's birth. Their second child was born a little over a year after Dylan.

References

Anderson, M. (1971a) 'Introduction', in M. Anderson (ed.), *Sociology of the Family*. Harmondsworth: Penguin. pp. 7–14.

Anderson, M. (ed.) (1971b) *Sociology of the Family*. Harmondsworth: Penguin.

Backett, K. (1982) *Mothers and Fathers: a Study of the Development and Negotiation of Parental Behaviour*. London: Macmillan.

Barker, F. (1984) *The Tremulous Private Body: Essays on Subjection*. London: Methuen.

Bauman, Z. (1996) 'From pilgrim to tourist – or a short history of identity', in S. Hall and P. du Gay (eds), *Questions of Cultural Identity*. London: Sage. pp. 18–36.

Beck-Gernsheim, E. (1996) 'Life as a planning project', in S. Lash, B. Szerszynski and B. Wynne (eds), *Risk, Environment and Modernity: Towards a New Ecology*. London: Sage. pp. 139–53.

Beck, U. (1992) *Risk Society: Towards a New Modernity*. London: Sage.

Beck, U. and Beck-Gernsheim, E. (1995) *The Normal Chaos of Love*. Cambridge: Polity Press.

Bell, A. (1991) *The Language of News Media*. Oxford: Blackwell.

Benjamin, J. (1994) 'The omnipotent mother: a psychoanalytic study of fantasy and reality', in D. Bassin, M. Honey and M. Kaplan (eds), *Representations of Motherhood*. New Haven, CT: Yale University Press. pp. 129–46.

Benjamin, O. and Sullivan, O. (1996) 'The importance of difference: conceptualising increased flexibility in gender relations at home', *Sociological Review*, 44 (2): 225–51.

Benvenuti, P., Marchetti, G., Niccheri, C. and Pazzagli, A. (1995) 'The psychosis of fatherhood: a clinical study', *Psychopathology*, 28 (2): 78–84.

Berger, P. and Luckmann, T. (1966) *The Social Construction of Reality*. Garden City, NY: Doubleday.

Berman, P. and Pedersen, F. (eds) (1987) *Men's Transitions to Parenthood: Longitudinal Studies of Early Family Experience*. Hillsdale, NJ: Lawrence Erlbaum.

Biddulph, S. (1994) *Manhood: a Book about Setting Men Free*. Sydney: Finch.

Blankenhorn, D. (1995) *Fatherless America: Confronting Our Most Urgent Social Problem.* New York: Basic Books.

Bly, R. (1990) *Iron John: a Book about Men.* New York: Addison-Wesley.

Bonner, F. and du Gay, P. (1992) 'Representing the enterprising self: thirty-something and contemporary consumer culture', *Theory, Culture and Society*, 9: 67–92.

Bordo, S. (1993) *Unbearable Weight: Feminism, Western Culture, and the Body.* Berkeley, CA: University of California Press.

Boukydis, Z. and Burgess, R. (1982) 'Adult physiological response to infant cries: effects of temperament of infant, parental status, and gender', *Child Development*, 53: 1291–8.

Bowen, S. and Miller, B. (1980) 'Paternal attachment behavior as related to presence at delivery and preparenthood classes: a pilot study', *Nursing Research*, 29 (5), 307–11.

Bowlby, J. (1969) *Attachment and Loss. Volume 1: Attachment.* London: Hogarth Press.

Bozett, F. and Hanson, S. (eds) (1991) *Fatherhood and Families in Cultural Context.* New York: Springer.

Braidotti, R. (1989) 'The politics of ontological difference', in T. Brennan (ed.), *Between Feminism and Psychoanalysis.* London: Routledge. pp. 89–105.

Brannen, J. and Moss, P. (1987) 'Fathers in dual-earner households – through mothers' eyes', in C. Lewis and M. O'Brien (eds), *Reassessing Fatherhood: New Observations on Fathers and the Modern Family.* London: Sage. pp. 126–43.

Brien, A. (1993) 'The extended father', in S. French (ed.), *Fatherhood.* London: Virago. pp. 13–26.

Brittan, A. (1989) *Masculinity and Power.* Oxford: Basil Blackwell.

Brown, M. (1986) 'Social support, stress, and health: a comparison of expectant mothers and fathers', *Nursing Research*, 35 (2): 72–6.

Burack, C. (1992) 'A house divided: feminism and object relations theory', *Women's Studies International Forum*, 15 (4): 499–506.

Burman, E. (1994) *Deconstructing Developmental Psychology.* London: Routledge.

Butler, J. (1990) *Gender Trouble: Feminism and the Subversion of Identity.* New York: Routledge.

Cain, M. (1993) 'Foucault, feminism and feeling: what Foucault can and cannot contribute to feminist epistemology', in C. Ramazanoglu (ed.), *Up against Foucault: Explorations of Some Tensions between Foucault and Feminism.* London: Routledge. pp. 73–96.

Cancian, F. (1987) *Love in America: Gender and Self-Development.* Cambridge: Cambridge University Press.

Chibucos, T. and Kail, P. (1981) 'Longitudinal examination of father–infant interaction and infant–father attachment', *Merrill-Palmer Quarterly*, 27 (2): 81–96.

Chodorow, N. (1978) *The Reproduction of Mothering.* Berkeley, CA: University of California Press.

Chodorow, N. (1989) *Feminism and Psychoanalytic Theory*. New Haven, CT: Yale University Press.

Chodorow, N. (1995a) 'Gender as a personal and cultural construction', *Signs*, 20 (3): 516–44.

Chodorow, N. (1995b) 'Individuality and difference in how women and men love', in A. Elliott and S. Frosh (eds), *Psychoanalysis in Contexts: Paths between Theory and Modern Culture*. London: Routledge. pp. 89–105.

Clark, A. (1992) 'Humanity or justice? Wifebeating and the law in the eighteenth and nineteenth centuries', in C. Smart (ed.), *Regulating Womanhood: Historical Essays on Marriage, Motherhood and Sexuality*. London: Routledge. pp. 187–206.

Cohen, D. (1990) *Being a Man*. London: Routledge.

Coltrane, S. and Allan, K. (1994) 'New' fathers and old stereotypes: representations of masculinity in 1980s television advertising', *Masculinities*, 2 (4): 43–66.

Connell, R. (1987) *Gender and Power*. Sydney: Allen and Unwin.

Connell, R. (1993) 'The big picture: masculinities in recent world history', *Theory and Society*, 22: 597–623.

Connell, R. (1995) *Masculinities*. Sydney: Allen and Unwin.

Cornwall, A. and Lindisfarne, N. (1994) 'Dislocating masculinity: gender, power and anthropology', in A. Cornwall and N. Lindisfarne (eds), *Dislocating Masculinity: Comparative Ethnographies*. London: Routledge. pp. 11–47.

Cosby, B. (1986) *Fatherhood*. New York: Dolphin Books.

Cosslett, T. (1994) *Women Writing Childbirth: Modern Discourses of Motherhood*. Manchester: Manchester University Press.

Cowan, C. and Cowan, P. (1987) 'Men's involvement in parenthood: identifying the antecedents and understanding the barriers', in P. Berman and F. Pedersen (eds), *Men's Transitions to Parenthood: Longitudinal Studies of Early Family Experience*. Hillsdale, NJ: Lawrence Erlbaum. pp. 145–74.

Cox, M., Owen, M., Henderson, V. and Margand, N. (1992) 'Prediction of infant–father and infant–mother attachment', *Developmental Psychology*, 28 (3): 474–83.

Crofts, S. (1995) 'Global *Neighbours*?', in R. Allen (ed.), *To Be Continued . . . Soap Operas around the World*. London: Routledge. pp. 98–121.

Crouch, M. and Manderson, L. (1995) 'The social life of bonding theory', *Social Science and Medicine*, 41 (6): 837–44.

Crouter, A., Perry-Jenkins, M., Huston, T. and McHale, S. (1987) 'Processes underlying father involvement in dual-earner and single-earner families', *Developmental Psychology*, 23 (3): 431–40.

Daly, K. (1993) 'Reshaping fatherhood: finding the models', *Journal of Family Issues*, 14 (4): 510–30.

Dearden, K., Hale, C. and Woolley, T. (1995) 'The antecedents of teen fatherhood: a retrospective case-control study of Great Britain youth', *American Journal of Public Health*, 85 (4): 551–4.

De Kanter, R. (1987) 'A father is a bag full of money: the person, the position and the symbol of the father', in T. Knijn and A.-C. Mulder (eds), *Unravelling Fatherhood*. Dordrecht, The Netherlands: Foris. pp. 6–26.

Dinnerstein, D. (1976) *The Mermaid and the Minotaur: Sexual Arrangements and Human Malaise*. New York: Harper and Row.

Donzelot, J. (1979) *The Policing of Families*. New York: Pantheon Books.

Dorsen, P. (1990) 'Man, husband, and father', in A. Pedersen and P. O'Mara (eds), *Being a Father: Family, Work, and Self*. Santa Fe, NM: John Muir. pp. 29–36.

Doucet, A. (1995) 'Gender equality and gender differences in household work and parenting', *Women's Studies International Forum*, 18 (3): 271–84.

Druck, K. (1990) 'Supporting the supporting father', in A. Pedersen and P. O'Mara (eds), *Being a Father: Family, Work, and Self*. Santa Fe, NM: John Muir. pp. 10–13.

Duden, B. (1991) *The Woman beneath the Skin: a Doctor's Patients in Eighteenth-Century Germany*. Cambridge, MA: Harvard University Press.

Duncombe, J. and Marsden, D. (1993) 'Love and intimacy: the gender division of emotion and "emotion work": a neglected aspect of sociological discussion of heterosexual relationships', *Sociology*, 27 (2): 221–41.

Ehrensaft, D. (1995) 'Bringing in fathers: the reconstruction of mothering', in J. Shapiro, M. Diamond and M. Greenberg (eds), *Becoming a Father: Contemporary, Social, Developmental, and Clinical Perspectives*. New York: Springer. pp. 43–59.

Elias, N. (1994) *The Civilizing Process*. Oxford: Blackwell.

Everingham, C. (1994) *Motherhood and Modernity*. Sydney: Allen and Unwin.

Fairclough, N. (1992) *Discourse and Social Change*. Cambridge: Polity Press.

Fein, R. (1978) 'Research on fathering: social policy and an emergent perspective', *Journal of Social Issues*, 34 (1): 122–35.

Ferketich, S. and Mercer, R. (1989) 'Men's health status during pregnancy and early fatherhood', *Research in Nursing and Health*, 12: 137–48.

Feuer, J. (1992) 'Genre study and television', in R. Allen (ed.), *Channels of Discourse, Reassembled*. London: Routledge. pp. 138–61.

Flax, J. (1993) 'Mothers and daughters revisited', in J. van Mens-Verhulst, K. Schreurs and L. Woertman (eds), *Daughtering and Mothering: Female Subjectivity Reanalysed*. London: Routledge. pp. 145–56.

Fost, D. (1996) 'The lost art of fatherhood', *American Demographics*, 18 (3): 16–18.

Foucault, M. (1984a) 'Truth and power', in P. Rabinow (ed.), *Foucault: a Reader*. New York: Pantheon Books. pp. 51–75.

Foucault, M. (1984b) 'The politics of health in the eighteenth century', in P. Rabinow (ed.), *The Foucault Reader*. New York: Pantheon Books. pp. 273–89.

Foucault, M. (1991) 'Governmentality', in G. Burchell, C. Gordon and P. Miller (eds), *The Foucault Effect: Studies in Governmentality*. Hempel Hempstead: Harvester Wheatsheaf. pp. 87–104.

Game, A. and Metcalfe, A. (1996) *Passionate Sociology*. London: Sage.

Garbarino, J. (1993) 'Reinventing fatherhood', *Families in Society*, January, 51–4.

Gatens, M. (1988) 'Towards a feminist philosophy of the body', in B. Caine, E. Grosz and M. de Lepervanche (eds), *Crossing Boundaries: Feminisms and the Critique of Knowledges*. Sydney: Allen and Unwin. pp. 59–70.

Geraghty, C. (1995) 'Social issues and realist soaps: a study of British soaps in the 1980s/1990s', in R. Allen (ed.), *To Be Continued . . . Soap Operas around the World*. London: Routledge. pp. 66–80.

Gerson, K. (1993) *No Man's Land: Men's Changing Commitments to Family and Work*. New York: Basic Books.

Gilligan, C. and Rogers, A. (1993) 'Reframing daughtering and mothering: a paradigm shift in psychology', in J. van Mens-Verhulst, K. Schreurs and L. Woertman (eds), *Daughtering and Mothering: Female Subjectivity Reanalysed*. London: Routledge. pp. 125–34.

Gillis, J. (1995) 'Bringing up father: British paternal identities, 1700 to present', *Masculinities*, 3 (3): 1–27.

Gordon, C. (1991) 'Government rationality: an introduction', in G. Burchell, C. Gordon and P. Miller (eds), *The Foucault Effect: Studies in Governmentality*. Hempel Hempstead: Harvester Wheatsheaf. pp. 1–52.

Gould, J. and Gunther, R. (1993) *Reinventing Fatherhood*. Blue Ridge Summit: TAB Books.

Graham, M. (1993) 'Parental sensitivity to infant cues: similarities and differences between mothers and fathers', *Journal of Pediatric Nursing*, 8 (6): 376–84.

Grbich, C. (1995) 'Male primary caregivers and domestic labour: involvement or avoidance?', *Journal of Family Studies*, 1 (2): 114–29.

Griswold, R. (1993) *Fatherhood in America: a History*. New York: Basic Books.

Grosz, E. (1994) *Volatile Bodies: Toward a Corporeal Feminism*. Sydney: Allen and Unwin.

Hall, E. (1995) 'From fun and excitement to joy and trouble: an explorative study of three Danish fathers' experiences around birth', *Scandinavian Journal of Caring Sciences*, 9: 171–9.

Hall, W. (1994) 'New fatherhood: myths and realities', *Public Health Nursing*, 11 (4): 219–28.

Hanson, S. and Bozett, F. (1987) 'Fatherhood and changing family roles', *Family Community Health*, 9 (4): 9–21.

Harrison, F. (1987) *A Winter's Tale*. London: Collins.

Hearn, J. (1996) 'Is masculinity dead? A critique of the concept of masculinity/masculinities', in M. Mac an Ghaill (ed.), *Understanding Masculinities*. Buckingham: Open University Press. pp. 202–17.

Heinowitz, J. (1990) 'Pregnant fathers', in A. Pedersen and P. O'Mara (eds), *Being a Father: Family, Work, and Self*. Santa Fe, NM: John Muir. pp. 3–9.

Henderson, A. and Brouse, A. (1991) 'The experiences of new fathers during the first three weeks of life', *Journal of Advanced Nursing*, 16: 293–8.

Henriques, J., Hollway, W., Urwin, C., Venn, C. and Walkerdine, V. (1984) *Changing the Subject: Psychology, Social Regulation and Subjectivity.* London: Methuen.

Hochschild, A. (with Machung, A.) (1989) *The Second Shift: Working Parents and the Revolution at Home.* New York: Viking.

Hoglund, G., Iselius, E. and Knave, B. (1992) 'Children of male spray painters: weight and length at birth', *British Journal of Industrial Medicine*, 49 (4): 249–53.

Hollway, W. (1984) 'Gender difference and the production of subjectivity', in J. Henriques, W. Hollway, C. Urwin, C. Venn and V. Walkerdine, *Changing the Subject: Psychology, Social Regulation and Subjectivity.* London: Methuen. pp. 227–63.

Hollway, W. (1989) *Subjectivity and Method in Psychology: Gender, Meaning and Science.* London: Sage.

Hollway, W. (1994) 'Beyond sex differences: a project for feminist psychology', *Feminism and Psychology*, 4 (4): 538–46.

Hollway, W. (1995) 'Feminist discourses and women's heterosexual desire', in S. Wilkinson and C. Kitzinger (eds), *Feminism and Discourse: Psychological Perspectives.* London: Sage. pp. 86–105.

Holstein, J. and Gubrium, J. (1994) 'Phenomenology, ethnomethodology, and interpretive practice', in N. Denzin and Y. Lincoln (eds), *Handbook of Qualitative Research.* Thousand Oaks, CA: Sage. pp. 262–73.

Hooper, C.-A. (1992) 'Child sexual abuse and the regulation of women: variations on a theme', in C. Smart (ed.), *Regulating Womanhood: Historical Essays on Marriage, Motherhood and Sexuality.* London: Routledge. pp. 53–77.

Horna, J. and Lupri, E. (1987) 'Fathers' participation in work, family life and leisure: a Canadian experience', in C. Lewis and M. O'Brien (eds), *Reassessing Fatherhood: New Observations on Fathers and the Modern Family.* London: Sage. pp. 54–73.

Horrocks, R. (1994) *Masculinity in Crisis.* New York: St Martin's Press.

Hyman, J. (1995) 'Shifting patterns of fathering in the first year of life: on intimacy between fathers and their babies', in J. Shapiro, M. Diamond and M. Greenberg (eds), *Becoming a Father: Contemporary, Social, Developmental, and Clinical Perspectives.* New York: Springer. pp. 256–67.

Hyssala, L., Rautava, P. and Sillanpaa, M. (1992) 'Health behaviour of fathers of young families expecting their first baby', *Scandinavian Journal of Social Medicine*, 20 (3): 165–72.

Jackson, D. (1990) *Unmasking Masculinity: a Critical Autobiography.* London: Unwin Hyman.

Jefferson, T. (1996) 'Introduction' (to special issue on masculinities, violence and crime), *British Journal of Criminology*, 36 (3): 337–47.

Jolly, H. (1981) *Book of Child Care* (third edition). London: George Allen and Unwin.

Jones, C. (1985) 'Father–infant relationships in the first year of life', in S. Hanson and F. Bozett (eds), *Dimensions of Fatherhood.* Beverly Hills, CA: Sage. pp. 92–114.

Jordan, J. (1993) 'The relational self: a model of women's development', in J. van Mens-Verhulst, K. Schreurs and L. Woertman (eds), *Daughtering and Mothering: Female Subjectivity Reanalysed*. London: Routledge. pp. 135–44.

Jordan, P. (1990) 'Laboring for relevance: expectant and new fatherhood', *Nursing Research*, 39 (1): 11–16.

Jordan, P. (1995) 'The mother's role in promoting fathering behavior', in J. Shapiro, M. Diamond and M. Greenberg (eds), *Becoming a Father: Contemporary, Social, Developmental, and Clinical Perspectives*. New York: Springer. pp. 61–71.

Kaplan, E.A. (1994) 'Sex, work, and motherhood: maternal subjectivity in recent visual culture', in D. Bassin, M. Honey and M. Kaplan (eds), *Representations of Motherhood*. New Haven, CT: Yale University Press. pp. 256–72.

Kimmel, M. (1987) 'Rethinking "masculinity": new directions in research', in M. Kimmel (ed.), *Changing Men: New Directions in Research on Men and Masculinity*. Newbury Park, CA: Sage. pp. 9–24.

Klein, M. (1979) *Envy and Gratitude and Other Works 1946–1963*. London: Hogarth Press.

Knijn, T. and Mulder, A.-C. (1987) 'Introduction', in T. Knijn and A.-C. Mulder (eds), *Unravelling Fatherhood*. Dordrecht, The Netherlands: Foris. pp. 1–5.

Kristeva, J. (1982) *Powers of Horror: an Essay on Abjection*. New York: Columbia University Press.

Kurki, T., Toivonen, L. and Ylikorkala, O. (1995) 'Father's heart beat responds to the birth of his child', *Acta Obstetricia et Gynecologica Scandinavia*, 74 (2): 127–8.

LaCerva, V. (1990) 'The importance of grief', in A. Pedersen and P. O'Mara (eds), *Being a Father: Family, Work, and Self*. Santa Fe, NM: John Muir. pp. 37–9.

Lamb, M. (1976) 'Interactions between eight-month-old children and their fathers and mothers', in M. Lamb (ed.), *The Role of the Father in Child Development*. New York: Wiley. pp. 307–27.

Lamb, M. (ed.) (1981) *The Role of the Father in Child Development* (second revised edition). New York: Wiley.

Lamb, M., Frodi, A., Hwang, C.-P., Frodi, M. and Steinberg, J. (1982) 'Mother– and father–infant interaction involving play and holding in traditional and nontraditional Swedish families', *Developmental Psychology*, 18 (2): 215–21.

Landerholm, E. and Scriven, G. (1981) 'A comparison of mother and father interaction with their six-month-old male and female infants', *Early Child Development and Care*, 7: 317–28.

LaRossa, R. (1988) 'Fatherhood and social change', *Family Relations*, 37: 451–7.

Leach, P. (1988) *Baby and Child: from Birth to Age Five* (second revised and updated edition). London: Penguin.

Leigh, B. (1990) 'A new father's field guide', in A. Pedersen and P. O'Mara (eds), *Being a Father: Family, Work, and Self*. Santa Fe, NM: John Muir. pp. 141–8.

Levy-Shiff, R. and Israelashvili, R. (1988) 'Antecedents of fathering: some further exploration', *Developmental Psychology*, 24 (3): 434–40.

Lewis, C. (1986) *Becoming a Father*. Milton Keynes: Open University Press.

Lewis, J. (1991) *The Ideological Octopus: an Exploration of Television and its Audience*. New York: Routledge.

Littman, H., Medendorp, S. and Goldfarb, J. (1994) 'The decision to breast-feed: the importance of a father's approval', *Clinical Pediatrics*, 33 (4): 214–9.

Lloyd, G. (1984) *The Man of Reason: 'Male' and 'Female' in Western Philosophy*. London: Methuen.

Lock, M. (1993) 'The politics of mid-life and menopause: ideologies for the second sex in North America and Japan', in S. Lindenbaum and M. Lock (eds), *Knowledge, Power and Practice: the Anthropology of Medicine and Everyday Life*. Berkeley, CA: University of California Press. pp. 330–63.

Mac an Ghaill, M. (ed.) (1996) *Understanding Masculinities*. Buckingham: Open University Press.

McBride, B. (1989) 'Stress and fathers' parental competence: implications for family life and parent educators', *Family Relations*, 38: 385–9.

McKee, L. and O'Brien, M. (1982) 'The father figure: some current orientations and historical perspectives', in L. McKee and M. O'Brien (eds), *The Father Figure*. London: Tavistock.

McMahon, M. (1995) *Engendering Motherhood: Identity and Self-Transformation in Women's Lives*. New York: Guilford Press.

Marshall, H. (1991) 'The social construction of motherhood: an analysis of childcare and parenting manuals', in A. Phoenix, A. Woollett and E. Lloyd, (eds), *Motherhood: Meanings, Practices and Ideologies*. London: Sage. pp. 66–85.

Marsiglio, W. (1993) 'Contemporary scholarship on fatherhood: culture, identity, and conduct', *Journal of Family Issues*, 14 (4): 484–509.

Mellen, J. (1978) *Big Bad Wolves: Masculinity in the American Film*. London: Elm Tree Books.

Mercer, R. and Ferketich, S. (1990) 'Predictors of parental attachment during early parenthood', *Journal of Advanced Nursing*, 15: 268–80.

Messner, M. (1993) '"Changing men" and feminist politics in the United States', *Theory and Society*, 22: 723–37.

Millar, R. (1990) 'How parenting civilizes us', in A. Pedersen and P. O'Mara (eds), *Being a Father: Family, Work, and Self*. Santa Fe, NM: John Muir. pp. 21–5.

Miller, P. and Rose, N. (1993) 'Governing economic life', in M. Gane and T. Johnson (eds), *Foucault's New Domains*. London: Routledge. pp. 75–105.

Morgan, D. (1992) *Discovering Men*. London: Routledge.

Morley, D. (1992) *Television, Audiences and Cultural Studies*. London: Routledge.

Moss, P. and Brannen, J. (1987) 'Fathers and employment', in C. Lewis and M. O'Brien (eds), *Reassessing Fatherhood: New Observations on Fathers and the Modern Family*. London: Sage. pp. 36–53.

Mumford, L. (1995) 'Plotting paternity: looking for dad on the daytime soaps', in R. Allen (ed), *To Be Continued . . . Soap Operas around the World*. London: Routledge. pp. 164–81.

Murcott, A. (1993) 'Purity and pollution: body management and the social place of infancy', in S. Scott and D. Morgan (eds), *Body Matters: Essays on the Sociology of the Body*. London: Falmer. pp. 122–34.

Nippert-Eng, C. (1996) *Home and Work*. Chicago: University of Chicago Press.

Oakley, A. (1974) *Housewife*. Harmondsworth: Penguin.

Osherson, S. (1992) *Wrestling with Love: How Men Struggle with Intimacy with Women, Children, Parents and Each Other*. New York: Fawcett Columbine.

Osherson, S. (1996) *The Passions of Fatherhood*. Sydney: Harper Perennial.

Parke, R. and Sawin, D. (1980) 'The family in early infancy: social interactional and attitudinal analyses', in F. Pedersen (ed.), *The Father–Infant Relationship*. New York: Praeger. pp. 44–70.

Parsons, T. (1964) *Essays in Sociological Theory*. New York: Free Press.

Parsons, T. and Bales, R. (1955) *Family, Socialization and Interaction Process*. New York: Free Press.

Pedersen, A. and O'Mara, P. (eds) (1990) *Being a Father: Family, Work, and Self*. Santa Fe, NM: John Muir.

Petersen, A. and Lupton, D. (1996) *The New Public Health: Health and Self in the Age of Risk*. Sydney and London: Allen and Unwin/Sage.

Philipson, I. (1981) 'Child rearing literature and capitalist industrialization', *Berkeley Journal of Sociology*, xxvi: 57–73.

Pleck, J. (1987) 'American fathering in historical perspective', in M. Kimmel (ed.), *Changing Men: New Directions in Research on Men and Masculinity*. Beverly Hills, CA: Sage. pp. 83–97.

Pollack, S. and Sutton, J. (1985) 'Fathers' rights, women's losses', *Women's Studies International Forum*, 8 (6): 593–9.

Popenoe, D. (1993) 'Parental androgyny', *Society*, 39 (6): 5–11.

Pouissant, A. (1995) 'Foreword', in J. Shapiro, M. Diamond and M. Greenberg (eds), *Becoming a Father: Contemporary, Social, Developmental, and Clinical Perspectives*. New York: Springer. pp. xix–xxii.

Probyn, E. (1993) *Sexing the Self: Gendered Positions in Cultural Studies*. London: Routledge.

Pruett, K. (1993) 'The paternal presence', *Families in Society*, January: 46–50.

Pruett, K. (1995) 'The paternal presence', in J. Shapiro, M. Diamond and M. Greenberg (eds), *Becoming a Father: Contemporary, Social, Developmental, and Clinical Perspectives*. New York: Springer. pp. 36–42.

Ramazanoglu, C. (1992) 'What can you do with a man? Feminism and the critical appraisal of masculinity', *Women's Studies International Forum*, 15 (3): 339–50.

Ramazanoglu, C. (ed.) (1993) *Up against Foucault: Explorations of some Tensions between Foucault and Feminism*. London: Routledge.

Reay, D. (1995) 'A silent majority? Mothers in parental involvement', *Women's Studies International Forum*, 18 (3): 337–48.

Ribbens, J. (1994) *Mothers and their Children: a Feminist Sociology of Childrearing*. London: Sage.

Riley, D. and Cochran, M. (1985) 'Naturally occurring childrearing advice for fathers: utilization of the personal social network', *Journal of Marriage and the Family*, May: 275–86.

Robinson, B. and Barret, R. (1986) *The Developing Father: Emerging Roles in Contemporary Society*. New York: Guilford Press.

Rose, N. (1989) 'Individualizing psychology', in J. Shotter and K. Gergen (eds), *Texts of Identity*. London: Sage. pp. 119–33.

Rose, N. (1996) *Inventing Our Selves: Psychology, Power, and Personhood*. Cambridge: Cambridge University Press.

Ross, E. (1993) *Love and Toil: Motherhood in Outcast London 1870–1918*. New York: Oxford University Press.

Rothman, B. (1994) 'Beyond mothers and fathers: ideology in a patriarchal society', in E. Glenn, G. Chang and L. Forcey (eds), *Mothering: Ideology, Experience, and Agency*. New York: Routledge. pp. 139–57.

Ruddick, S. (1989) *Maternal Thinking: Towards a Politics of Peace*. London: The Women's Press.

Ruddick, S. (1994) 'Thinking mothers/conceiving birth', in D. Bassin, M. Honey and M. Kaplan (eds), *Representations of Motherhood*. New Haven, CT: Yale University Press. pp. 29–45.

Russell, G. (1978) 'The father role and its relation to masculinity, femininity, and androgyny', *Child Development*, 49: 1174–81.

Russell, G. (1987) 'Problems in role-reversed families', in C. Lewis and M. O'Brien (eds), *Reassessing Fatherhood: New Observations on Fathers and the Modern Family*. London: Sage. pp. 161–79.

Rustia, J. and Abbott, D. (1993) 'Father involvement in infant care: two longitudinal studies', *International Journal of Nursing Studies*, 30 (6): 467–76.

Sampson, E. (1989) 'The deconstruction of the self', in J. Shotter and K. Gergen (eds), *Texts of Identity*. London: Sage. pp. 1–10.

Schnitzer, P., Olshan, A. and Erickson, J. (1995) 'Paternal occupation and risk of birth defects in offspring', *Epidemiology*, 6 (6): 577–83.

Schwartz, A. (1994) 'Taking the nature out of mother', in D. Bassin, M. Honey and M. Kaplan (eds), *Representations of Motherhood*. New Haven, CT: Yale University Press. pp. 240–55.

Sears, W. (1990) 'Foreword', in A. Pedersen and P. O'Mara (eds), *Being a Father: Family, Work, and Self*. Santa Fe, NM: John Muir. pp. vii–xi.

Segal, L. (1990) *Slow Motion: Changing Masculinities, Changing Men*. London: Virago.

Shapiro, J., Diamond, M. and Greenberg, M. (1995) 'Introduction', in J. Shapiro, M. Diamond and M. Greenberg (eds), *Becoming a Father:*

Contemporary, Social, Developmental, and Clinical Perspectives. New York: Springer. pp. 3–14.

Shilling, C. (1993) *The Body and Social Theory*. London: Sage.

Shotter, J. (1989) 'Social accountability and the social construction of "you"', in J. Shotter and K. Gergen (eds), *Texts of Identity*. London: Sage. pp. 133–51.

Shotter, J. and Gergen, K. (1989) 'Preface and introduction', in J. Shotter and K. Gergen (eds), *Texts of Identity*. London: Sage. pp. ix–xi.

Skeffington, H. (1990) 'Weathering the storm together', in A. Pedersen and P. O'Mara (eds), *Being a Father: Family, Work, and Self*. Santa Fe, NM: John Muir. pp. 77–9.

Smith, P. and Daglish, L. (1977) 'Sex differences in parent and infant behavior', *Child Development*, 48: 1250–4.

Sparks, R. (1996) 'Masculinity and heroism in the Hollywood "blockbuster": the culture industry and contemporary images of crime and law enforcement', *British Journal of Criminology*, 36 (3): 348–60.

Spock, B. (1989) *Parenting*. London: Michael Joseph.

Spock, B. and Rothenberg, M. (1992) *Dr. Spock's Baby and Child Care* (sixth revised edition). New York: Pocket Books.

Stearns, P. (1991) 'Fatherhood in historical perspective: the role of social change', in F. Bozett and S. Hanson (eds), *Fatherhood and Families in Cultural Context*. New York: Springer. pp. 28–52.

Surrey, J. (1993) 'The mother–daughter relationship: themes in psychotherapy', in J. van Mens-Verhulst, K. Schreurs and L. Woertman (eds), *Daughtering and Mothering: Female Subjectivity Reanalysed*. London: Routledge. pp. 114–24.

Terry, D. (1991) 'Predictors of subjective stress in a sample of new parents', *Australian Journal of Psychology*, 43 (1): 29–36.

Terry, D., McHugh, T. and Noller, P. (1991) 'Role dissatisfaction and the decline in marital quality across the transition to parenthood', *Australian Journal of Psychology*, 43 (3): 129–32.

Theweleit, K. (1987) *Male Fantasies. Volume 1: Women, Floods, Bodies, History*. Cambridge: Polity Press.

Tiedje, L. and Darling-Fisher, C. (1993) 'Factors that influence fathers' participation in child care', *Health Care for Women International*, 14 (1): 99–107.

Tosh, J. (1996) 'Authority and nurture in middle-class fatherhood: the case of early and mid-Victorian England', *Gender and History*, 8 (1): 48–64.

Urwin, C. (1985) 'Constructing motherhood: the persuasion of normal development', in C. Steedman, C. Urwin and V. Walkerdine (eds), *Language, Gender and Childhood*. London: Routledge and Kegan Paul. pp. 164–202.

Verheyen, C. (1987) 'Mother knows best: for him the play, for her the rest', in T. Knijn and A.-C. Mulder (eds), *Unravelling Fatherhood*. Dordrecht, The Netherlands: Foris. pp. 37–47.

Vincent-Buffault, A. (1991) *The History of Tears: Sensibility and Sentimentality in France*. Houndsmills: Macmillan.

Walkerdine, V. (1984) 'Developmental psychology and the child-centred pedagogy: the insertion of Piaget into early education', in J. Henriques, W. Hollway, C. Urwin, C. Venn and V. Walkerdine, *Changing the Subject: Psychology, Social Regulation and Subjectivity*. London: Methuen. pp. 153–202.

Walkerdine, V. and Lucey, H. (1989) *Democracy in the Kitchen: Regulating Mothers and Socialising Daughters*. London: Virago.

Walters, S. (1992) *Lives Together/Worlds Apart: Mothers and Daughters in Popular Culture*. Berkeley, CA: University of California Press.

Walzer, S. (1996) 'Thinking about the baby: gender and divisions of infant care', *Social Problems*, 43 (2): 219–34.

Weedon, C. (1992) *Feminist Practice and Poststructuralist Theory*. Oxford: Blackwell.

White, N. (1994) 'About fathers: masculinity and the social construction of fatherhood', *Australian and New Zealand Journal of Sociology*, 30 (2): 119–31.

Woollett, A. and Phoenix, A. (1991) 'Psychological views of mothering', in A. Phoenix, A. Woollett and E. Lloyd (eds), *Motherhood: Meanings, Practices and Ideologies*. London: Sage. pp. 28–46.

Yacovone, D. (1990) 'Abolitionists and the "language of fraternal love"', in M. Carnes and C. Griffen (eds), *Meanings for Manhood: Constructions of Masculinity in Victorian America*. Chicago: University of Chicago Press. pp. 85–95.

Young, A. (1996) 'In the frame: crime and the limits of representation', *Australian and New Zealand Journal of Criminology*, 29 (2): 81–101.

Young, I. (1990) *Throwing Like a Girl and Other Essays in Feminist Philosophy and Social Theory*. Bloomington, IN: Indiana University Press.

Index